Baseball's Retired Numbers

Baseball's Retired Numbers

Major and Minor Leagues

Thomas W. Brucato

McFarland & Company, Inc., Publishers
Jefferson, North Carolina, and London

LIBRARY OF CONGRESS CATALOGUING-IN-PUBLICATION DATA

Brucato, Thomas W.
    Baseball's retired numbers : major and minor leagues / Thomas W. Brucato.
       p.   cm.
    Includes bibliographical references and index.

    ISBN 0-7864-1762-5 (softcover : 50# alkaline paper) ∞

    1. Baseball uniforms — Numbers — United States — History.
2. Baseball players — United States — Biography.
I. Title.
GV879.7.B78   2004
796.357'02 — dc22   2004000405

British Library cataloguing data are available

©2004 Thomas W. Brucato. All rights reserved

No part of this book may be reproduced or transmitted in any form or by any means, electronic or mechanical, including photocopying or recording, or by any information storage and retrieval system, without permission in writing from the publisher.

Manufactured in the United States of America

Cover photograph: ©2004 Corbis Images

McFarland & Company, Inc., Publishers
  Box 611, Jefferson, North Carolina 28640
    www.mcfarlandpub.com

To Kathryn —
I'll always be your biggest fan.

Acknowledgments

As always, I want to acknowledge my wife and executive research assistant, Julie Brucato, for her support and assistance.

I would also like to acknowledge the following individuals and organizations for their invaluable contributions: Sean Aronson, Director of Media Relations/Broadcasting, Allentown Ambassadors; Fred Baker, Boise Hawks Booster Club; Paul Barbeau, Vice President–General Manager, Spokane Indians; Beverly, Amarillo Dillas; Travis Brower, Director of Operations, Idaho Falls Padres; Mark Bryant, Assistant General Manager, Capital City Bombers; Josh Buchholz, Fargo-Moorhead RedHawks; Christian Carlson, General Manager, South Bend Silver Hawks; Greg Coleman, General Manager, Modesto A's; Greg Detter, Communications Manager/Radio Broadcaster, Sioux Falls Canaries; Dave Echols, Brockton Rox; David Flemming, Radio Broadcaster and Assistant Director of Community Affairs, Pawtucket Red Sox; John Frey, General Manager, Erie SeaWolves; Jonathan Green, Director of Communications, Winnipeg Goldeyes; Jason Griffin, Public/Media Relations, Toledo Mud Hens; Chuck Hinkel, Director of Media Relations, Rochester Red Wings; Huntsville Stars; Bill Lee, President, Frontier League; Steve Lenox, Director of Broadcasting and Media Relations, Wilmington Blue Rocks; Todd Marlin, Assistant General Manager, Nashua Pride; Mark Moehlenkamp, Vice President, O'Brien Field and the Peoria Chiefs; New Jersey Cardinals; New Jersey Jackals; Reading Phillies; Bob Richmond, President, Arizona League; Gabe Ross, Director of Public Relations, Colorado Springs Sky Sox; Joe Santry, Historian, Columbus Clippers; Scott, Canadian Baseball Hall of Fame and Museum; Scranton/Wilkes-Barre Red Barons; Paul Stiritz, Assistant General Manager, Inland Empire 66ers; Dave Wright, Director of Public Relations/

Internet, St. Paul Saints; Jill Yde, Administrative Assistant, Orlando Rays; and Alan York, Director of Broadcasting/Media Relations, Winston-Salem Warthogs.

I owe the greatest thanks to God for all of His great and glorious gifts.

Contents

Acknowledgments	vii
Introduction	1

PART I: Major Leagues

1. List of Players	9
2. Team-by-Team List	223
3. Numerical List	228

PART II: Minor Leagues

4. List of Players	235
5. Team-by-Team List	258
6. Numerical List	277
Bibliography	281
Index	283

Introduction

The concept of retiring a uniform number to honor a player likely began with the New York Yankees. The Yankees, while not the first team to wear uniform numbers to identify players (a few others had experimented with the idea earlier), were the first to don them permanently, in 1929. Other teams quickly followed suit, and by mid–1932 every team in major league baseball was using numbers. The practice eventually spread to other team sports, and the use of numbers is now standard in most.

Numbers are worn at all levels — professional, semipro, amateur, college, high school, and even elementary school and earlier — and retired numbers permeate most, if not all, of these levels. This book focuses exclusively on professional baseball, and thus includes both the major and minor leagues.

Major Leagues

When Yankees first baseman Lou Gehrig stepped down in 1939 because he had contracted amyotrophic lateral sclerosis, the team decided to honor him by retiring his number 4. Retiring numbers has now become a rather popular way of honoring players in many sports. While popular, however, the honor remains a rare one. Amazingly, it is easier for a player to get into the Hall of Fame than to get his number retired, although that disparity may be mitigated somewhat by the fact that numbers were not worn regularly before 1929.

The idea behind retiring a number seems to center on the concept that no one else is worthy of wearing the number once borne by the honored player. In practice, however, a specific player's number often is not retired until several others have worn it. At least nine Yankees, for example, wore Babe Ruth's number 3 after the Sultan of Swat himself had left the team. In many cases, a team does not decide to retire a number until a specific player has added to his achievements with another team, or until he has been inducted into the Hall of Fame.

Neither the National League nor the American League has a policy regarding the retirement of numbers, so teams are free to employ their own as they see fit. Most clubs have no hard and fast rules regarding eligibility, although the Boston Red Sox require that an individual finish his career with the team in some capacity. Most teams do display their retired numbers somewhere in their ballparks.

The honor of having a number retired is not restricted to players. Coaches and managers have had numbers retired, and symbolic retirements have been bestowed upon owners and other executives. The latter is a somewhat controversial practice, as many question the propriety of retiring a uniform number for someone who never wore a uniform. The practice is far more common in the minor leagues than it is in the majors, however.

Six umpires — three in the National League and three in the American League — also had their numbers retired at a time when the two leagues maintained separate umpire rosters. In 2000, the league offices were shut down and operations were assumed by Major League Baseball. The previously retired umpires' numbers came back into use at that time.

Two teams — the San Francisco Giants and the Philadelphia Phillies — have chosen to honor men who never wore numbers in the same way as those who did, placing their names on the ballpark displays alongside those who have had numbers retired, with old team logos to represent their respective eras. While those four men (Christy Mathewson, John McGraw, Grover Cleveland Alexander, and Chuck Klein) were not technically honored with number retirements, they are usually included in lists of retired numbers and they do appear here.

Teams retire numbers for a variety of reasons. Most often, the individual in question has achieved some level of greatness with the team retiring his number, and longevity is often, though not always, a factor. In some cases, an individual's death prompts a number retirement, and in some, greatness achieved with another team plays a role.

As previously mentioned, teams often wait until at least several years after a player's retirement before retiring that player's number. As a result, two teams felt that a specific pair of players who wore the same number deserved number retirements. Thus, the Yankees have retired number 8 for both Bill Dickey and Yogi Berra, and the Montreal Expos have retired number 10 for both Rusty Staub and Andre Dawson.

Eight men have had numbers retired by more than one team. Six have had numbers retired by two teams — Hank Aaron, Rod Carew, Rollie Fingers, Carlton Fisk, Frank Robinson, and Casey Stengel. Only one, Nolan Ryan, had his number retired by three teams. In 1997, in honor of the fiftieth anniversary of Jackie Robinson's breaking the color barrier, Major League Baseball decreed that all teams would retire the number 42 that Robinson wore with the Brooklyn Dodgers. He is the only individual to have been so honored in any sport. Somewhat curiously, that decree also extended to the minor league teams affiliated with Major League Baseball.

Fisk and Ryan are the only individuals to have had two different numbers retired. The highest retired number is the number 85 that the St. Louis Cardinals retired symbolically for August A. Busch, Jr. The highest retired number that was actually worn, however, was the 72 retired by the Chicago White Sox for Carlton Fisk.

The Yankees have retired the most numbers (16, honoring a total of 17 men), while several teams have not retired any, except, of course, for Robinson's. The most commonly retired numbers are the numbers 1 and 4, each of which has been retired for eight individuals. Three Robinsons have had numbers retired (Brooks, Frank, and Jackie), and the Baltimore Orioles are in the unique position of having retired numbers for all three.

In the section of this book devoted to major leaguers, each individual's name is followed by his retired number and the name of the team that retired it, plus the year in which it was retired. Next appears the role that that individual played in the major leagues, e.g., a position on the diamond, coach, manager, umpire, owner, etc. Positions listed are those that were a player's primary position for at least one season, even if that player's season was abbreviated. Finally listed are the names of the individual's teams (or, in the case of umpires, leagues) with which he was affiliated and the years of his major league career. The book then presents a short history of the individual's career, followed by any major awards or honors he won. Specifically, these awards and honors include the Rookie of the Year Award, the League Award (indicating a Most Valuable Player from 1922–29), the Most Valuable Player Award, Gold Gloves, the Cy Young Award, the Rolaids Relief Man Award, the Manager of the Year Award (of which there are two — those awarded by the Associated Press are noted parenthetically by "AP," those awarded by the Baseball Writers Association of America by "BBWAA"), and Hall of Fame induction. Unless otherwise specified, the term "Hall of Fame" in this book refers to the National Baseball Hall of Fame in Cooperstown, New York.

Some awards were originally given to only one player per year, rather than to one player from each league. This fact explains why, in certain listings, the term "American League" or "National League" does not appear before a specific award. Similarly, Gold Gloves for outfielders were originally awarded specifically to left fielders, center fielders, and right fielders, but were later combined into simply "outfielders."

Following the histories, the reader will find team-by-team and numerical lists of honored individuals.

Minor Leagues

The minor leagues have a different attitude concerning retired numbers. A player who excels in the minor leagues is not usually with a team for long, because he usually gets promoted and may soon reach the major leagues. Longevity, therefore, is rarely a factor, and achievement is often based on what a player accomplishes overall rather than with a specific team. Popularity is also a motivating element, and so is death. Sometimes a team will retire the number of its first player to reach the major leagues.

Minor league teams that relocate seldom admit to their previous identities. A team switching from one city to another usually promotes itself as a "new" team, and if it had retired numbers in its previous city, it does not usually honor those in its new location. Indeed, retired numbers in the minor leagues are often more connected to a city than to a franchise, and in many cases, a team will retire numbers for individuals who played with previous teams in the same location.

Some minor league teams do not issue the numbers that have been retired by their major league parent clubs. This is especially true of teams whose uniforms are issued by their parent teams. (For example, the Elizabethton Twins receive their uniforms from the Minnesota Twins, and therefore will not receive jerseys bearing numbers that the Minnesota Twins have retired.) Those situations are not listed in this book, since the numbers are not truly retired at the minor league level and the teams in question, if they were simply to switch affiliations, could begin to reissue those numbers.

Symbolic retirements abound in the minor leagues, and even encompass individuals who excelled in other sports. Thirteen individuals with retired numbers in the major leagues have also had numbers retired by minor league teams. Some of these retirements are symbolic as well, and in those cases the number retired is usually the one the individual wore in the major leagues. As previously mentioned, the retirement of Jackie

Robinson's number 42 extends to those minor league teams that are affiliated with Major League Baseball. It does not, however, include the independent leagues, although the Nashua Pride of the Atlantic League chose to retire it anyway.

Other than Jackie Robinson, Luke Easter is the only individual to have had numbers retired by more than one minor league team. The highest number retired in the minor leagues puts to shame the number 85 that major league baseball claims as its highest. That "honor" goes to the number 8222, retired symbolically by the Rochester Red Wings for Morrie Silver and the team's original shareholders. The Colorado Springs Sky Sox have retired the most numbers among minor league teams, with seven.

In the section of this book devoted to minor leaguers, each individual's name is followed by the name of the team that retired it, and then by a brief description of the significance of that individual. Following these descriptions, the reader will find team-by-team and numerical lists of honored individuals.

Franchise shifts and name changes occur annually in the minor leagues. Teams included in this book are those that were active as of the 2003 baseball season. The team-by-team list also gives each club's league affiliation, current as of the 2003 baseball season.

The Arizona Fall League — which is temporarily stocked each year by major league clubs, and which does not technically even have its own uniforms — and leagues based outside the United States are not included.

Part I

Major Leagues

List of Players

Hank Aaron

Retired Number: 44 (Milwaukee Brewers, 1976; Atlanta Braves, 1977)
Outfielder/Designated Hitter
Playing Career: Milwaukee Braves 1954–65; Atlanta Braves 1966–74; Milwaukee Brewers 1975–76

Born Henry Louis Aaron in Mobile, Alabama, on February 5, 1934, the player who would create his legacy as "Hammerin' Hank" began playing semipro ball at the tender age of 15. By 1950 he was the shortstop for the Indianapolis Clowns of the Negro American League, and in 1952 was purchased by the Milwaukee Braves for the paltry sum of $7500.

The Braves called Aaron up to the big club in 1954 to fill in for Bobby Thomson, who had broken a leg in spring training, and Hank never looked back. In his rookie season he batted .280 and slugged 13 home runs and 27 doubles, but that performance was the merest shadow of what was to come.

The following year he hit .314, adding 27 home runs and tying for the National League lead with 37 doubles. In 1956 he won his first batting title with a .328 average, leading the league with 200 hits and 34 doubles. In 1957 he earned the league's Most Valuable Player Award when he led the circuit with 44 roundtrippers, 132 runs batted in, and 118 runs scored.

Aaron won his second batting title in 1959 when he hit .355, and although that would be the last time he led the league in batting average, he batted over .300 fourteen times in his 23-year career. He led the league in home runs four times, but ironically, the man who would become baseball's all-time home run king never hit more than 47 in a single season.

Aaron was the model of consistency. Between 1957 and 1973 he hit fewer than 30 home runs in a season only twice, and from 1955 through 1973 fell below 90 RBIs but three times.

When the Braves left Milwaukee for Atlanta in 1966, Aaron went with them, playing another nine seasons in the Georgia city. He collected his 3000th career hit on May 17, 1970, on an infield single off Wayne Simpson of the Cincinnati Reds at Crosley Field in the second game of a doubleheader, but the crowning point of his career — and the achievement for which he is most famous — was his pursuit of Babe Ruth's all-time home run record. Aaron finished the 1973 season with 713 lifetime homers, only one shy of the record, and having endured several years of derogatory remarks and even death threats from those who did not want to see the Babe's mark eclipsed — and from those whose racist tendencies came brazenly to the fore — he would have to wait yet another winter before continuing his assault.

On Opening Day of 1974, Aaron hit number 714 in Cincinnati off Jack Billingham, then slugged the record-breaker on April 8 in Atlanta off Al Downing of the Los Angeles Dodgers.

Aaron had always expressed a desire to return to Milwaukee, and as he neared the end of his career, the Braves obliged him by trading him to the Milwaukee Brewers following the 1974 campaign for Dave May and minor leaguer Roger Alexander. While Hank's best days were behind him — he batted .234 and .229 in his two seasons with the Brewers, and collectively hit but 22 home runs — he truly went out in style, having amassed 755 home runs and 2297 RBIs in his remarkable career, both all-time major league records, while also accumulating 3771 hits.

Aaron's bat obviously spoke for itself, but what many people do not realize is that the outfielder was also an outstanding defensive specialist. He won three consecutive Gold Gloves in his storied career, from 1958 through 1960, all while playing right field for the Braves.

Aaron wore number 5 when he first joined the Braves in 1954, but he expressed a preference for a repetitive two-digit number. Number 44 was available, and Aaron took it in 1955. Hank was so lean in those years that his teammates were said to have joked that there was no room on his back for a two-digit number. Aaron is one of only eight men to have his number retired by more than one team. While Hank spent 21 years with the Braves and only 2 with the Brewers, it was the Brewers who actually retired his number first. They put it to rest in 1976, the same year Aaron himself retired, and the Braves followed suit the following year. While some have questioned the appropriateness of retiring a number for someone who spent only two years with a team, suffice it to say that the Brewers realized the historical importance of the man who donned their uniform for the final two seasons of his illustrious career. This was no ordinary superstar — if there is such a thing — but major league baseball's all-time home run king, a title that does not come lightly or easily.

In 1999 Major League Baseball created the Hank Aaron Award in commemoration of the twenty-fifth anniversary of Aaron's breaking Babe Ruth's home run record. The award is designed to honor the best overall hitter in each league by assessing a certain number of points for each hit, home run, and RBI.

Aaron's brother Tommie played with Hank for seven years on the Braves — three in Milwaukee and four in Atlanta.

Awards/Honors

1957 National League Most Valuable Player
1958 National League Gold Glove Right Fielder
1959 National League Gold Glove Right Fielder
1960 National League Gold Glove Right Fielder
1982 Hall of Fame

Grover Cleveland Alexander

Retired Number: None (Philadelphia Phillies, 2001)
Pitcher
Playing Career: Philadelphia Phillies 1911–17, 1930; Chicago Cubs 1918–26; St. Louis Cardinals 1926–29

Also known as Pete Alexander, Grover was an epileptic and an alcoholic who was nevertheless one of the greatest pitchers in major league history. Born in 1887 in Elba, Nebraska, he was hit in the head by a throw in 1909 while trying to break up a double play in the minor leagues, and ended up unconscious for two days. When he finally awoke, he suffered from double vision for the rest of the year. The following season he was back to normal and won 29 games for the Syracuse Stars of the New York State League, and had his contract purchased by the Philadelphia Phillies in 1911 for a mere $750.

In his first seven seasons with the Phillies, Alexander won at least 20 games six times, and the one time he failed he won 19. He led the National League with 28 wins in 1911, 27 in 1914 (tied with Dick Rudolph of the

Boston Braves), 31 in 1915, 33 in 1916, and 30 in 1917. His league-leading earned run average in 1915 was a microscopic 1.22, and in 1916 was 1.55, also the best in the circuit.

Complete games were the norm rather than the exception for starting pitchers in that era, but even so, Alexander's numbers were stellar. He led the league in that category five of his initial seven years with Philadelphia, and had 438 in his career. He consistently led the league in several other areas as well, including starts, innings pitched, strikeouts (more often than not recording over 200), and shutouts. His 16 shutouts in 1916, in fact, remain the single-season record for a pitcher, and his lifetime total of 90 puts him second on the all-time list.

Throughout his career he struggled with both epilepsy and alcoholism, and his epilepsy was often mistaken for drunkenness. Neither disease seemed to affect him on the mound, however, as he dominated National League hitters year after year with apparent ease. He slowed down only a little when he was traded to the Chicago Cubs in 1918, winning over 20 games with Chicago twice and with the St. Louis Cardinals once. His 27 wins with the Cubs in 1920 led all National League pitchers, as did his 1.72 ERA in 1919 and his 1.91 mark the following year.

His strikeout totals dropped severely, although his 173 led the league in 1920. After that he would never again strike out more than 77 batters in a season, yet he continued to amass victories.

After his stints with the Cubs and the Cardinals, Alexander returned to the Phillies in 1930, but he was 43 years old and his drinking was finally taking its toll. He appeared in only nine games for Philadelphia that year, and his ERA ballooned to 9.14.

His 373 lifetime victories place him in a tie for third place on the all-time list with Christy Mathewson. He totaled 2199 strikeouts, and his career ERA was 2.56.

Grover Cleveland Alexander is one of several players who never wore a uniform number, but who have been honored by their teams in the same way as those who did. The Phillies, in fact, did not adopt numbers until 1932, two years after Alexander left the major leagues for good. In 2001, when the Phillies retired Jim Bunning's number 14, they also placed on the outfield wall two block-like *P*'s that had adorned Phillies' uniforms in the early part of the twentieth century. One was for Alexander, the other for Chuck Klein.

Grover Cleveland Alexander died in St. Paul, Nebraska, in 1950.

Awards/Honors

1938 Hall of Fame

Walter Alston

Retired Number: 24 (Los Angeles Dodgers, 1977)
First Baseman/Manager
Playing Career: St. Louis Cardinals 1936
Managerial Career: Brooklyn Dodgers 1954–57; Los Angeles Dodgers 1958–76

Walter Alston's major league playing career consisted of but a single at-bat. On September 27, 1936, the St. Louis Cardinals called upon him to replace Johnny Mize during a game. Mize had earlier been ejected. In his only at-bat, Alston struck out.

Born in Venice, Ohio, in 1911, the man who would be known as "Smokey" had a rather successful career playing in the minor leagues before becoming a full-time manager. He led the Mid-Atlantic League with 35 home runs in 1936, only his second professional season, the same year he experienced his one and only major league appearance. He would continue in the minor leagues for 11 more seasons, leading the league with 28 home runs in 1940 while with the Portsmouth Cubs of the Piedmont League. He was the player/manager for Portsmouth that year, and led the circuit in both home runs and runs batted in the following two seasons. He became player/manager with the Trenton Packers in the Brooklyn Dodgers' organization in mid–1944, and over the next nine years he gradually moved up through the ranks. By 1949 he was the skipper of the Montreal Royals, the top minor league club in the Brooklyn system, and the team never finished lower than second place during his tenure.

On November 24, 1953, he was offered the helm of the Dodgers by Branch Rickey, and for the next 23 years he was the major league club's field commander.

Alston was a fixture in Brooklyn through 1957, and moved with the Dodgers to Los Angeles in 1958. In his 23 years his teams finished first seven times and finished second another eight. On only four occasions did they finish lower than fourth place.

In 1954, his first year at the helm, his squad finished second, and the following year they captured the National League pennant and then defeated the New York Yankees, four games to three, in the World Series. They repeated their league championship in 1956, but this time the Yankees captured the series by an identical 4–3 margin.

After a disturbing seventh-place finish in 1958, the team's first year in Los Angeles, Alston's Dodgers came back to capture the flag again in 1959, and this time they defeated the Chicago White Sox in the World

Series, four games to two. The Associated Press named Alston its National League Manager of the Year. The Dodgers finished four games behind the Cincinnati Reds in 1961, then tied the San Francisco Giants in the standings in 1962 and forced a best-of-three playoff series. The Giants took that series two games to one, but the Dodgers came back to capture the pennant in 1963 and then swept the Yankees in the World Series.

The club fell to sixth in 1964, but rebounded with consecutive pennants the next two seasons, winning the 1965 World Series in seven games over the Minnesota Twins, but being swept by the Baltimore Orioles in 1966. The AP named Alston its NL Manager of the Year both seasons. Over the next 11 years Alston's team finished second five times, but won only one more pennant, in 1974, defeating the Pittsburgh Pirates three games to one in the League Championship Series, but losing the World Series to the Oakland Athletics in five games. The AP once again named Walter the NL Manager of the Year.

Alston won 2040 games as a manager throughout his major league career against 1613 losses, for an impressive .558 winning percentage. In total his teams won seven pennants and four World Championships, including Brooklyn's only title in 1955.

Alston retired at the end of the 1976 season. He had worn number 21 in his single game with the Cardinals, but bore 24 during his entire tenure with the Dodgers. The Dodgers retired that number the year following his retirement. Alston died in Oxford, Ohio, in 1984.

Awards/Honors

1959 National League Manager of the Year (AP)
1965 National League Manager of the Year (AP)
1966 National League Manager of the Year (AP)
1974 National League Manager of the Year (AP)
1983 Hall of Fame

Luis Aparicio

Retired Number: 11 (Chicago White Sox, 1984)
Shortstop
Playing Career: Chicago White Sox 1956–62, 1968–70; Baltimore Orioles 1963–67; Boston Red Sox 1971–73

A native Venezuelan, Luis Aparicio played only two seasons in the minor leagues before being called up to the Chicago White Sox in 1956 at the age of 21. Nicknamed "Little Looie," he followed in his father's footsteps by playing shortstop in the Venezuelan League, and with the Chisox he quickly became known as one of the best-fielding shortstops of all time.

During the 1956 season Aparicio batted .266 and led the American League by stealing 21 bases, and his play earned him the league's Rookie of the Year Award. He revived the stolen base as a true offensive weapon in the circuit, leading the league in that category every one of his first nine seasons. He topped 50 steals four times during that period, his high mark being 57 in 1964 with the Baltimore Orioles, and when he retired he had accumulated 506 lifetime.

Aparicio hit .300 only once in his career, batting .313 in 1970 during his second stint with the White Sox. His lifetime average was an unspectacular but respectable .262, but it was not his bat for which he was most famous. It was his speed on the bases and his truly awesome glovework, coupled with a powerful arm, that garnered him the honors that were his due.

Luis won nine Gold Gloves during his career, capturing five in a row from 1958–62. He led all American League shortstops eight consecutive years in fielding percentage, seven times in assists, four times in putouts, twice in total chances per game, and twice in double plays. With Nellie Fox, who manned second base, he helped form one of the most deadly defensive combinations up the middle in major league history.

When the White Sox hired a new general manager in 1963, Aparicio was dealt to the Orioles along with Al Smith for Hoyt Wilhelm, Pete Ward, Ron Hansen, and Dave Nicholson. He spent five years with Baltimore, continuing to lead the league in stolen bases his first two seasons there and winning two more Gold Gloves.

In 1967 the White Sox brought him back, sending Don Buford, Bruce Howard, and Roger Nelson to the Orioles in exchange for Aparicio, Russ Snyder, and John Matias. He spent an additional three seasons in Chicago, and his season batting average climbed each year, from .264 to .280 to his personal best of .313. His speed had begun to wane, however, and he stole but eight bases in 146 games in 1970. He won his last Gold Glove during that 1970 campaign, and after that season the White Sox dealt him to the Boston Red Sox, where he played three more seasons before retiring.

In 18 major league seasons encompassing 2599 games, Aparicio never played a single inning at any position other than shortstop. In fact, he holds the all-time record for most games played at shortstop with 2581 (games during which he pinch hit or pinch ran are not counted), as well as American League records for assists with 8016, total chances with 12,564, and putouts with 4548. He participated in two World Series: His 1959

White Sox lost to the Los Angeles Dodgers, four games to two, a Series during which Aparicio batted .308, and his 1966 Orioles defeated those same Dodgers, four games to none.

Aparicio wore number 11 throughout his career, with all three teams with whom he played, and the White Sox retired it in 1984, the same year he was inducted into the Hall of Fame.

Awards/Honors

1956 American League Rookie of the Year
1958 American League Gold Glove Shortstop
1959 American League Gold Glove Shortstop
1960 American League Gold Glove Shortstop
1961 American League Gold Glove Shortstop
1962 American League Gold Glove Shortstop
1964 American League Gold Glove Shortstop
1966 American League Gold Glove Shortstop
1968 American League Gold Glove Shortstop
1970 American League Gold Glove Shortstop
1984 Hall of Fame

Luke Appling

Retired Number: 4 (Chicago White Sox, 1975)
Shortstop/Third Baseman/Coach/Manager
Playing Career: Chicago White Sox 1930–43, 1945–50
Coaching Career: Detroit Tigers 1960; Cleveland Indians 1960–61; Baltimore Orioles 1963; Kansas City Athletics 1964–67; Chicago White Sox 1970–71
Managerial Career: Kansas City Athletics 1967

Luke Appling was nicknamed "Old Aches and Pains" because of his penchant for complaining about various ailments, whether real or imagined. He did suffer some broken bones that were very real, but he was also one of the best hitters in Chicago White Sox history.

Born in High Point, North Carolina, in 1907, Appling broke in with Chicago in 1930. He played in only six games because of a broken finger, but he hit .308, and by 1932 he had established himself as the club's regular shortstop and had embarked on a solid 20-year career, all of which was with the White Sox.

During those 20 years, he hit over .300 a total of 16 times. He batted .322 in 1933, and his average would not fall under .300 until 1942, when he hit .262.

In 1936 he won the American League batting title with a .388 average, his personal best. He became the first White Sox player ever to lead the league in batting average, and amassed 204 hits along the way. In 1943 he won the title again, this time hitting .328, and he would not again fail to bat at least .301 until his final season of 1950.

He missed the entire 1944 season and most of 1945 because he was serving in the Army. He returned to play but 18 games in 1945, but his bat had not missed a beat, as he hit .362 during his limited playing time.

From 1946–49 he was his usual self at the plate, finishing with averages of .309, .306, .314, and .301. In 1950, at the age of 42, he appeared in only 50 games, and his average dropped to .234. He then retired as a player for good.

Appling's fielding was atrocious at first and adequate later; he was known primarily for his offense. He did, however, set major league records for games played and double plays turned by a shortstop, as well as American League records for putouts and assists by a shortstop. All of those records were eventually broken by Luis Aparicio, who, ironically, played most of his career with the White Sox as well. Appling retired with a lifetime .310 batting average and 2749 hits.

When Appling retired as a player he became a minor league manager, winning a pennant with the Memphis Chicks of the Southern Association in 1953. He became a coach for the Detroit Tigers in 1960 and for the Cleveland Indians in 1960 and '61, then managed the Indianapolis Indians of the American Association in 1962 and won the pennant there. He became a coach with the Baltimore Orioles in 1963 and the Kansas City Athletics in 1964, and was elected to the Hall of Fame that same year. He continued as a coach in Kansas City until 1967, and temporarily replaced Alvin Dark as manager there during the 1967 campaign. His managerial record was a less-than-impressive 10–30, although the club had been foundering long before he took the reins.

He returned to the White Sox as a coach from 1970–71, then retired from baseball for good. He had never been a power hitter, slugging but 45 home runs in his 20-year playing career, but in 1982, at the age of 75, he connected for a long one off Warren Spahn in Washington, D.C. at an old-timers' game.

When Appling debuted in 1930 the White Sox did not wear uniform numbers. When the club adopted them in 1931, Luke first wore number 5, then switched to number 8 the following year. He did not don his familiar number 4 until 1933, and he then wore it for the rest of his career. As a coach and manager he wore various numbers with other clubs, but he was once again given number 4 when he returned to Chicago in 1970. The White Sox retired the number for him in 1975.

Appling died in Cumming, Georgia, in 1991.

Awards/Honors

1964 Hall of Fame

Richie Ashburn

Retired Number: 1 (Philadelphia Phillies, 1979)
Outfielder
Playing Career: Philadelphia Phillies 1948–59; Chicago Cubs 1960–61; New York Mets 1962

Richie Ashburn was a farm boy from Tilden, Nebraska, who broke in with the Philadelphia Phillies in 1948. He was only 21 years old when he made his debut, and he immediately made an impression. In 117 games he batted .333 and led the National League with 32 stolen bases during his rookie season. He was the only rookie on the National League All-Star team.

The consummate leadoff hitter, "Whitey," as he came to be known, hit over .300 nine times in his 15-year career. In 1949, his second season, he hit .284, and with the 1950 Whiz Kids, his 14 triples paced the circuit, although he batted only .176 in the World Series as the Phillies were swept by the New York Yankees.

In 1951 Ashburn's 221 hits led the league as he batted .344, and he led again with 205 hits in 1953. He also had an excellent eye at the plate, as evidenced by his league-leading 125 walks in 1954. The following year he won the first of two batting titles with a .338 average, and in 1957 tied for the league lead with Johnny Temple of the Cincinnati Redlegs with 94 walks.

His best season was 1958, when he won his second batting title with a .350 batting average and also led the league with 215 hits, 13 triples, and 97 walks. He spent only one more season in Philadelphia, however, as the Phillies traded him to the Chicago Cubs prior to the 1960 campaign.

Ashburn spent two seasons in Chicago, hitting .291 in 1960 and leading the league with 116 walks. In 1961 his average dropped significantly, and the Cubs sold him to the expansion New York Mets for 1962.

Richie hit .306 in his only season with New York, which was also his last year as an active player. He was the only All-Star that year for a club that finished a dismal last with an incredible 120 losses against but 40 wins.

Ashburn retired with a lifetime .308 batting average; he had been the prototypical singles hitter, as singles accounted for fully 86 percent of all of his hits. Those hits totaled 2574, and he had also accumulated 1198 walks and scored 1322 runs.

In addition to his impressive offensive statistics, Ashburn was solid defensively as a center fielder. He set major league records by leading the league in chances nine times, garnering 500 or more putouts in a season four times, and collecting 400 or more putouts in a season nine times. His better-than-average speed allowed him to get to balls many center fielders would have been unable to track down.

When he retired from the Mets following the 1962 season, the Phillies immediately called and offered him a job as a broadcaster. Ashburn accepted, and for the next 35 years he worked as a color commentator on both television and radio. He spent many of them beside the legendary Harry Kalas, and was well known for his wit and his dry brand of humor.

The Phillies retired his number 1 in 1979, although Richie was not inducted into the Hall of Fame until 1995.

Ashburn died of a heart attack in a hotel in 1997 at the age of 70. Only hours before, he had broadcast a game between the Phillies and the Mets.

Awards/Honors

1995 Hall of Fame

Gene Autry

Retired Number: 26 (Anaheim Angels, 1982)
Owner
Team Ownership: Los Angeles Angels 1961–64; California Angels 1965–98

Orvon Gene Autry was born in Tioga, Texas, on September 29, 1907, although he always called Oklahoma his home. The eventual owner of the Los Angeles/California Angels, Autry is one of three men to have a major league uniform number retired without having actually worn a uniform.

Autry is famous for a singing and acting career, a career that, according to legend, began in 1926 when he worked as a telegraph operator. The story goes that he was strumming his guitar and singing in order to pass the time at his job, when a man came in intending to send a telegram. The stranger heard Autry singing and asked him to continue. The man turned out to be Will Rogers, and Rogers advised Gene to try a career in radio.

Autry took Will Rogers' advice and ended up in Tulsa two years later performing as Oklahoma's Yodeling Cowboy on radio station KVOO. In 1929 he made his first recording for Victor Records and signed a recording contract with American Record Corporation, a division of Columbia Records.

Autry's first hit, "That Silver-Haired Daddy of Mine," came in 1932. He received the first of over a dozen gold records for that song in 1933, and the following year he went to Hollywood and made his film debut in *In Old Santa Fe*. His first starring role was in *The Phantom Empire* in 1935, a science fiction Western serial.

In 1940 he began performing on a radio show called *The Melody Ranch*, and was heard weekly over the CBS Radio Network until 1956. In 1943 he recorded "There's a Star Spangled Banner Waving Somewhere," "Home on the Range," and "When the Lights Go On Again" for the War Department. He enlisted for World War II service on the air, and from 1943–45 he flew cargo planes in China, Burma, and India. After the war he toured with a USO troupe in the South Pacific before resuming his movie career in 1946.

Many of his movies were based upon his hit songs, including *South of the Border* and *Mexicali Rose* in 1939, *Back in the Saddle* in 1941, *The Last Round-Up* in 1947 (which was also the first film made under Gene Autry Productions), and *Strawberry Roan* in 1948. He recorded "Here Comes Santa Claus" in 1947, and his 1949 hit "Rudolph the Red-Nosed Reindeer" was the first record ever to go platinum.

Autry made his television debut in 1950 on CBS with *The Gene Autry Show*, and also produced other series such as *Annie Oakley*, *The Range Rider*, *Buffalo Bill Jr.*, and *The Adventures of Champion*. He made his last feature film, *Last of the Pony Riders*, in 1953, but continued with *The Gene Autry Show* until 1955. He made his last record in 1964 and then retired from show business, although he would return with his old sidekick Pat Buttram in 1987 to host The Nashville Network's *Melody Ranch Theatre*, which featured 65 of his old Western films.

In his career in entertainment Autry appeared in 93 feature films and made 635 recordings. He wrote or co-wrote over three hundred of those songs himself. He was inducted into the Country Music Hall of Fame in 1969, and was later inducted into the Nashville Songwriters' Hall of Fame, the National Cowboy Hall of Fame, and the National Association of Broadcasters Hall of Fame. He is the only entertainer to have five stars on the

Hollywood Walk of Fame, boasting one each for motion pictures, radio, music recording, television, and live theater. In 1988 he opened the Autry Museum of Western Heritage in Los Angeles.

Autry had a great love of baseball, and in 1960 a group headed by Autry and by former football star Bob Reynolds was awarded an expansion franchise in the American League. In 1961 the Los Angeles Angels took the field for the first time. The team was renamed the California Angels in 1965 in an effort to attract a wider fan base and in anticipation of the club's eventual move to Anaheim. The Walt Disney Company purchased 25 percent of the team and management control in 1996. In 1997, the team was renamed the Anaheim Angels.

A major league baseball roster consists of 25 players, and as owner, Autry was seen as the 26th man who made the team a success. The Angels therefore retired uniform number 26 in his honor in 1982.

One of Autry's greatest desires had been to see his Angels make it to the World Series, but unfortunately that dream was never realized. The team advanced to the American League Championship Series three times under Gene's ownership but could not win the pennant, losing to the Baltimore Orioles in 1979, three games to one, to the Milwaukee Brewers in 1982, three games to two, and to the Boston Red Sox in 1986, four games to three. Autry died in Studio City, California, in 1998; the Angels finally made their first World Series appearance — and won the World Championship — in 2002.

Earl Averill

Retired Number: 3 (Cleveland Indians, 1975)
Outfielder
Playing Career: Cleveland Indians 1929–39; Detroit Tigers 1939–40; Boston Braves 1941

Howard Earl Averill was born in Snohomish, Washington, in 1902, and eventually became known as the "Earl of Snohomish." He played most of a 13-year career with a mediocre Cleveland Indians' team and thus received little recognition, except perhaps for the fact that he was named to each of the first six All-Star Games (1933–38).

Averill's debut came in 1929, and he batted a more-than-solid .331 with 199 hits. He would, in fact, hit over .300 each of his first six seasons, and would do so eight times total in his career. In 1931 he collected 209 hits and belted 32 home runs with 143 runs batted in; the next year he again hit 32 homers, and he finished in the top five in that category four times throughout the decade. In 1936 he hit .378, his career high, and he led the league that year with 232 hits while tying for the league lead with 15 triples and slugging 28 home runs.

He batted .330 in 1938, and that year the team celebrated "Earl Averill Day" and presented him with a new Cadillac among other gifts. In 1939, however, after he had played only 24 games, the Indians traded him to the Detroit Tigers for pitcher Harry Eisenstat and cash. Averill was hitting .273 at the time, and he would hit only .262 in 87 games for the Tigers the rest of the season, finishing with a collective mark of .264, while Eisenstat would go only 6–7 for the Indians with a composite earned run average of 4.12.

Averill was relegated to part-time duty in Detroit in 1940 with the American League champions, but he did bat .280 in 64 games. He pinch hit three times in the World Series that season as the Tigers lost in seven games to the Cincinnati Reds, but he did not collect a hit. Averill signed with the Boston Braves in 1941, but he appeared in only eight games and was batting a minuscule .118 when he retired.

He finished his career with an impressive .318 lifetime batting average, having accumulated 2020 hits in 13 years. At the time of his retirement he led the Indians in lifetime runs scored, triples, home runs, RBIs, total bases, extra-base hits, and slugging percentage. He was the first Indian to amass a thousand RBIs, although many of his records have since been broken.

The Indians did not yet wear uniform numbers when Averill first made his debut, but when the club adopted them in 1931, Earl was given number 3 and continued to wear that number throughout his career with the Tribe. He wore the same number with the Braves, but wore number 24 with the Tigers in 1939 and number 27 with them in 1940.

The Indians retired his number 3 in 1975, the same year he was inducted into the Hall of Fame.

Averill's son, Earl Douglas Averill, had a seven-year major league career with the Indians, Chicago Cubs, Chicago White Sox, Los Angeles Angels, and Philadelphia Phillies.

Averill died in Everett, Washington, on August 16, 1983.

Awards/Honors

1975 Hall of Fame

Harold Baines

Retired Number: 3 (Chicago White Sox, 1989)
Outfielder/Designated Hitter

Playing Career: Chicago White Sox 1980–89, 1996–97, 2000–01; Texas Rangers 1989–90; Oakland Athletics 1990–92; Baltimore Orioles 1993–95, 1997–99, 2000; Cleveland Indians 1999

It is perhaps no wonder that Little League baseball is becoming more and more of a media event, considering the fact that Harold Baines was discovered that way by Chicago White Sox' owner Bill Veeck. Impressed by the youngster's ability when Baines was but 12 years of age, Veeck kept an eye on his career and made him Chicago's first pick in the 1977 June draft.

Baines was born in Easton, Maryland, in 1959, and was a mere 20 years old when he made his debut for the White Sox in 1980. He hit only .255 that first year, but showed some potential by hitting 13 home runs. In 1981 he appeared in only 82 games, but he began to hit his stride in 1982, slugging 25 home runs with 105 runs batted in while batting a respectable .271.

Baines followed that season with another like it, hitting at a .280 clip in 1983 while connecting for 20 home runs and driving in 99. The White Sox made it to the American League Championship Series that year, although they lost to the Baltimore Orioles and Baines batted a mere .125 in the postseason.

In 1984 he hit .304 and led the American League with a .541 slugging percentage. His 29 home runs were the most of his career, and he drove in 94. On May 9 of that year, he participated in the longest game by time in major league history, and the longest by innings in American League history. The game, which pitted the White Sox against the Milwaukee Brewers, went on for eight hours and six minutes, and its 25 innings were only one short of the major league record. Harold's home run in the twenty-fifth inning proved to be the deciding factor as the White Sox defeated the Brewers, 4–3.

In 1986 Baines suffered a knee injury that would affect him the rest of his career, although he still appeared in 145 games and batted .296 with 21 homers and 88 RBIs.

It was at that point that he became more of a designated hitter than an outfielder, and his knee problems seemed to have no effect on his performance at the plate. He hit .293 in 1987, belting 20 homers and driving in 93 runs, and in 1989 he was batting .321 when the White Sox traded him to the Texas Rangers for Scott Fletcher, Wilson Alvarez, and Sammy Sosa.

The White Sox did a rather odd thing later that year. When the Rangers came to town to play the Chisox on August 20, the Sox honored

Baines by retiring the number 3 he had worn during his 10 years with the team ... even though he was still an active player.

Baines became something of a journeyman for the rest of his career, although he would continue to produce and would last another 12 seasons. In 1990 the Rangers traded him to the Oakland Athletics late in the season, and that move got him into the postseason. He hit .357 in Oakland's sweep of the Boston Red Sox in the American League Championship Series, but faltered as the A's were in turn swept by the Cincinnati Reds in the World Series.

The A's went to the playoffs in 1992, and Baines ripped Toronto pitching at a .440 clip although the Blue Jays defeated Oakland in six games.

The Athletics traded Baines to the Baltimore Orioles prior to the 1993 season, and Harold responded by hitting .313 for the O's with 20 home runs. He clubbed 24 homers in 1995, then he became a free agent and was signed by none other than the Chicago White Sox.

Bringing his own number out of retirement in 1996, Baines hit .311 with 22 home runs, and was hitting .305 in 1997 when the White Sox traded him back to the Orioles. He stung the ball at a .400 clip in the American League Division Series against the Seattle Mariners, and hit .353 in the battle for the pennant as the O's lost to the Cleveland Indians.

In 1998 the Orioles traded him to the Indians. That guaranteed yet another postseason appearance, in which the Tribe lost the American League Division Series to the Boston Red Sox despite Baines' .357 batting average.

Following the 1999 season, Baines signed with the Orioles as a free agent, his third stint with that club. In July of 2000, the O's traded him back to the White Sox. In his third go-round with Chicago — during which he once again brought his own number out of retirement — Baines appeared in a mere 24 games for the remainder of the 2000 season. He did play in the American League Division Series, which the Sox lost to the Mariners, then batted only .131 in 32 games in 2001.

In his career Baines played in 2830 games, finishing with a lifetime batting average of .289 with 384 lifetime home runs and 1628 career RBIs. He hit a cumulative .324 in postseason play.

Ernie Banks

Retired Number: 14 (Chicago Cubs, 1982)
Shortstop/First Baseman/Coach
Playing Career: Chicago Cubs 1953–71
Coaching Career: Chicago Cubs 1967–69, 1972–73

Known affectionately as "Mr. Cub," Ernie Banks played his entire career with Chicago's National League entry and became the first Cub to have his uniform number retired. He was also the first black player to join the club.

Born in 1931 in Dallas, Texas, Ernie was destined for greatness from the age of 17, when he began to play baseball for a Negro League barnstorming team for $15 a game. In 1950 Cool Papa Bell signed him to play for the Kansas City Monarchs of the Negro American League, a team that won the Western Division title and had the best overall record in the league. He spent 1951 and 1952 in the Army, then returned to the Monarchs in 1953.

The Cubs signed him at the end of that season, and he appeared in 10 games for Chicago, debuting at shortstop and hitting .314. As the Cubs' regular shortstop the following year he hit 19 home runs, then exploded in 1955, crushing 44 home runs with 117 runs batted in. Those 44 homers were the most ever hit by a shortstop in a season up to that time. Two years later he clubbed 43 roundtrippers and knocked in 102 runs, then in 1958 put together the first of two consecutive Most Valuable Player seasons.

Banks led the league with 47 home runs and 129 RBIs during that campaign, while also pacing the circuit with a .614 slugging average. He hit .313 and scored a career-high 119 runs in the process. In 1959 he continued his torrid hitting, batting .304, belting 45 home runs, and once again leading the National League with 143 RBIs. In 1960 his 41 home runs led the league, and that would be the fifth and last time he would hit at least 40 in a season. He also proved himself to be no slouch in the field that season, winning the league's Gold Glove award at his shortstop position.

Between 1955 and 1960 Banks hit more home runs than anyone in the major leagues. Following the 1961 season he switched from shortstop to first base because injuries to his legs had begun to affect his range. His production at the plate continued, however, as he whacked 29 home runs in 1961 and another 37 in 1962 with 104 RBIs.

By the time he retired in 1971 he had amassed 512 home runs, 1636 RBIs, 407 doubles, 90 triples, and a .274 lifetime batting average.

Banks played his entire career with the Cubs, three of them — 1967–69 — as a player/coach. He returned as a coach from 1972–73. His love for the game is evidenced by the phrase that has made him as much a legend as his incredible offensive feats: "Let's play two!"

Ernie was inducted into the Hall of Fame in 1977. He had worn number 14 throughout his career, and the Cubs retired the number in 1982.

Awards/Honors

1958 National League Most Valuable Player
1959 National League Most Valuable Player
1960 National League Gold Glove Shortstop
1977 Hall of Fame

Carl Barger

Retired Number: 5 (Florida Marlins, 1993)
President
Team President: Pittsburgh Pirates 1987–91; Florida Marlins 1991–92

Carl Barger is one of three men to have a major league uniform number retired without having actually worn a uniform.

As an athlete Barger played basketball with Shippensburg University in Pennsylvania from 1949–52. The university considered his to be one of their eight greatest success stories.

Barger ran a successful law firm in Pittsburgh, and when the Pirates went up for sale in the late 1980s he made an offer of free legal counsel to anyone who would buy the team and keep it in Pittsburgh. In 1987, he was named president of the team.

Carl's close friend was Wayne Huizenga, and when Major League Baseball announced plans to expand by 1993, Barger encouraged Huizenga to pursue a franchise for Miami. Huizenga followed Carl's advice and began to aggressively pursue a team for South Florida, and on June 10, 1991, Major League Baseball granted him the franchise.

Huizenga chose the name Florida Marlins for his team because of his great love of fishing, and he also followed a tradition in the area because three previous minor league teams had been called the Miami Marlins. Huizenga hired Barger away from the Pirates to be the Marlins' first team president.

Barger was charged with overseeing the search for a general manager, as well as with building the club's minor league system and participating in the major league expansion draft on November 17, 1992. Carl's choice for the very first Marlins player was Nigel Wilson, whom he selected from the Toronto Blue Jays.

Barger pursued his responsibilities with a passion, and even named the team's mascot Billy the Marlin after his brother. He had an almost fanatic love of baseball, and the Marlins were a dream come true for him.

On December 9, 1992, four months before the team's inaugural Opening Day, Barger was attending an owners' meeting when he collapsed and died of a ruptured aneurysm. The team he had built so lovingly would see its first light without him.

To honor Barger, the Marlins created the Carl Barger Player Development Person of the Year Award, which is given to the individual who most makes an impact on nurturing the franchise's young talent in a given year. They also named the Carl Barger Baseball Complex after him, a facility that is located in Melbourne, Florida, approximately three hundred yards from Space Coast Stadium.

Barger's favorite player had been Joe DiMaggio of the New York Yankees. Since DiMaggio had worn uniform number 5, the Marlins also honored their first president by retiring that same number in his name during their inaugural 1993 season.

Huizenga eventually sold the Marlins to John Henry in 1998. Many speculate that, if Barger had still been alive, Huizenga would not have sold the team.

Al Barlick

Retired Number: 3 (National League Umpires)
Umpire
Umpiring Career: National League 1940–43, 1946–55, 1958–71

Many people never notice that umpires wear numbers on their sleeves. Umpires do wear numbers, and, like ballplayers, they can be honored by having those numbers retired.

Al Barlick is one of six umpires to receive such an accolade. Born April 2, 1915, in Springfield, Illinois, he was a coal miner who started umpiring sandlot games at a dollar a game during a miners' strike. In 1936 he became a professional umpire in the Northeast Arkansas League, and moved to the Piedmont League later that same year. In 1938 he joined the Eastern League, then was promoted to the International League in 1939.

Toward the end of the 1940 season, Barlick was elevated to the National League, having climbed from what was then Class D to the major leagues within a five-year period. In 1940 he was 25 years of age and thus became one of the youngest umpires ever to reach the majors.

Barlick served in the Coast Guard during World War II. Returning to the National League in 1946, he eventually worked in a record seven All-Star Games. He was the first base umpire when Jackie Robinson played his first game for the Brooklyn Dodgers, and was behind the plate when Enos Slaughter scored from first base later that same year to win the 1946 World Series for the St. Louis Cardinals against the Boston Red Sox. He was the home plate umpire during the 1970 All-Star Game in Cincinnati when Pete Rose bowled over Ray Fosse to win the game for the National League.

Barlick also worked seven World Series, and throughout his career he was greatly respected by players and fellow umpires alike. He had a grandiose style, making his calls loudly and using clear and emphatic hand signals that left no doubt as to his judgment on plays. He was known for his consistent and fair calling of balls and strikes, as well as for his ability to defuse potentially explosive situations.

After his retirement from umpiring in 1971, he became a consultant for the National League, and he was elected to the Hall of Fame by the Veterans Committee in 1989.

His number 3 was eventually retired by the National League office along with the numbers of Bill Klem and Jocko Conlan. The number came back into use, however, when the National League and American League offices were shut down and the umpires from those leagues came under the joint aegis of Major League Baseball in 2000.

Barlick died in Springfield on December 27, 1995.

Awards/Honors

1989 Hall of Fame

Johnny Bench

Retired Number: 5 (Cincinnati Reds, 1984)
Catcher/First Baseman/Third Baseman
Playing Career: Cincinnati Reds 1967–83

Many consider Johnny Bench to have been the best catcher of all time. Of the few who do not, the vast majority would consider him to have been in at least the top two or three.

Born in Oklahoma City, Oklahoma, on December 7, 1947, Bench dreamed of being a major league baseball player from a young age. His father reasoned that catching was the most direct path to that goal, and he turned out to be prophetic. In high school Johnny won all-state honors, and after playing for Peninsula in 1966 and Buffalo for most of 1967, he made his debut with the Cincinnati Reds in August of '67. He played in only 26 games for Cincinnati that year and had a rather inauspicious start, batting only .163 with but a single home run, but the Reds recognized his potential and kept him around for the entire 1968 season, making him their regular catcher.

Bench responded with a .275 average and 15 home runs, setting a record for catchers by hitting 40 doubles and winning the National League Rookie of the Year Award. In 1969 he proved that his rookie season had been no fluke, as he raised his average to .293 and belted 26 home runs with 90 runs batted in.

In 1970 he duplicated his .293 average of the previous season, but also led the league with 45 home runs and 148 RBIs, adding 35 doubles to the mix. His performance was good enough to win him the league's Most Valuable Player Award. In the National League Championship Series he hit a home run as the Reds defeated the Pittsburgh Pirates, then in the World Series, which the Reds lost to the Baltimore Orioles, he hit another.

In 1972 Bench led the league with 40 home runs and 125 RBIs. The Reds defeated the Pirates again for the National League pennant, and Bench contributed a .333 average, while also adding a homer in Cincinnati's seven-game loss to the Oakland Athletics in the World Series. Once again, Johnny earned MVP honors.

He would never again hit 40 home runs, but his numbers stayed above 20 for the next eight seasons except for 1976, when he hit 16. He had 104 RBIs in 1973, 129 in 1974 to lead the National League, 110 in 1975, and 109 in 1977. He had a .333 average in the LCS in 1976 against the Philadelphia Phillies, and pounded the New York Yankees to the tune of a .533 average with two home runs and six RBIs in the World Series.

In his 17 years with the Reds, Bench hit .267 with 389 lifetime home runs and 1376 career RBIs. He was one of the most vital cogs in the Big Red Machine that, throughout the 1970s, won six division titles, four pennants, and two consecutive World Championships. He was known as much for his defense as for his offense, displaying a unique one-handed catching style behind the plate and throwing out would-be basestealers at a prodigious rate. He won 10 consecutive Gold Gloves, and was sometimes called "The Little General" because of his ability to direct fielders on where to play defensively for specific hitters. His calling of pitches was equally astute. He set a record by catching 100 games or more for 13 consecutive years.

Bench tired late in his career and was moved to first base for the 1981 season. He played only 52 games in that strike-shortened year, although he hit .309, and played third base in 1982 and his final year of 1983.

The Reds honored their 12-time All-Star with "Johnny Bench Night" in 1983, and he responded in dramatic fashion by hitting a home run in that game. The Reds retired his number 5 the following year, and Bench was elected to the Hall of Fame in 1989.

Awards/Honors

1968 National League Rookie of the Year
1968 National League Gold Glove Catcher
1969 National League Gold Glove Catcher
1970 National League Most Valuable Player
1970 National League Gold Glove Catcher
1971 National League Gold Glove Catcher
1972 National League Most Valuable Player
1972 National League Gold Glove Catcher
1973 National League Gold Glove Catcher
1974 National League Gold Glove Catcher
1975 National League Gold Glove Catcher
1976 National League Gold Glove Catcher
1977 National League Gold Glove Catcher
1989 Hall of Fame

Yogi Berra

Retired Number: 8 (New York Yankees, 1972)
Catcher/Outfielder/Coach/Manager
Playing Career: New York Yankees 1946–63; New York Mets 1965
Coaching Career: New York Yankees 1963, 1976–83; New York Mets 1965–71; Houston Astros 1986–92
Managerial Career: New York Yankees 1964, 1984–85; New York Mets 1972–75

Lawrence Peter Berra had a long and storied career in major league baseball. Born in St. Louis, Missouri, in 1925, he became as famous for his unique sayings, or "Yogi-isms," as for his success on the playing field.

Berra received his nickname from a childhood friend who thought he resembled a Hindu yogi. In 1942 he was signed by the New York Yankees organization and began his minor league career in Norfolk. When he turned 18 he joined the Navy and served in World War II, participating in the D-Day invasion at Omaha Beach and also spending time in North Africa and Italy. Returning to the United States after the war, he resumed his baseball career and rose rapidly through the minor leagues, debuting with the Yankees in late 1946 and playing seven games with the big club, batting .364.

Berra had originally been an outfielder, but converted to catching and spent the vast majority of his career behind the plate. He hit .305 in 1948, and in 1950 batted .322 with 28 home runs and 124 runs batted in. In 1951 he won the first of three American League Most Valuable Player Awards, batting .294 with 27 homers and 88 RBIs. In 1954 he won his second, contributing a .307 average with 22 homers and 125 knocked in. His third came the following year, when he batted .272 with 27 home runs and 108 RBIs.

In his 19-year career, Berra hit at least 20 home runs 11 times, and hit 19 one other. He collected at least 90 RBIs nine times, and finished his career with a .285 lifetime batting average, 358 home runs, and 1430 RBIs. Oddly, he never led the league in a single major offensive category.

He also played in 14 World Series, however, contributing to 10 championships. When he retired he held the World Series records for most games played with 75, most at-bats with 259, most hits with 71, and most doubles with 10. He also scored 41 runs, drove in 39, hit 12 home runs, and drew 32 walks. His Yankees won World Championships in 1947, 1949–53, 1956, 1958, and 1961–62.

In the 1953 Series he batted .429 against the Brooklyn Dodgers, and hit .417 against them in 1955. In all he hit over .300 in five World Series, and he was the catcher in 1956 when Don Larsen pitched the only perfect game in World Series history against Brooklyn.

Yogi began to play more games in the outfield late in his career, and in 1961 he played 87 at that position and only 15 as a catcher. In 1962 he was relegated even more to part-time duty, playing 31 games as a backstop and 28 in the outfield.

In 1963 Berra served as a player/coach for the Yankees, and in 1964 he retired from playing and was made the team's manager. He guided the team to the American League pennant in 1964 by a single game over the Chicago White Sox, but the club lost a close World Series to the St. Louis Cardinals in seven games. Curiously, the Yankees fired him after that loss.

In 1965 the New York Mets signed him as a player/coach. As a player with the National League team he appeared in only four games and hit .222. He retired once again as a player but continued with the Mets as a full-time coach through the 1971 season. In 1972 the team made him its manager, and he guided them to a third-place finish that year and to the National League pennant in 1973. The Mets lost the World Series to the Oakland Athletics in seven games. During the 1975 season, the Mets fired Yogi, and in 1976 he would return to the Yankees as a coach.

Berra continued his coaching career through the 1983 season, and the following year the Yankees once again appointed him to be their manager. The team finished third that year, and in 1985 they were off to a 6–10 start when the Yankees replaced him with Billy Martin.

Yogi was hired as a coach by the Houston Astros in 1986, and he would remain with them until 1992, when he retired for good.

Berra was noted as a talker behind the plate, and many opposing players complained about his efforts to distract them. He also became famous for his many "Yogi-isms," including such quotes as, "It ain't over 'til it's over," "It's deja vu all over again," "I didn't really say everything I said," "If the people don't want to come out to the ballpark, nobody's going to stop them," and, "When you come to a fork in the road, take it."

When Yogi first joined the Yankees in 1946 he wore number 38, and he switched to number 35 in 1947. He switched to number 8 in 1948 and wore it the rest of his career, not only with the Yankees but with the Mets and Astros as well. Bill Dickey had worn the number before him, and had still been wearing it in 1946, his final year as a player. When Dickey returned to the Yankees as a coach in 1949, he wore number 33 because Berra had taken 8. In 1972, the year Berra was inducted into the Hall of Fame, the Yankees retired number 8 for *both* men, the only team other than the Montreal Expos to retire the same number for two different players.

Yogi's son, Dale Berra, had an 11-year career in the major leagues with the Pittsburgh Pirates, the Yankees, and the Astros.

Awards/Honors

1951 American League Most Valuable Player
1954 American League Most Valuable Player
1955 American League Most Valuable Player
1972 Hall of Fame

Wade Boggs

Retired Number: 12 (Tampa Bay Devil Rays, 2000)
First Baseman/Third Baseman/Coach
Playing Career: Boston Red Sox 1982–92; New York Yankees 1993–97; Tampa Bay Devil Rays 1998–99
Coaching Career: Tampa Bay Devil Rays 2001

Wade Boggs actually played far less of his career with the Tampa Bay Devil Rays than he had with the Boston Red Sox and the New York Yankees, and yet it was the Devil Rays who retired his number.

Born in Omaha, Nebraska, in 1958, Boggs was a perennial hitting machine who, in 18 major league seasons, batted *under* .300 only three times. He broke in with Boston in 1982 as a backup first baseman and third baseman, and when he hit .349 in 104 games, the Red Sox knew they had to make room for him on a more permanent basis. So they traded third baseman Carney Lansford, who had won the American League batting title in 1981, and gave Boggs that position. Wade did not disappoint, winning the 1983 batting title himself with a .361 average and 210 hits. He followed that performance with a .325 average and 203 hits in 1984, then in 1985 won the first of four consecutive batting titles.

In those four years he hit .368, .357, .363, and .366. He led the league in 1985 with 240 hits, in 1986 with 105 walks, and in 1988 with 45 doubles, 128 runs scored, and 125 walks. He made it to the World Series for the first time in 1986, but the Red Sox lost in seven games to the New York Mets. In 1987 he hit 24 home runs, the only time he would hit more than 11 in a season.

In 1989 he batted .330, led the American League once again with 51 doubles, and tied with Rickey Henderson with 113 runs scored. From 1983 through 1988 he became the first major leaguer to collect at least 200 hits in six consecutive seasons, and he followed that with a seventh in 1989 when he garnered 205.

In 1992 his average inexplicably fell to .259 as the Red Sox finished in last place for the first time since 1939.

Boggs signed with the Yankees in 1993 and rebounded with a .302 average. In 1994 and 1995 he batted .342 and .324, respectively, and also proved his adeptness as a fielder by winning back-to-back Gold Gloves at third base. In his second World Series in 1996 he helped the Yankees defeat the Atlanta Braves, four games to two. In 1997, his last season in New York, he also pitched one inning, walking a batter and striking out one while not giving up a hit or a run.

At the age of 39 he signed with the Tampa Bay Devil Rays for the 1998 season, and his average declined to .280. He hoped to reach the 3000-hit plateau, however, and was 78 hits shy at the conclusion of that campaign. He played his final season in 1999 for Tampa Bay and collected hit number 3000 on August 7, the day after Tony Gwynn had reached the same milestone with the San Diego Padres. Boggs' 3000th hit was a rare home run, which he hit off Chris Haney of the Cleveland Indians in the sixth inning. He also pitched for the second time in his career that season, totaling an inning and a third and surrendering three hits and one run, which was earned, while also striking out a batter.

Wade retired with a .328 lifetime batting average, 3010 hits, and 1014 RBIs. He briefly became a coach for the Devil Rays in 2001.

Boggs had worn number 26 throughout his career with the Red Sox, and wore number 12 only in his five years with the Yankees and his two with the Devil Rays. The Devil Rays retired the number in his honor when they opened the 2000 season.

Awards/Honors

1994 American League Gold Glove Third Baseman
1995 American League Gold Glove Third Baseman

Lou Boudreau

Retired Number: 5 (Cleveland Indians, 1970)
Third Baseman/Shortstop/Manager
Playing Career: Cleveland Indians 1938–50; Boston Red Sox 1951–52
Managerial Career: Cleveland Indians 1942–50; Boston Red Sox 1952–54; Kansas City Athletics 1955–57; Chicago Cubs 1960

Born in 1917 in Harvey, Illinois, Lou Boudreau rose through the minor leagues as a third baseman/catcher. His official major league debut came in 1938 with the Cleveland Indians, but he would play only a single game that year in the big leagues — at third base — and would spend nearly all of the rest of his career as a shortstop.

He became the Indians' regular shortstop in 1940. Only 22 years of age at the beginning of the season, he turned in a solid .295 batting average and, despite hitting only 9 home runs, collected 101 runs batted in.

In 1941 he led the American League with 45 doubles, and the following year the Indians named him their player/manager. Only 24 at the time, he became the youngest person to manage an entire season in major league history.

He continued as player/manager for the Tribe through the 1950 season. Along the way he had a major influence on the game he loved, playing an instrumental role in converting Bob Lemon from a third baseman/outfielder into a pitcher and devising the defensive shift against Ted Williams that was soon put into use around the league.

In 1944 he won the American League batting title with a .327 average, also leading the circuit once again with 45 doubles. He hit .306 in 1945, and in 1947 contributed a .307 average while leading the league for the third time with 45 doubles.

In 1948 he turned in the most impressive season of his career, although, strangely, he did not lead the league in a single category. He did hit an incredible .355 with 34 doubles, 18 home runs (the most of his career) and 106 RBIs. He also scored 116 runs, garnered 199 hits, and walked 98 times, all while striking out on only 9 occasions. His performance was enough to win him the league's Most Valuable Player Award. The Indians tied with the Boston Red Sox in the standings that year, and in a one-game playoff Boudreau slammed two home runs and collected two singles as Cleveland defeated the Red Sox by a score of 8–3. In the World Series the Indians went on to best the Boston Braves, four games to two.

Following the 1950 season Boudreau signed solely as a player with the Boston Red Sox. In 1952 he became the player/manager of the Sox, although he appeared in only four games and did not manage a hit.

He retired as a player but continued as Boston's manager through the 1954 season, although his teams never finished higher than fourth. In 1955 he became the manager of the Kansas City Athletics, and those squads fared even worse, finishing sixth and eighth and being mired in eighth place in 1958 when Boudreau was replaced by Harry Craft. He piloted one final season in 1960 with the Chicago Cubs, managing only a seventh-place finish, then he became a broadcaster in Chicago.

The Indians retired his number in 1970, the same year he was inducted into the Hall of Fame, and the city renamed the street outside the club's ballpark Boudreau Boulevard.

Awards/Honors

1948 American League Most Valuable Player
1970 Hall of Fame

Ken Boyer

Retired Number: 14 (St. Louis Cardinals, 1984)
Third Baseman/Outfielder/First Baseman/Coach/Manager
Playing Career: St. Louis Cardinals 1955–65; New York Mets 1966–67; Chicago White Sox 1967–68; Los Angeles Dodgers 1968–69
Coaching Career: St. Louis Cardinals 1971–72
Managerial Career: St. Louis Cardinals 1978–80

One of three Boyer brothers to play in the major leagues (the others were Cloyd and Clete), Ken Boyer was born in Liberty, Missouri, in 1931. He was a third baseman who played most of one season in center field, and who was switched to first base for the very few games he played at the end of his career.

Boyer was a perennial high-average hitter with good power. Debuting with St. Louis in 1955, he contributed a .264 average with 18 home runs, then increased his output to the tune of .306, 26 home runs, and 98 runs batted in the following season. In 1957 he was moved to center field and did not enjoy his stay there, but he did belt 19 home runs. When the Cardinals obtained center fielder Curt Flood for the 1958 campaign, Boyer was shifted back to the hot corner and would stay there for most of his career.

In 1958 he hit .307 with 23 home runs and 90 RBIs, topping that with a .309 average in 1959 with 28 homers and 94 knocked in. Back at his third base position in '58, he would also win the first of four consecutive and five total Gold Gloves.

His 32 home runs in 1960 were a career high. He also added 97 RBIs, although he would top that total three times in later years. In 1961 he batted a career-high .329, and would hit exactly 24 home runs that year and for the next three after that. His RBI totals, in the meantime, would climb from 95 to 98 to 111 to a career-high and league-leading 119 in 1964. Boyer won the National League Most Valuable Player Award that year, also contributing a .295 average with 24 home runs, 100 runs scored, and 70 walks. He hit for the cycle for the second time (the first was in 1961) and played a major role in the World Series as the Cardinals defeated the New York Yankees in seven games. He hit a grand slam in the fourth game off Al Downing, claiming responsibility for all of the Redbirds' runs in a 4–3 victory, then homered off Steve Hamilton in the seventh game as the Cardinals came out on the top of a 7–5 score to win the World Championship.

The Cardinals traded him to the New York Mets following the 1965 season, and his numbers began to decline. The Mets traded him to the Chicago White Sox in the midst of the 1967 season, then he went from Chicago to the Los Angeles Dodgers early in 1968. After hitting .271 for L.A. in 1968 — and .257 overall — he would play only 25 games for them in 1969 before retiring as a player.

In 1971 he returned to the Cardinals as a coach and stayed with them for two seasons. In early 1978 he was named the team's manager, and although the club finished fifth, he guided them to a third-place finish in 1979. With an 18–33 record in 1980, he was replaced by Whitey Herzog.

Boyer died of lung cancer in 1982. Two years later, the Cardinals retired his number 14 on what would have been his fifty-third birthday.

Awards/Honors

1958 National League Gold Glove Third Baseman
1959 National League Gold Glove Third Baseman
1960 National League Gold Glove Third Baseman
1961 National League Gold Glove Third Baseman
1963 National League Gold Glove Third Baseman
1964 National League Most Valuable Player

Nick Bremigan

Retired Number: 2 (American League Umpires)
Umpire
Umpiring Career: American League 1974–89

Nick Bremigan was one of six major league umpires to have his number retired.

He worked his way up through the Florida State League, the Eastern League, the International League, and even the Florida Winter Instructional League and the Puerto Rican Winter League before reaching the American League in 1974. Thereafter he became one of the most respected umpires in American League history, and was renowned as one of the best rule interpreters in baseball. He authored a system for understanding the basic rules of baseball, and called his system *Rules for Idiots*.

Bremigan umpired two All-Star Games, four American League Championship Series, and the 1980 World Series during his distinguished career. He also became a syndicated columnist on baseball and gave clinics to American armed forces in Spain, England, and Germany.

Tragically, he died of a heart attack on March 28, 1989, while he was still on the umpiring staff of the American League.

The league office eventually retired his number 2, but the number came back into use when the National League and American League offices were shut down and the umpires from those leagues came under the joint aegis of Major League Baseball in 2000.

George Brett

Retired Number: 5 (Kansas City Royals, 1994)
Third Baseman/First Baseman/Designated Hitter
Playing Career: Kansas City Royals 1973–93

George Brett was one of those increasingly rare players who played his entire career with a single team — in his case, a 21-year career.

Born in West Virginia in 1953, Brett made his debut with the Kansas City Royals on August 2, 1973, at a mere 20 years of age. He had hit a solid but unspectacular .281 in over three seasons in the minor leagues, and in 13 games with Kansas City his first year he batted only .125. He hit .282 in 1974, his first full season in the major leagues, and hit only two home runs. In 1975, however, he would begin to show his true colors. That year he batted .308, led the American League with 195 hits, and tied Mickey Rivers for the league lead with 13 triples.

He turned it up a notch in 1976, winning the first of three batting titles with a .333 average and once again leading the league in hits with 215 and in triples with 14. Those kinds of numbers were to become the norm for Brett as he established himself as a true franchise player for Kansas City.

He hit .312 in 1977 and led the league with 45 doubles in 1978. The Royals lost the American League Championship Series for three consecutive seasons — from 1976 through 1978 — but it was no fault of Brett's, as he batted .444, .300, and .389 in those series, respectively.

In 1979 he contributed a .329 average while leading the league with 212 hits and 20 triples. His best season would come in 1980, however, as he flirted with a .400 average the entire year and finished at an incredible .390 to win his second batting crown. He also led the league with a .664 slugging percentage, and belted 24 home runs with 118 runs batted in, winning the American League's Most Valuable Player Award in the process. He hit .375 in the World Series, but the Royals lost to the Philadelphia Phillies in six games.

He hit over .300 during four of the next five seasons, while also leading the circuit in slugging percentage in 1983 and 1985. He won a Gold Glove for his work at third base in '85, having come a long way from the days when he led the California League in errors in only his second professional season. He finally won a World Series ring that year as well, as his Royals won the American League Championship Series in seven games over the Toronto Blue Jays and took the World Championship in another seven over the St. Louis Cardinals. Brett hit .348 with three home runs against Toronto, and contributed a .370 mark against St. Louis.

George won his third batting title in 1990 with a .329 average, becoming the only player to win the crown in three different decades. He also tied for the league lead with Jody Reed of the Boston Red Sox with 45 doubles that year. On September 30, 1992, he collected his 3000th hit off Tim Fortugno of the California Angels at Anaheim Stadium.

Brett retired following the 1993 season, and he stepped down as the only player to collect more than 3000 hits, 300 home runs, 600 doubles, 100 triples, and 200 stolen bases. His lifetime average was .305, and he amassed 3154 hits, 665 doubles, 137 triples, and 201 stolen bases. He had a .373 World Series batting average.

Brett actually wore number 25 during his first two seasons with the Royals, and switched to his famous number 5 in 1975. He wanted the number because he admired Brooks Robinson, who wore the same number with the Baltimore Orioles, and Joe DiMaggio, who had worn it with the New York Yankees. The Royals retired the number the season following his retirement. George was inducted into the Hall of Fame in 1999.

His brother, Ken Brett, had a long career with many teams. With his brother Bobby, George later became one of the owners of the Class A Spokane Indians of the Northwest League.

Awards/Honors

1980 American League Most Valuable Player
1985 American League Gold Glove Third Baseman
1999 Hall of Fame

Lou Brock

Retired Number: 20 (St. Louis Cardinals, 1979)
Outfielder
Playing Career: Chicago Cubs 1961–64; St. Louis Cardinals 1964–79

Louis Clark Brock hailed from El Dorado, Arkansas, where he was born in 1939, and would become one of the most prolific basestealers in baseball history.

Signed out of Southern University by the Chicago Cubs in 1961, Brock appeared in four games for Chicago that year. By 1963 he had become a regular in the Cubs' outfield, although in 1962 and '63 he was mediocre at the plate. He did steal 16 and 24 bases, however. On June 15, the Cubs traded him, along with Jack Spring and Paul Toth, to the St. Louis Cardinals for Ernie Broglio, Bobby Shantz, and Doug Clemens. It would prove to be one of the best deals in Cardinals history.

Brock hit .348 for St. Louis for the rest of that season, finishing up with a cumulative average of .315, and along the way he stole 43 bases. He also batted .300 in the World Series as the Cards bested the New York Yankees in seven games.

He stole 63 more bases in 1965, and in 1966 led the National League for the first of four consecutive times with 74. One of his best seasons was 1967, when he batted .299, led the league with 52 stolen bases, and tied Hank Aaron with 113 runs scored. He also belted 21 home runs and thus became the first player to hit at least 20 homers and steal at least 50 bases in the same season. In the postseason he won his second World Series ring as he hit .414 and swiped seven bases en route to a seven-game Series victory over the Boston Red Sox.

In 1968 he again led the league in stolen bases with 62, and also topped the circuit in doubles with 46 and in triples with 14. He batted

.464 in the World Series and stole another seven bases, although the Redbirds lost this time in seven games to the Detroit Tigers.

He led the league again in 1969 with 53 steals.

Brock batted over .300 for the next three seasons. His 51 steals in 1970 were second to the 57 of Cincinnati's Bobby Tolan, but beginning in 1971 he would again lead the league for four years in a row. He swiped 64 in 1971, while also leading the league with 126 runs scored, stole 63 in 1972, another 70 in 1973, and a then-record 118 in 1974, which shattered Maury Wills' single-season record of 104. He also batted .306 that year, and hit .309 and .301 the next two seasons.

On August 13, 1979, Brock singled off Dennis Lamp of the Cubs for his 3000th career hit. He retired following the 1979 season with a lifetime batting average of .293. His 938 career stolen bases were a record at the time of his retirement, although that record has since been broken by Rickey Henderson. He also accumulated 3023 hits, 486 doubles, 141 triples, and 149 home runs. His .391 World Series average was second all-time (and is now third), his 14 World Series stolen bases tied for first with Eddie Collins.

Brock wore number 24 with the Cubs, but number 20 during his entire career in St. Louis. The Cardinals retired his number 20 in 1979, and he was inducted into the Hall of Fame during his first year of eligibility in 1985.

Awards/Honors

1985 Hall of Fame

Jim Bunning

Retired Number: 14 (Philadelphia Phillies, 2001)
Pitcher
Playing Career: Detroit Tigers 1955–63; Philadelphia Phillies 1964–67, 1970–71; Pittsburgh Pirates 1968–69; Los Angeles Dodgers 1969

A product of Southgate, Kentucky, Jim Bunning was born in 1931 and was a major leaguer by the time he was 23.

He opened a 17-year career in 1955 with the Detroit Tigers, and would actually pitch more years for Detroit than for any of the other three teams with whom he played. He was unimpressive in 1955, but improved the next year. In 1957 he became a 20-game winner for the only time in his career, although he would win 19 on four other occasions. His 20 wins tied for the American League lead with Billy Pierce that year, and his record was 20–8 as he posted an earned run average of 2.69. He also led the league in innings pitched with 267⅓.

In 1958 he pitched a no-hitter for the Tigers, and in 1959 he won 17 games and led the league with 201 strikeouts, a mark he would duplicate in 1960 as he once again topped the circuit. He had an impressive 17–11 record in 1961, then went 19–10 in 1962.

Following the 1963 season the Tigers traded him to the Philadelphia Phillies, and Bunning had a spectacular season in 1964. He finished with a 19–8 record, a sparkling 2.63 ERA, and 248 strikeouts, but the highlight of the season — and of his career — came on Father's Day, when he pitched a perfect game against the New York Mets at Shea Stadium. He thus became one of the few pitchers to hurl a no-hitter in both leagues, and the perfect game was the first pitched in the National League since 1880.

He went 19–9 in 1965, and on May 5 won a 1–0 game against the Mets when he hit a home run off Warren Spahn to account for the game's only run.

In 1966 he was 19–14 with a 2.41 ERA and led the league with 5 shutouts. The following season he won 17, and his ERA improved even further to 2.29 as he led the league with 302⅓ innings pitched, 253 strikeouts, and 6 shutouts.

In spite of that performance, the Phillies traded him to the Pittsburgh Pirates after the season for Don Money, Woodie Fryman, Bill Laxton, and minor leaguer Hal Clem. He faltered in 1968 with Pittsburgh, going 4–14, but during his first win he recorded his 1000th strikeout in the National League and thus became the first pitcher since Cy Young to strike out at least 1000 batters in each league.

He was 10–9 for the Pirates in 1969 when they dealt him to the Los Angeles Dodgers, and he finished the season at 13–10 with a 3.69 ERA.

Bunning returned to the Phillies in 1970 and pitched two more seasons, although his numbers declined during those years. He retired with a 224–184 lifetime record, a 3.27 career ERA, 2855 strikeouts, and 40 shutouts. As of 2003 he was one of only six pitchers to win at least 100 games in each league, winning 118 in the American League and 106 in the National League.

The Phillies retired his number 14 in 2001 at Veterans Stadium before their home opener. At that time they also placed on the outfield wall two block-like *P*'s that had adorned Phillies' uniforms in the early part of the twentieth century; one was for Grover Cleveland Alexander, the other for Chuck Klein, both of whom had played for Philadelphia before the Phillies adopted uniform numbers. Speaking of the honor, Bunning was quoted as saying, "What else could you get done? I'm in the Hall of Fame. My number is retired. The next thing to do is die."

After his retirement he launched a successful political career, serving for several years in the U.S. House of Representatives and, in 1998, being elected a United States Senator representing Kentucky.

Awards/Honors

1996 Hall of Fame

August A. Busch, Jr.

Retired Number: 85 (St. Louis Cardinals, 1984)
Owner
Team Ownership: St. Louis Cardinals 1953–89

August A. Busch, Jr., or "Gussie," is one of three men to have a major league uniform number retired without having actually worn a uniform. A native of St. Louis, Busch was born on March 28, 1899, and inherited a brewing empire that continues to sell the number one brand of beer in the United States to this day — Budweiser.

It was his great-grandfather, Eberhard Anheuser, who had purchased the troubled Bavarian Brewery in 1860 and begun the family business. Eberhard's son-in-law, Adolphus Busch, joined him and became a full partner in 1869. Budweiser was introduced as the United States' first national beer brand in 1876. Eberhard died in 1880, and Adolphus became president. In 1896 Budweiser created the Michelob brand, and the company eventually passed into the hands of Adolphus' son, August Anheuser Busch, Sr.

August A. Busch, Jr. entered the family brewing business, now known as Anheuser-Busch, in 1924, and by 1931 was Second Vice President and a member of the company's board of directors. Prohibition had gone into effect in 1919, and the company survived by manufacturing yeast, corn and malt syrups, and ice cream, among other products. August Busch, Jr. had a great love of horses, especially Clydesdales. When Prohibition ended in 1933, he surprised his father by presenting him with a team of six of the horses and a Budweiser beer wagon. To celebrate the end of Prohibition, this team was sent to New York to formally deliver two cases of beer to Governor Al Smith in front of the Empire State Building, then on a tour of New England and the mid–Atlantic regions. Along the way they stopped at the White House and delivered two cases of beer to President Franklin D. Roosevelt. The Clydesdales remain a distinctive symbol of Budweiser beer to this day.

August Busch, Sr. died shortly after the repeal of Prohibition, and his son, Adolphus Busch III, took over the company's reins. In 1942 August Busch, Jr. was commissioned a major in the Ordnance Corps, and during World War II he served on various committees to help industry and the Ordnance Corps work together toward the war effort. In 1946 he took over Anheuser-Busch when his brother Adolphus died, and annual sales gradually increased from 3 million barrels to 34 million barrels. He introduced Busch beer, which joined Budweiser and Michelob among the company's brands, and by 1957 Anheuser-Busch was the country's leading brewer in terms of production and Budweiser was the nation's top-selling brand.

In 1953 he convinced the brewery to purchase the St. Louis Cardinals and to renovate Sportsman's Park, which was later renamed Busch Stadium. Under his leadership the team won the World Championship in 1964. He was instrumental in the building of a new ballpark for the club, and when the stadium opened in 1966, it, too, was called Busch Stadium. The Cardinals won the World Championship again in 1967, and the National League pennant in 1968.

August retired from having an active role at Anheuser-Busch in 1975, turning the business over to his son, August A. Busch III. He still owned the Cardinals, however, and the team went on to win the World Series in 1982 and National League pennants in 1985 and 1987.

In 1984, the team retired the number 85 in his honor in conjunction with his eighty-fifth birthday. The number is the highest to be retired by any major league team.

In 1989 August Busch, Jr. died at the age of 90.

Roy Campanella

Retired Number: 39 (Los Angeles Dodgers, 1972)
Catcher
Playing Career: Brooklyn Dodgers 1948–57

Roy "Campy" Campanella was born in Philadelphia in 1921 and enjoyed a successful career in the Negro Leagues, especially with the Baltimore Elite Giants of the Negro National League, before being signed by Branch Rickey and making his way through the Brooklyn Dodgers system. He joined the Dodgers part-way through the 1948 season, and that would be the beginning of a 10-year career in Brooklyn.

Campanella was a solid catcher with a cannon for an arm and great adeptness at handling pitchers. He was solid at the plate as well, always hitting for a respectable average and putting up good power numbers.

His first full season was 1949, when he appeared in 130 games and batted .287, slugging 22 home runs at the same time. In 1950 he belted 31 long ones and accumulated 89 runs batted in.

In 1951 he won the first of three National League Most Valuable Player Awards, batting a career-high .325 with 33 home runs and 108 RBIs, adding 33 doubles and scoring 90 runs along the way.

In 1953 he won his second MVP Award, hitting .312 for the Dodgers and swatting a career-high 41 home runs, which at the time set a new record for catchers. His 142 RBIs led the National League and were also a record for catchers, and he contributed 26 doubles and scored 103 runs.

Campanella suffered a hand injury in spring training of 1954, and that injury limited him to 111 games for the season. His average tailed off to .207, and he hit only 19 home runs.

He rebounded in 1955. Appearing in 123 games, he batted .318 with 32 home runs and 107 RBIs, a performance that netted him his third National League MVP Award. For the fourth time during his days in Brooklyn, the Dodgers went to the World Series, and for the only time, they won, defeating the New York Yankees in seven games. Campanella contributed two home runs to the effort.

The next year his hand once again began to bother him, and his average dropped to .219. He hit 20 home runs and drove in 73, and although the Dodgers won the National League pennant, they lost the World Series to the Yankees.

In January of 1958 Roy was involved in an automobile accident that damaged his spinal cord and left him permanently disabled. His baseball career was abruptly over, but his lifetime numbers were good enough for Hall of Fame induction. In 10 years he had hit .276 and accumulated 242 home runs, 856 RBIs, and 178 doubles. He had appeared in five World Series and contributed four home runs.

Campanella had worn numbers 33, 56, and 39 in his rookie 1948 season with the Dodgers, but then stuck with 39 for the rest of his career. The Dodgers retired that number in his honor on June 4, 1972, the same day they retired the numbers of Jackie Robinson and Sandy Koufax.

Roy was inducted into the Hall of Fame in 1969. He died in California in 1993.

Awards/Honors

1951 National League Most Valuable Player
1953 National League Most Valuable Player
1955 National League Most Valuable Player
1969 Hall of Fame

Rod Carew

Retired Number: 29 (Minnesota Twins, 1987; Anaheim Angels, 1991)
Second Baseman/First Baseman/Coach
Playing Career: Minnesota Twins 1967–78; California Angels 1979–85
Coaching Career: California Angels 1992–96; Anaheim Angels 1997–99; Milwaukee Brewers 2000–01

Rod Carew is one of only eight men to have his number retired by more than one team. Born on a train in Panama in 1945, he moved to the United States with his mother at age 17. The Minnesota Twins signed him out of high school in 1964, and after three years in the minor leagues, he jumped directly to the major leagues from what was then Class C.

Carew was the consummate hitter, batting over .300 for 15 consecutive seasons and winning 7 batting titles, a mark topped only by Ty Cobb, Honus Wagner, and Tony Gwynn, and equaled only by Rogers Hornsby and Stan Musial.

Carew hit .292 in his first season with the Twins, connecting for 150 hits and winning the American League Rookie of the Year Award. In 1969 he started his incredible run of .300 seasons. He hit .332 that year and won his first batting title, although he faltered in the League Championship Series with an .071 average as Minnesota lost to the Baltimore Orioles.

He suffered a knee injury in 1970 and was limited to 51 games, but he made those 51 count as he batted .366. The Twins once again advanced to the American League Championship Series, which they once again lost to the Orioles, and Carew pinch hit twice and did not manage a hit.

He was back to full-time action in 1971, and in 1972 he won the first of four consecutive batting titles with a .318 average. In 1973 he not only topped the circuit with a .350 average, but with 203 hits as well, while tying Al Bumbry with 11 triples. He continued to dominate in 1974 with a .364 batting average, also leading the American League with 218 hits, and won his fourth title in 1975 with a .359 average.

In 1976 his .331 mark was third in the league, although it was only two percentage points behind George Brett's .333 and one behind Hal McRae's .332. He also collected 200 hits that year. In 1977 he won his sixth batting crown with a career-high mark of .388, leading the league with 239 hits, 16 triples, and 128 runs scored, and his performance earned him the American League Most Valuable Player Award. He won his seventh and last batting title in 1978 when he hit .333.

The Twins dealt their batting champion to the California Angels for four players prior to the 1979 season, and while Carew never won another batting championship, he usually finished somewhere in the top five. He batted .318 in his first year with the Angels, and from 1980–83 hit between .305 and .339. In the 1979 ALCS he hit .412 for California, although the Angels lost to the Orioles, and in 1982 he hit only .176 in the series as they fell to the Milwaukee Brewers.

On August 4, 1985, Rod singled off Frank Viola of the Minnesota Twins in the third inning to reach the 3000-hit plateau. Carew retired following the 1985 season with a .328 lifetime batting average, 3053 hits, and 112 triples. The Twins retired his number 29 in 1987, and the Angels followed suit in 1991, the same year he was inducted into the Hall of Fame.

In 1992 Rod returned to the Angels as a coach, and he remained with them through 1999. From 2000–01 he served as a coach with the Brewers.

Awards/Honors

1967 American League Rookie of the Year
1977 American League Most Valuable Player
1991 Hall of Fame

Steve Carlton

Retired Number: 32 (Philadelphia Phillies, 1989)
Pitcher
Playing Career: St. Louis Cardinals 1965–71; Philadelphia Phillies 1972–86; San Francisco Giants 1986; Chicago White Sox 1986; Cleveland Indians 1987; Minnesota Twins 1987–88

One of the best left-handers ever to take the mound, Steve Carlton was born in Miami, Florida, in 1944. The St. Louis Cardinals signed him out of Miami-Dade Community College in 1963, and he was pitching in the major leagues two years later.

Carlton appeared in 15 games for the Cardinals in 1965, although he started only 2 of them. While he did not earn a decision, he finished the year with a sparkling 2.52 earned run average.

He pitched much of the 1966 season at AAA, but was recalled late in the season and started 9 games for St. Louis, going 3–3 with a 3.12 ERA. In 1967 he became a regular in the rotation and won 14 games, also celebrating his first World Championship as the Cardinals took the Boston Red Sox in seven games, then won 13 more in 1968. The following year his record was 17–11, his ERA a minuscule 2.17.

His success led him to a contract dispute with the Cardinals prior to the 1970 season, and he ended up sitting out spring training. Whether or not that led to his control problems that year is questionable, but the fact is that his record plummeted to 10–19, and those 19 losses led the National League. He bounced back mightily in 1971, however, achieving the first of six 20-win seasons with a 20–9 record, and that prompted him to ask Cardinals management for a raise.

Instead of rewarding him, however, the Redbirds' brass traded him to the Philadelphia Phillies for Rick Wise. Carlton responded with his first of four Cy Young seasons in 1972 as he won the pitching Triple Crown with a 27–10 record, a microscopic 1.97 ERA, and 310 strikeouts, while also topping the loop with 30 complete games and 346⅓ innings pitched. And he did all this for a Phillies team that finished in last place and that managed only 59 wins all season; Carlton's 27 accounted for an incredible 45.8 percent of the club's victories.

Steve led the league with 20 losses in 1973, going 13–20, but he still tied Tom Seaver with 18 complete games and tied Jack Billingham with 293⅓ innings pitched, while also striking out 223 batters. His Phillies were still limping along in last place.

His record improved to 16–13 in 1974, and he led the league with 240 strikeouts. The Phillies as a whole were also improving, and by 1976 they were good enough to win the National League Eastern Division crown. Carlton won 20 games for the third time, going 20–7 for a league-leading .741 winning percentage, although Philadelphia was swept by the Cincinnati Reds in the National League Championship Series.

In 1977 Carlton's 23 wins once again led the league as he claimed his second Cy Young Award. The Phillies again won their division, but again lost the pennant, this time to the Los Angeles Dodgers.

In 1980 Steve had another sensational season, leading the league with 24 wins against only 9 losses, and also leading with 304 innings pitched and 286 strikeouts. His ERA was 2.34, and his season was good enough to win him his third Cy Young Award. He also won two games in the World Series as the Phillies defeated the Kansas City Royals.

In the strike-shortened 1981 season Carlton was 13–4 and won his only Gold Glove. The following year he led the National League with 23 wins, 19 complete games, 295⅔ innings pitched, 286 strikeouts, and 6 shutouts. Those numbers netted him his fourth and final Cy Young Award.

In 1983 he led the league in innings pitched with 283⅔ and in strikeouts with 275. The Phillies went to the World Series again, but lost to the Baltimore Orioles.

After 1984 Carlton's numbers began to drop. Injuries limited him to

16 games and a 1–8 record in 1985, and he would never be the same pitcher. After stints with the San Francisco Giants and Chicago White Sox in 1986, the Cleveland Indians in 1987, and the Minnesota Twins from 1987–88, he brought his 24-year career to an end with a lifetime 329–244 record. His 329 career victories were second only to Warren Spahn's 363 for left-handers, and his 4136 career strikeouts were second only to Nolan Ryan overall.

Carlton wore number 32 throughout his career with every team except the Twins, who gave him number 38 because Dan Gladden was wearing 32.

The Phillies retired the number for him in 1989, and he was inducted into the Hall of Fame in 1994, his first year of eligibility.

Awards/Honors

1972 National League Cy Young Award
1977 National League Cy Young Award
1980 National League Cy Young Award
1981 National League Gold Glove Pitcher
1982 National League Cy Young Award
1994 Hall of Fame

Gary Carter

Retired Number: 8 (Montreal Expos, 1993)
Catcher/Outfielder
Playing Career: Montreal Expos 1974–84, 1992; New York Mets 1985–89; San Francisco Giants 1990; Los Angeles Dodgers 1991

Gary "Kid" Carter was born in Culver City, California, on April 8, 1954. He had a lot of personality, but only once did he lead the league in any offensive category. At the same time he was durable and talented behind the plate and had a penchant for coming through in clutch situations.

Carter was originally an outfielder who was converted to a catcher by the Montreal Expos. He made his major league debut by playing in nine games for the Expos in 1974; six of them were behind the plate, two in the outfield, and one as a pinch hitter. He made the most of his 27 at-bats, as he posted a .407 batting average.

In 1975 he played 144 games in Montreal, 92 of them in the outfield, 66 catching, and even one at third base. He was injured prior to the 1976 season when he ran into an outfield wall chasing a fly ball in spring training, and as a result he appeared in only 91 games, two-thirds of them as a backstop, the rest in the outfield.

By 1977 he was the Expos' regular catcher, and he responded with a .284 average, 31 home runs, and 84 runs batted in. On April 20 he homered in three consecutive at-bats. He hit 20 home runs in 1978, 22 in 1979, and 29 in 1980 with 101 RBIs. From 1977 through 1980, he hit a home run in four consecutive Opening Day games. He also won the first of three consecutive Gold Gloves in 1980 for his work behind the plate.

In 1981 he hit two home runs in the All-Star Game and won the Most Valuable Player Award for that contest. He also hit .421 in the National League divisional playoffs and .438 in the National League Championship Series, although the Expos lost the pennant to the Los Angeles Dodgers, three games to two. He hit 29 home runs in 1982 and knocked in 97, and in 1984 slugged 27 roundtrippers with a league-leading 106 RBIs (tied with Mike Schmidt). He hit another home run in the All-Star Game and once again won All-Star MVP honors.

After the 1984 season the Expos traded him to the New York Mets for four players, and he hit a career-high 32 home runs with the Mets that season and drove in 100 runs. He followed that performance with 24 homers in 1986, adding 105 RBIs, and he won a World Series ring as the Mets defeated the Boston Red Sox in seven games.

Carter played with the Mets through the 1989 season, then went to the San Francisco Giants in 1990 and to the Dodgers in 1991 before returning to the Expos for a last hurrah in 1992. He retired having caught 2056 games, second only to Carlton Fisk and Bob Boone, with 324 lifetime home runs, 1225 RBIs, and 10 career grand slams.

Carter wore number 57 when he first debuted with the Expos in 1974, but he donned number 8 for the rest of his career with all four teams with whom he played. The Expos retired the number the year following his retirement from baseball.

Gary became a broadcaster when his playing days were over. He was inducted into the Hall of Fame in 2003.

Awards/Honors

1980 National League Gold Glove Catcher
1981 National League Gold Glove Catcher
1982 National League Gold Glove Catcher
2003 Hall of Fame

Orlando Cepeda

Retired Number: 30 (San Francisco Giants, 1999)
First Baseman/Outfielder/Designated Hitter

Playing Career: San Francisco Giants 1958–66; St. Louis Cardinals 1966–68; Atlanta Braves 1969–72; Oakland Athletics 1972; Boston Red Sox 1973; Kansas City Royals 1974

Orlando "The Baby Bull" Cepeda hailed from Ponce, Puerto Rico, where he was born in 1937, the son of Perucho "The Bull" Cepeda, one of the greatest baseball players in Puerto Rican history. He would follow in his father's footsteps, but would do so in the major leagues beginning in 1958.

Orlando debuted in a big way with the San Francisco Giants that year, becoming their regular first baseman and hitting .312 with 25 home runs, 96 runs batted in, and a league-leading 38 doubles. He even hit a home run in his first game in the big leagues, and his season performance netted him the National League's Rookie of the Year Award. He followed that up with a .317 season in 1959, slugging 27 home runs with 105 RBIs.

Cepeda hit at least 20 home runs during each of his first seven seasons in the major leagues, his high mark coming in 1961 when he led the National League with 46 and with 142 RBIs, batting .311 for the season. In 1962 he continued his onslaught, hitting .306 while slugging 35 homers and knocking in 114. The Giants made it to the World Series, but lost in seven games to the New York Yankees.

Cepeda batted .316 and .304 the next two seasons, cracking 34 and 31 home runs, respectively. He garnered 97 RBIs both seasons. He suffered a knee injury in 1965 and was limited to a mere 33 games. Early in the 1966 season, the Giants traded him to the St. Louis Cardinals for Ray Sadecki. He batted .303 for St. Louis from that point on and finished at .301 for the season, winning the Comeback Player of the Year Award.

It was the following year, however, that made the Giants truly regret parting with him. He hit to the tune of a .325 average with 25 home runs, 37 doubles, and a league-leading 111 RBIs, a performance good enough to win him the National League Most Valuable Player Award. The Cardinals went to the World Series, and although Orlando went only 3-for-29 (a .103 average), the Cardinals defeated the Boston Red Sox in seven games.

Two years later the Cardinals traded Cepeda to the Atlanta Braves for Joe Torre. Orlando responded with 22 home runs for the Braves in 1969, but turned it up a notch in 1970 by hitting .305 with 34 home runs and 111 RBIs.

His numbers slowly began to fade after that, and the Braves traded him to the Oakland Athletics for Denny McLain midway through the 1972 season. Cepeda played only three games for Oakland, however, then signed with the Red Sox in 1973 and with the Kansas City Royals in 1974.

He retired with a .297 lifetime batting average, 379 home runs, 417 doubles, and 1365 RBIs.

The Giants retired his number 30 in 1999, the same year he was inducted into the Hall of Fame.

Awards/Honors

1958 National League Rookie of the Year
1967 National League Most Valuable Player
1999 Hall of Fame

Roberto Clemente

Retired Number: 21 (Pittsburgh Pirates, 1973)
Outfielder
Playing Career: Pittsburgh Pirates 1955–72

Roberto Clemente emerged from Carolina, Puerto Rico, where he was born in 1934, to become one of the greatest players of all time. A speedy outfielder with a prolific bat, a more-than-steady glove, and a rocket for an arm, he made his mark on the game for 18 years, all of them with the Pittsburgh Pirates.

Clemente's first season was 1955, which was somewhat mediocre, but he turned it on the following year and hit .311. After falling to .253 in 1957, his average slowly began to climb again, and from 1960 on, he would fail to hit .300 only one other time.

He hit .314 in 1960 and batted .310 in the World Series as the Pirates defeated the New York Yankees in seven games. He had a monster season in 1961 as he won the first of four batting championships. His .351 average was accompanied with 201 hits, 23 home runs, 89 RBIs, and 100 runs scored, and he also won the first of 12 consecutive Gold Gloves.

Clemente kept on hitting, winning his second batting crown in 1964 with a .339 average while also tying with Curt Flood for the league lead with 211 hits and collecting 40 doubles. He repeated as batting champion the following year with a .329 average, amassing 194 hits in the process. In 1966 his .317 mark was fifth in the league, but with career highs of 29 home runs, 119 RBIs, and 105 runs scored, plus 202 hits, 31 doubles, and his sixth consecutive Gold Glove, he won the National League's Most Valuable Player Award.

He won his fourth and final batting championship in 1967 as he led the league with a .357 batting average — a career high — and 209 hits. He also hit 23 home runs with 110 RBIs, and two years later he hit .345 and led the NL with 12 triples.

In 1971 Roberto contributed a .341 average to the Pirates' pennant drive with 29 doubles and 86 RBIs, and the Bucs captured the National League flag by defeating the San Francisco Giants, three games to one. Clemente had an awesome World Series as he batted .414 with 12 hits, including two home runs, helping Pittsburgh defeat the Baltimore Orioles in seven games. For his efforts he won the Series MVP Award.

In 1972 Clemente hit .312, the thirteenth time he had batted over .300, although he appeared in only 102 games. On September 30 he stroked a double off Jon Matlack of the New York Mets at Three Rivers Stadium for the 3000th hit of his career. It would also be his last.

On New Year's Eve of 1972, Clemente was aboard a plane that was bringing supplies to earthquake victims in Nicaragua when the plane crashed just off the coast of Puerto Rico, killing everyone on board. He was only 38 years old at the time.

His lifetime batting average was .317, and he had amassed exactly 3000 hits along with 240 home runs, 1305 RBIs, 440 doubles, and 1416 runs scored. In two World Series he had a cumulative average of .362.

Because of Clemente's death, the Hall of Fame waived the customary five-year waiting period required for induction and admitted him in 1973.

Roberto wore number 13 when he first debuted with the Pirates in 1955, but switched to number 21 the same year and wore that number for the rest of his career. The Pirates retired the number in 1973.

Awards/Honors

1961 National League Gold Glove Outfielder
1962 National League Gold Glove Outfielder
1963 National League Gold Glove Outfielder
1964 National League Gold Glove Outfielder
1965 National League Gold Glove Outfielder
1966 National League Most Valuable Player
1966 National League Gold Glove Outfielder
1967 National League Gold Glove Outfielder
1968 National League Gold Glove Outfielder
1969 National League Gold Glove Outfielder
1970 National League Gold Glove Outfielder
1971 National League Gold Glove Outfielder
1972 National League Gold Glove Outfielder
1973 Hall of Fame

Jocko Conlan

Retired Number: 2 (National League Umpires, 1995)
Outfielder/Umpire
Playing Career: Chicago White Sox 1934–35
Umpiring Career: National League 1941–64

Jocko Conlan is one of six umpires to have his number retired. His is also a rather rare case where a major league player became an umpire.

Born in Chicago in 1899, Conlan had a brief two-year playing career as a part-time outfielder with the Chicago White Sox. He broke in 1934 and batted .249 in 63 games, then raised his average to a much more respectable .286 in 65 games in 1935. He never hit a home run, but did have 18 career doubles, 4 triples, and 31 runs batted in. His cumulative average was .263. In a game against the St. Louis Browns in 1935, American League umpire Red Ormsby was overcome by heat and had to leave the field, and Conlan filled in for the rest of the game. That was his first experience with umpiring, and he would make a career of it shortly thereafter.

Jocko became a National League umpire in 1941 and was soon noted for his polka-dot tie and his balloon chest protector, as well as for his fairness and accuracy in making calls. He was respected by peers and players alike, and eventually umpired several World Series and All-Star Games. He was also the only umpire to work each of the first four National League pennant playoffs (in 1946, 1951, 1959, and 1962).

During a New York Giants game in 1941 at the Polo Grounds, Conlan halted play for 45 minutes so that the crowd could listen to a radio speech given by President Franklin D. Roosevelt concerning World War II.

Conlan had a sunny disposition, but would not hesitate to go toe-to-toe with a disagreeable player, manager, or coach. He had many such run-ins with the more fiery personalities around the league, and on one occasion ended up in a kicking match with Los Angeles Dodgers coach Leo Durocher.

During a game in 1955, he was suffering from such a severe attack of arthritis that he could not get low enough to call some pitches. He called a strike on Jackie Robinson that caused the Dodgers player to look at him in complete shock. Jocko noted that Robinson's expression was one of such honest surprise that he knew he must have erred, and he left the field for the rest of the game so that he would not make another such mistake.

Conlan retired in 1964, and was inducted into the Hall of Fame as an umpire in 1974, the fifth arbiter to be so honored. He died in Scottsdale, Arizona, in 1989. His number 2 was eventually retired by the National League office along with the numbers of Al Barlick and Bill Klem, but the number came back into use when the National League and American League offices were shut down and the umpires from those leagues came under the joint aegis of Major League Baseball in 2000.

Awards/Honors

1974 Hall of Fame

Joe Cronin

Retired Number: 4 (Boston Red Sox, 1984)
Second Baseman/Shortstop/Third Baseman/First Baseman/Manager
Playing Career: Pittsburgh Pirates 1926–27; Washington Nationals 1928–34; Boston Red Sox 1935–45
Managerial Career: Washington Nationals 1933–34; Boston Red Sox 1935–47

A 1906 native of San Francisco, California, Joe Cronin made his major league debut not at the shortstop position for which he is most famous, but rather at the keystone sack. It was primarily there that he emerged with the Pittsburgh Pirates for 38 games in 1926 and for 12 more in 1937, although he did man shortstop for a few games and even first base for one. The Pirates already had a regular shortstop by the name of Arky Vaughan.

Cronin went to the Washington Nationals in 1928, and it was there that he would begin to blossom. He became Washington's regular shortstop in 1929, but it would take him until 1930 to show his true colors. He hit .346 that year, the first of 11 times he would bat over .300 in his 20-year career. He also hit 13 home runs and had 126 runs batted in, while scoring 127 himself. He added 41 doubles and had 203 hits.

In 1931 he hit .306 and had another 126 RBIs, scoring 103 runs and stroking 44 doubles and 13 triples. He followed that up with a .318 mark in 1932 with 116 RBIs, and his 18 triples led the American League.

Nationals' owner Clark Griffith named Cronin player/manager in 1933, and although Cronin was only 27 years old at the time, he took Washington to the World Series as the team won 99 games and finished 7 ahead of the New York Yankees. They lost in five games to the New York Giants, but Cronin had made his mark. He also hit .309 for the season with 118 RBIs, and led the American League with 45 doubles. He hit .318 in the World Series.

In 1934 the Nationals dropped to seventh place, winning only 66 games and finishing 34 behind the Detroit Tigers. Griffith had introduced Cronin to his niece, Mildred Robertson, that year, and the two were married before the year was out. At the end of the season, however, Griffith traded Joe to the Boston Red Sox for Lyn Lary and $225,000.

The Red Sox installed Cronin as *their* player/manager, and Joe would manage four second-place finishes for them in the next 11 years. He continued his hot hitting, batting .307 in 1937 with 110 RBIs, .325 in 1938 as he led the league with 51 doubles, and .308 in 1939 with 107 RBIs.

In 1940 his average fell off a bit, but he would bat over .300 during each of the next three seasons. By 1942 he had become a part-time player, mostly serving as a pinch hitter and third baseman. He set a record in 1943 by hitting a pinch-hit home run in each game of a doubleheader.

In 1945 he was batting .375 in three games when he broke his leg, and the injury ended his playing career, although he continued to manage for two more seasons. In 1946 he took the Red Sox to the World Series, but they lost in seven games to the St. Louis Cardinals.

After a third-place finish in 1947, Cronin moved to Boston's front office, and he would remain there through 1959. He was inducted into the Hall of Fame while he was there, in 1956. When he left the Red Sox front office he began the first of two terms as American League president.

As a player he had a .301 lifetime batting average with 2285 hits, 1424 RBIs, and 515 doubles.

Cronin wore number 4 throughout his career with both the Nationals and the Red Sox, although he switched to number 6 for one season with Boston, in 1936. The Red Sox retired his number 4 in May of 1984, and Joe died three months later.

Awards/Honors

1956 Hall of Fame

Jose Cruz

Retired Number: 25 (Houston Astros, 1992)
Outfielder/Designated Hitter/Coach
Playing Career: St. Louis Cardinals 1970–74; Houston Astros 1975–87; New York Yankees 1988
Coaching Career: Houston Astros 1997–

Jose Cruz was born in Puerto Rico in 1947, and was one of three brothers to reach the major leagues. (The others were Hector and Tommy.) Jose began his big-league career with the St. Louis Cardinals in 1970, and in six games hit .353. A solid outfielder, he yet did nothing to dazzle the Cardinals over the next four seasons, and immediately following the 1974 season St. Louis sold him to the Houston Astros.

Cruz was mediocre in his first year with Houston, but then batted .303 in 1976 with 21 doubles and 28 stolen bases. He hit .299 the following season, cracking 31 doubles, and swiped a career-high 44 bases.

In 1980 Cruz hit .302 as the Astros won the National League Western Division crown, and in the League Championship Series against the Philadelphia Phillies he hit .400, although the Phillies took the series, three games to two.

In 1983 he batted .318 and tied with Andre Dawson for the National League lead with 189 hits, also stroking 28 doubles and stealing 30 bases.

His numbers began to fall off in 1986; he managed only three steals in 141 games, but the Astros once again went to the playoffs and this time lost to the New York Mets, four games to two. Cruz went just 5-for-26 in that series.

Prior to the 1988 season Jose signed with the New York Yankees, where he was used as a designated hitter, outfielder, and pinch hitter in only 38 games.

That would be the end of a 19-year career that concluded with a .284 lifetime batting average, 391 doubles, and 317 stolen bases. During most of his years with the Astros he either led the team or placed in the top two or three in batting average, home runs, and runs batted in. He appeared in 2353 games in his career, most of them with Houston, and hit over .300 seven times and stole at least 30 bases five times. In 1997 he became a coach with the Astros.

Cruz wore number 38 with the Cardinals and number 21 with the Yankees, but number 25 throughout his career with the Astros. The Astros retired the number in his honor four years after his retirement as a player, in 1992.

Jose's son, Jose Cruz, Jr., has launched a successful major league career with several teams.

Andre Dawson

Retired Number: 10 (Montreal Expos, 1997)
Outfielder
Playing Career: Montreal Expos 1976–86; Chicago Cubs 1987–92; Boston Red Sox 1993–94; Florida Marlins 1995–96

Born in Miami, Florida, on July 10, 1954, Andre Dawson made his first major league appearance late in the 1976 season with the Montreal

Expos. He was called up for only 24 games, but he was back in 1977 and posted a .282 average with 19 home runs and 21 stolen bases, a performance that earned him the National League Rookie of the Year Award.

The award was no fluke, as Dawson hit 25 home runs in each of the next two seasons, stealing 28 and 35 bases, respectively, and in 1980 he batted .308 with 17 homers and 34 stolen bases and also won his first Gold Glove. It would be the first of five times he would hit over .300 in his 21-year career, and the first of six consecutive and eight overall Gold Gloves that he would win.

In 1978 he had led the league in being hit by pitches, and he duplicated that feat in 1980, 1981, and 1983. He finished second in that category in 1982.

Dawson batted .302 in 1981, and his 24 home runs were second in the league during that strike-shortened season. The Expos went to the National League Championship Series, but lost, three games to two, to the Los Angeles Dodgers. Dawson hit a mere .150 in that series.

He had a career-high 39 steals in 1982, then in 1983 tied Jose Cruz for the National League lead with 189 hits. He also hammered 32 home runs with 113 runs batted in, and stole 25 bases.

His numbers began to decline after that, possibly due to knee problems he was experiencing caused by playing on the artificial turf at Olympic Stadium. Following the 1986 season, he became a free agent and signed with the Chicago Cubs, and that move rejuvenated his career. In 1987, his first year in Chicago, he won the National League Most Valuable Player Award by hitting .287 with a league-leading 49 home runs and 137 RBIs, both career highs. He hit 24 home runs the next year and 21 the year after that as the Cubs won the 1989 National League Eastern Division title and advanced to the League Championship Series. They lost to the San Francisco Giants, four games to one, and Andre could manage only a .105 average in that series.

In 1990 Dawson batted a career-high .310 with 27 homers and 100 RBIs, then hit 31 roundtrippers and knocked in 104 runs in 1991. The following year his numbers began to fall, and he became a free agent following the season and signed with the Boston Red Sox.

He was limited to only 121 games due to a broken wrist in 1993, and by 1994 was being used only in a part-time role. He signed with the Florida Marlins for 1995 and 1996, then retired with a .279 average, 2774 hits, 503 doubles, 438 home runs, and 314 stolen bases.

The year following his retirement, the Expos did something unusual and retired the number 10 he had worn during his playing days in Montreal. What made it unusual was the fact that they had already retired the number in 1993 for Rusty Staub. Dawson's name was simply added to the number alongside Staub's, and the Expos thus became the only team other than the New York Yankees to retire the same number for two different players.

Awards/Honors

1977 National League Rookie of the Year
1980 National League Gold Glove Outfielder
1981 National League Gold Glove Outfielder
1982 National League Gold Glove Outfielder
1983 National League Gold Glove Outfielder
1984 National League Gold Glove Outfielder
1985 National League Gold Glove Outfielder
1987 National League Most Valuable Player
1987 National League Gold Glove Outfielder
1988 National League Gold Glove Outfielder

Dizzy Dean

Retired Number: 17 (St. Louis Cardinals, 1974)
Pitcher/Coach
Playing Career: St. Louis Cardinals 1930, 1932–37; Chicago Cubs 1938–41; St. Louis Browns 1947
Coaching Career: Chicago Cubs 1941

Jay Hanna Dean, as he was born in 1911 in Lucas, Arkansas, was nicknamed "Dizzy" by one of his sergeants when he was in the Army, and the nickname stuck. He and his brother Paul, who was nicknamed "Daffy," pitched together for four seasons for the St. Louis Cardinals.

Dizzy made his major league debut in 1930 on the last day of the season. He pitched a complete game, giving up only three hits to the Pittsburgh Pirates as the Cardinals beat them, 3–1. Dean would spend the entire 1931 season in the minor leagues with the Houston Buffaloes, but his 26 victories and 303 strikeouts made him a Cardinal again in 1932.

During that season Dean won 18 games with a 3.30 earned run average, leading the National League with 286 innings pitched and 191 strikeouts and finishing in a three-way tie with 4 shutouts. He won 20 games the following season and led the league with 48 games pitched, 26 complete games (tied with Lon Warneke), and 199 strikeouts.

His best season was 1934, when he won the National League Most Valuable Player Award by winning an incredible 30 games. His brother Paul won 19, so the Dean brothers accounted for 49 St. Louis victories between them. Dizzy's 30 wins paced the National League, as did his .811 winning percentage (his record was 30–7), his 24 complete games, his 195 strikeouts, and his 7 shutouts. The Cardinals won the World Championship by defeating the Detroit Tigers in seven games, and Dean went 2–1 in the Series with 17 strikeouts and a 1.73 ERA.

Dizzy nearly duplicated these feats in 1935 as he led the league with 28 victories, 29 complete games, 325⅓ innings pitched, and 190 strikeouts. The following season he was 24–13 and paced the circuit with 28 complete games and 315 innings pitched, while also tying Paul Derringer with 51 games pitched.

In 1937 Dean suffered an injury that affected the rest of his career. During the All-Star Game he was hit in the toe by a line drive off the bat of Earl Averill. The toe was broken, and Dizzy attempted to come back before it was fully healed. As a result he favored it while he was on the mound, and the resulting change in his pitching delivery caused bursitis in his arm. He would never be the same pitcher, and would never again pitch a full season.

He went 13–10 in 1937, then was traded to the Chicago Cubs for three players and $185,000. In Chicago he managed only 16 wins over the next three seasons. He pitched only a single inning in 1941, giving up three hits and two earned runs, then did some coaching with the Cubs. He retired at the age of 30 and became a broadcaster for the St. Louis Browns.

That was the beginning of a broadcasting career that would last more than twenty years. In 1947, however, disgusted with the Browns' pitching, Dean took the mound himself for one game against the Chicago White Sox. He pitched four innings and gave up three hits and one walk but did not allow a run. He came to the plate one last time and got a base hit, officially batting 1.000 for the season with a 0.00 ERA.

Dean's lifetime record was 150–83, his ERA 3.02. He amassed 1163 strikeouts and 154 complete games in 12 seasons, only 5 of them "full" seasons.

Dizzy died in July of 1974 in Reno, Nevada. In September, the Cardinals retired his number 17.

Awards/Honors

1934 National League Most Valuable Player
1953 Hall of Fame

Bill Dickey

Retired Number: 8 (New York Yankees, 1972)
Catcher/Manager/Coach
Playing Career: New York Yankees 1928–43, 1946
Managerial Career: New York Yankees 1946
Coaching Career: New York Yankees 1949–57, 1960

Bill Dickey was a Louisiana native who was born in 1906. He spent his entire career with the New York Yankees, first as a catcher, then briefly as a player/manager, then as a coach.

Dickey was an outstanding catcher who was a mainstay on a Yankees' club that participated in eight World Series and won seven of them. In his 17-year playing career, he hit over .300 eleven times.

His 1928 debut consisted of only 10 games, but in 1929 he played 130 and batted .324, a mark he would surpass the next two seasons. In 1931 he became the first catcher to go an entire season without allowing a passed ball. In the 1932 World Series he batted a commanding .438 as the Yanks swept the Chicago Cubs.

While he was hitting for these high averages, Dickey was seldom striking out. He struck out only 13 times in 1932 in 423 at-bats, and he would never strike out more than 37 times in a single season. He usually whiffed somewhere between 11 and 22 times a year.

The next two seasons he capped a string of six consecutive .300-plus campaigns. Two years later, in 1936, he hit a career-high .362 with 22 home runs and 107 runs batted in. He had a relatively poor World Series, but the Yankees defeated the New York Giants anyway.

In 1937 he continued his torrid pace with a .332 average, 29 home runs, and 133 RBIs, all while striking out only 22 times. The Yankees won another World Championship over the Giants. In 1938 Dickey hit .400 in the World Series as New York once again swept the Cubs. The following season he hit .302 with 24 roundtrippers and 105 RBIs, the tenth time in 11 full seasons that he had hit over .300 and the fourth consecutive time he had topped 100 RBIs.

Dickey's numbers began to drop drastically in 1940, and he would hit .300 only one more time and his nine home runs would be the high for the remainder of his career.

He played only 85 games in 1943, and at the conclusion of that season he enlisted in the Navy and would not return until 1946, when World War II was over. He played only 54 games that year, but became the Yankees' player/manager 35 games into the season. He guided the Bronx

Bombers to a 57–48 record before being replaced by Johnny Neun for the final 14 games. The Yankees finished third, 17 games behind the Boston Red Sox.

Dickey's playing days, as well as his managing days, were over, but he returned as a coach in 1949 and remained in that role through 1957. Along the way, in 1954, he was inducted into the Hall of Fame. He scouted for the Yankees in 1959, returned again as a coach in 1960, and then retired for good.

He retired with a lifetime batting average of .313, and he had set an American League record by catching over 100 games for 13 years in a row. His 38 World Series games caught is a major league record.

When the Yankees became the first team to regularly issue uniform numbers in 1929, Dickey was given number 10. He switched to number 8 in 1930 and wore that number for the rest of his playing career. When he returned as a coach in 1949, however, Yogi Berra was wearing number 8, so Dickey switched to number 33.

In 1972 the Yankees retired number 8 for both Dickey *and* Berra. They are thus the only team other than the Montreal Expos to retire the same number for two different players.

Dickey's brother, George Dickey, had a brief career as a catcher with the Red Sox and Chicago White Sox.

Bill Dickey died in Arkansas in 1993.

Awards/Honors

1954 Hall of Fame

Larry Dierker

Retired Number: 49 (Houston Astros, 2002)
Pitcher/Manager
Playing Career: Houston Colt .45s 1964; Houston Astros 1965–76; St. Louis Cardinals 1977
Managerial Career: Houston Astros 1997–2001

Larry Dierker was a highly successful pitcher with the Houston Astros who became a successful broadcaster and then a successful manager.

Born in Hollywood, California, in 1946, Dierker appeared in three games in 1964 for the team that was then called the Houston Colt .45s. He was 0–1 with an earned run average of 2.00. In 1965 the club became the Astros and Dierker became a solid part of the pitching staff, appearing in 26 games and starting 19 of them. His 7–8 record belied his ability, because this was a Houston team that was still very new, and that finished second-to-last in the standings and second-to-last in team batting. The Houston club had been formed in 1962, and in the days before free agency, expansion teams took a little time to ripen.

Dierker won 10 games in 1966, and in a 14-year career would record double-digit wins in 9 seasons. Only three times did his ERA crack the 4.00 barrier, and two of those were partial seasons.

In 1967 he appeared in only 15 games because he spent time in military service, but in 1969 he became a 20-game winner. His 20–13 record was accompanied with a 2.33 ERA and a whopping 232 strikeouts, a career high.

Dierker won 16 games the next year and then 12 the next with a 2.72 ERA. In 1972 he was 15–8, but he suffered a shoulder injury the following season and appeared in only 14 games. He was back to form in 1974, as he started 33 games and went 11–10 with a 2.89 ERA.

Dierker had flirted with no-hitters four times but had never managed to complete one. That changed on July 9, 1976, when he blanked the Montreal Expos. Nevertheless, the Astros traded him to the St. Louis Cardinals shortly after the season ended.

Larry pitched only one season with St. Louis, the worst of his career, then he retired and took up a new vocation in the broadcast booth.

In 1997 the Astros hired him to be their manager, although he had had no prior professional managerial experience in the major *or* minor leagues. He responded by taking Houston to the National League Central Division title, finishing five games ahead of the Pittsburgh Pirates in the standings. Unfortunately, the Astros were swept in the Division Series by the Atlanta Braves in three games.

In 1998 Dierker again guided Houston to the division crown, this time besting the Chicago Cubs by 12½ games. For his efforts, the Baseball Writers Association of America awarded him the National League Manager of the Year Award. Once again, however, his club lost the Division Series, this time by a 3–1 margin to the San Diego Padres.

In 1999 Dierker took the Astros to the division title for the third straight time, finishing a game and a half up on the Cincinnati Reds. In the Division Series, they were bested by the Braves, three games to one.

The team fell to fourth in 2000, and that would prove to be the only time Dierker failed to finish first. It was an ugly season for Houston, as they lost 90 games and finished 23 behind the Cardinals. But they were back on pace in 2001 as they won the division crown for the fourth time in five years, tying for first place with the Cardinals and being awarded the division championship by virtue of their winning season record against St. Louis. The Redbirds were awarded the Wild Card and advanced to the playoffs as well. In the Division Series, the Astros followed an all-too-familiar pattern and were swept by the Braves in three games.

Dierker was fired following the 2001 season, his all-time managerial record consisting of 448 wins against 362 losses for a winning percentage of .553.

One night when Dierker was 12 years old, his 9-year-old brother Rick, with whom he shared a bunk, began to chant, "Forty-nine ... forty-nine ... forty-nine..." for no apparent reason. Six years later, when he was called up to the Astros for the first time, the 18-year-old Larry Dierker chose that to be his uniform number ... *and* he became Houston's manager at the age of 49.

Recognizing his talents as a manager as well as his abilities as a player, the Astros retired his number 49 in 2002. Recalling the fact that two previous Astros — Jim Umbricht and Don Wilson — had had their numbers retired posthumously, Dierker commented, "Well, this is a real honor. And I'm glad I'm not dead like some of these guys."

Awards/Honors

1998 National League Manager of the Year (BBWAA)

Joe DiMaggio

Retired Number: 5 (New York Yankees, 1952)
Outfielder/Coach
Playing Career: New York Yankees 1936–42, 1946–51
Coaching Career: Oakland Athletics 1968–69

Joe DiMaggio, a California native born in 1914, established himself on the West Coast with the minor league San Francisco Seals before signing with the New York Yankees. With the Seals, in fact, he put together a 61-game hitting streak in 1933, a record that eclipsed the major league record he would establish almost a decade later.

DiMaggio actually signed with the Yankees in 1934, and his contract allowed him to play with the Seals in 1935 before reporting to New York the following season. He became a bonafide Yankee in 1936, and thus began one of the greatest careers in major league history.

DiMaggio hit .323 his first season in New York with 29 home runs and 125 runs batted in, while finishing in a three-way tie for the American League lead with 15 triples. In his 13 major league seasons, he would fail to hit .300 only twice, would fail to hit at least 20 home runs only twice, and would fail to drive in 100 runs only four times.

In 1937 he hit .346 and led the league with a .673 slugging average, 46 home runs, and 151 runs scored. He also drove in an incredible 167 runs, but Hank Greenberg had 183 that year. The following season "Joltin' Joe" batted .324 and smashed 32 homers with 140 RBIs.

In 1939 he won both the batting title and the American League Most Valuable Player Award, hitting .381 with 30 home runs and 126 RBIs. In 1940 he repeated as batting champion with a .352 average, slugging 31 home runs and driving in 133. In 1941 he set a major league record by hitting in 56 consecutive games, a feat that riveted the nation for a month and a half. He hit .357 for the season and led the league with 125 RBIs, winning his second Most Valuable Player Award despite the fact that Ted Williams hit .406 that year.

After the 1942 season, DiMaggio went off to war. World War II would rob him of three complete seasons while he was in the prime of his career, but he returned in 1946 as if he had never been away. He hit .290 that year, then .315 the next. DiMaggio had always been much more than a hitter, however; his fielding excellence was well documented, his hustle and speed on the bases beyond question. In 1947 he committed only a single error, and he made more than ten on only three occasions. He won his third and final MVP Award that season.

In 1948 he cranked up his offense, hitting .320 and leading the American League with 39 home runs and 155 RBIs. The following season a heel injury limited him to only 76 games, although he hit .346, but in 1950 he led the league with a .585 slugging average. He retired after the 1951 season with a .325 lifetime batting average, 361 home runs, and 1537 RBIs. Between 1936 and 1951, "The Yankee Clipper" helped drive his team to 10 American League pennants and 9 World Championships, finishing his career with World Series totals of 51 games played, 54 hits, 8 home runs, 30 RBIs, and 27 runs scored.

DiMaggio also gained fame for his marriage to actress Marilyn Monroe, a marriage that put him in the spotlight as surely as did his Yankee pinstripes. For two seasons, 1968 and 1969, he returned to his California roots and served as a coach with the Oakland Athletics.

When he first joined the Yankees in 1936, DiMaggio wore uniform number 9, but he switched to number 5 the following year and wore that number for the rest of his career. The Yankees retired the number in 1952, the season following his retirement. Several other Hall of Fame players have donned that number because of DiMaggio, among them George Brett and Brooks Robinson. The Florida Marlins retired number 5 for their late first president, Carl Barger, after Barger died, because DiMaggio had been Barger's favorite player.

Joe's brother Dom had an 11-year career with the Boston Red Sox, and his brother Vince had a 10-year career with several teams in the National League.

Joe DiMaggio died in 1999 in, somewhat poetically, perhaps, Hollywood, Florida.

Awards/Honors

1939 American League Most Valuable Player
1941 American League Most Valuable Player
1947 American League Most Valuable Player
1955 Hall of Fame

Lou DiMuro

Retired Number: 16 (American League Umpires)
Umpire
Umpiring Career: American League 1963–82

Lou DiMuro was one of six major league umpires to have his number retired.

He became an umpire because of a broken finger he suffered while playing baseball in the Air Force. Not able to play and yet not willing to give up the game he loved, he saw umpiring as a suitable alternative. The rest is history.

DiMuro, known as "Pops" to those close to him, worked in two World Series, three American League Championship Series, and four All-Star Games.

He began his major league career in 1963. A little accident-prone, in 1979 he suffered an injury when Cliff Johnson of the New York Yankees collided with him during a play at the plate; the injury caused him to miss most of the season.

In 1981 he sprained his back in Milwaukee when he slipped in the visitors' dugout during a rain delay at a Brewers game. Then, on June 8, 1982, shortly after umpiring a game between the Texas Rangers and the Chicago White Sox in Arlington, Texas, he was struck by a car and killed while leaving a restaurant. He was 51 years of age.

DiMuro's son, Mike, became an American League umpire in 1999. His son Ray became an umpire in the Pacific Coast League.

The league office retired his number 16, but the number came back into use when the National League and American League offices were shut down and the umpires from those leagues came under the joint aegis of Major League Baseball in 2000.

Larry Doby

Retired Number: 14 (Cleveland Indians, 1994)
Second Baseman/Outfielder/Coach/Manager
Playing Career: Cleveland Indians 1947–55, 1958; Chicago White Sox 1956–57, 1959; Detroit Tigers 1959
Coaching Career: Montreal Expos 1971–73, 1976; Cleveland Indians 1974; Chicago White Sox 1977–78
Managerial Career: Chicago White Sox 1978

Larry Doby was the first black player in the American League, but he was much more than that. An outstanding hitter and a perennial All-Star, he put together a 13-year career and became the first black player to lead his league in home runs, the first to hit a home run in the World Series, and the first to celebrate a World Championship.

Doby was born in Camden, South Carolina in 1924, and he had a successful career with the Newark Eagles of the Negro National League before joining the Cleveland Indians. He was partly responsible for the Eagles' NNL championship in 1946.

Doby joined Cleveland late in 1947, the same year Jackie Robinson broke the color barrier with his own Brooklyn Dodger debut. Larry appeared in only 29 games for the Indians that year, but hit .301 the next in 121 games. The Indians tied in the standings with the Boston Red Sox in 1948, and they won a one-game playoff by an 8–3 score to advance to the World Series. They then defeated the Boston Braves, four games to two, to take the title, and Doby contributed a .318 batting average with a home run in the six games.

In 1949 he hit 24 home runs, then hit 25 the next year with a .326 batting average, 102 runs batted in, and 110 runs scored. Two years later he led the American League with a .541 slugging average, 32 roundtrippers, and 104 runs scored, but also with 111 strikeouts. His 104 RBIs were only one behind teammate Al Rosen.

In 1953 Doby hit 29 home runs with 102 knocked in, but he again led the league in strikeouts with 121. It was a tradeoff the Indians were willing to make, however, as he once again led the American League in 1954 with 32 homers and 126 RBIs. He finished second to Yogi Berra in voting for the league's Most Valuable Player Award. The Indians went to the World Series again, but this time were swept by the New York Giants.

Following the 1955 season the Tribe traded him to the Chicago White Sox. Doby hit 24 home runs for Chicago and drove in 102 runs, but he began to decline the next year. In 1957 the White Sox traded him to the Baltimore Orioles, but he would never appear in a regular-season game in a Baltimore uniform, because just prior to the start of the 1958 season the O's traded him back to the Indians.

He hit 13 home runs in only 89 games for Cleveland that year, but prior to the 1959 campaign the Indians traded him to the Detroit Tigers. After only 18 games with the Tigers, he was sold back to the White Sox, and he retired after that season with a .283 lifetime batting average, 253 home runs, and 969 RBIs. In 1962, he and Don Newcombe became the first former major leaguers to play professionally in Japan, as they were both signed by the Chunichi Dragons.

Doby returned to coach the Montreal Expos for several seasons beginning in 1971, then coached the Indians in 1974, the Expos again in 1976, and the White Sox in 1977 and '78. Midway through the 1978 season the White Sox named him manager to replace Bob Lemon, and he guided them to a 37–50 record as they finished in fifth place, 20½ games behind the Kansas City Royals.

Larry had endured many of the same racist attacks that had been aimed at Jackie Robinson earlier in his debut season, but such injustices were largely ignored by the media. As Doby pointed out, the press unfortunately did not want to "repeat the same story."

Doby briefly wore numbers 37 and 6 before switching to 14. In 1994 the Indians retired his number 14, and in 1998 he was inducted into the Hall of Fame. Larry passed away in 2003.

Awards/Honors

1998 Hall of Fame

Bobby Doerr

Retired Number: 1 (Boston Red Sox, 1988)
Second Baseman/Coach
Playing Career: Boston Red Sox 1937–44, 1946–51
Coaching Career: Boston Red Sox 1967–69; Toronto Blue Jays 1977–81

Robert Pershing Doerr was born on April 7, 1918, in Los Angeles, California. His middle name was inspired by General John J. Pershing, a

World War I hero. Just 13 days past his nineteenth birthday, Doerr had crossed from the West Coast to the East and made his major league debut at second base for the 1937 Boston Red Sox.

In that debut Doerr went 3-for-5, but he made only 55 appearances for the Bosox that season and hit just .224. During the rest of his 14-year career, however, he would bat below .270 only once.

Doerr was a quiet leader for the Red Sox who always hit for a respectable average and had decent power. After hitting .289 in 1938, his first full season, he batted .318 in 1939, one of three times he would top the .300 mark.

In 1940 he slugged 22 home runs with 105 runs batted in, and two years later he drove in 102 runs. One of his best seasons came in 1944, when he hit a career-high .325 and led the American League with a .528 slugging percentage, belting 15 home runs and driving home 82 along the way.

He missed the 1945 season because of military service, but came back in 1946 with 18 home runs and 116 RBIs. The Red Sox went to the World Series that year, and in a seven-game losing effort against the St. Louis Cardinals Doerr contributed a .409 batting average with a home run and three RBIs.

In 1948 Bobby hit a career-high 27 homers with 111 RBIs. The 1950 season was probably his best ever, as he hit .294 with a .519 slugging percentage while tying his career high of 27 home runs and adding a career-high 120 RBIs. That was the sixth and last time he would drive in at least 100 runs. He also finished in a three-way tie for the American League lead with 11 triples.

Doerr retired following the 1951 season with a .288 lifetime batting average, 223 home runs, and 1247 RBIs. He had appeared in nine All-Star Games.

Bobby returned to the Red Sox as a coach in 1967 and spent three years in that role, then had a similar five-year stint with the Toronto Blue Jays beginning in 1977. He was inducted into the Hall of Fame in 1986.

Doerr had worn number 9 with the Red Sox when he made his debut in 1937, but in 1938 he traded with Ben Chapman, who wore number 1. Chapman wore number 9 in 1938, then Ted Williams took it over the following season. Doerr wore number 1 for the rest of his playing career, although he donned number 31 during his tenure as a coach because first Joe Foy and then Joe Azcue was wearing number 1. The Red Sox retired number 1 for Doerr in 1988, two years after his Hall of Fame induction.

Awards/Honors

1986 Hall of Fame

Don Drysdale

Retired Number: 53 (Los Angeles Dodgers, 1984)
Pitcher
Playing Career: Brooklyn Dodgers 1956–57; Los Angeles Dodgers 1958–69

A California native who was born in 1936, Don Drysdale made his debut with the Brooklyn Dodgers in 1956 as a fireballing right-handed pitcher. He served notice in 1957 by going 17–9 with a 2.69 earned run average.

He was with the team when it moved from Brooklyn to Los Angeles, and pitched the first game for the Dodgers in their new West Coast location. They lost to the San Francisco Giants in that contest, and Drysdale had a rough season as his record fell to 12–13 and his ERA soared to 4.17, but he would not experience another such campaign for 11 years. He did make a good showing at the plate, as he hit .227 and belted seven home runs.

In 1959 he won 17 games and led the National League with 242 strikeouts while finishing in a seven-way tie with 4 shutouts. In 1960 his 246 whiffs paced the loop, and in 1962 he won the Cy Young Award — which was given to only a single pitcher at that time rather than to one from each league — with a 25–9 record and a 2.83 ERA. His 25 victories were tops in the league that season, as were his 314⅓ innings pitched and his 232 strikeouts.

Drysdale led the league in starts for four seasons in a row beginning that year, and in 1964 also led with 321⅓ innings pitched. Between 1959 and 1965 he failed to strike out 200 batters only once. In 1961 he even hit five home runs.

He became a 20-game winner again in 1965 as he went 23–12 with a 2.77 ERA and 210 strikeouts. He also hit .300, the only Dodger to do so that year, and he tied his own personal high by slugging seven home runs. He was frequently used as a pinch hitter. That was the last time he would win 20 games and the last time he would strike out 200 batters, but in 1968 he set a then–National League record by pitching 58⅔ consecutive scoreless innings, a record that spanned six straight shutouts and stood for 20 years.

Drysdale pitched only one more season, as an arm injury limited him to only 12 games and caused him to retire at the age of 32. He was the last Brooklyn Dodger playing in Los Angeles.

His lifetime record was 209–166, his ERA 2.95. He struck out 2486 batters in his career, but also hit 154 of them, a National League record. He hit 29 home runs as a batter, second only to Warren Spahn among pitchers in NL history. He also pitched in five World Series for the Dodgers, experiencing the ultimate championship in 1959, 1963, and 1965. His World Series record was 3–3 with a 2.95 ERA and 36 strikeouts.

Drysdale appeared on several television shows, including *The Donna Reed Show* and *The Brady Bunch*, and following his retirement he became a broadcaster for the California Angels and the Chicago White Sox before going back to work for the Dodgers.

The Dodgers retired his number in 1984, the same year he was inducted into the Hall of Fame. Drysdale died in Montreal, Quebec, in 1993.

Awards/Honors

1962 Cy Young Award
1984 Hall of Fame

Bob Feller

Retired Number: 19 (Cleveland Indians, 1957)
Pitcher
Playing Career: Cleveland Indians 1936–41, 1945–56

"Rapid Robert" Feller hailed from Van Meter, Iowa, where he was born in 1918 and where, as he was growing up, he practiced pitching on the family farm. He was signed for one dollar by a Cleveland Indians scout, and would become one of the greatest pitchers ever to play the game.

Feller debuted with Cleveland toward the end of the 1936 season and got into 14 games. On August 25 he made his first start and struck out 15 St. Louis Browns as the Indians prevailed, 4–1. There was much, much more to come.

Bob became a regular starter in 1937, and in 1938 he won 17 games and led the American League with 240 strikeouts. He was also wild, however, pacing the circuit with 208 walks as well. In his career he would lead the league in strikeouts seven times, and in bases on balls four times.

In 1939 Feller led the league with 24 victories, and he also paced the loop with 24 complete games (tied with Bobo Newsom), 296⅔ innings pitched, and 246 strikeouts. On April 16, 1940, Opening Day for the Indians, he pitched a no-hitter against the Chicago White Sox at Comiskey Park. It was the first of three no-hitters he would pitch in his storied career. He won the pitching Triple Crown that season with 27 wins, a 2.61 earned run average, and 261 strikeouts, and also led with 43 games pitched, 31 complete games, and 320⅓ innings pitched, as well as finishing in a three-way tie with 4 shutouts.

He again led the league in 1941 with 25 wins, and with 44 games pitched, 343 innings pitched, 260 strikeouts, and 6 shutouts. After that season he joined the Navy and served throughout World War II, earning five combat ribbons and eight battle stars and not returning to baseball until 1945.

During his next two full seasons, 1946 and 1947, he won 26 and 20 games, respectively, leading the league each time (although he tied with Hal Newhouser in '46). He also led in innings pitched, strikeouts, and shutouts both years, as well as in games pitched and complete games (36) in '46. His 348 strikeouts that year were a career high, as were his 10 shutouts, and he pitched his second no-hitter against the New York Yankees.

In 1948 he won 19 games and led the American League with 164 strikeouts. The Indians went to the World Series, where they defeated the Boston Braves, four games to two, although Bob lost both of his starts.

In 1951 he led the league in victories as he went 22–8, as well as in winning percentage at .733. His numbers declined after that, although he continued to pitch through the 1956 season and retired with 266 lifetime victories, a 3.25 ERA, and 2581 strikeouts ... all while missing nearly four seasons due to military service.

Feller had worn number 9 during his first season with the Indians and number 14 for the next two, but in 1939 he switched to number 19 and wore that for the rest of his career. The Indians retired the number the year following his retirement. He was the first Cleveland player to be so honored. In 1962 he was inducted into the Hall of Fame.

Awards/Honors

1962 Hall of Fame

Rollie Fingers

Retired Number: 34 (Milwaukee Brewers, 1992; Oakland Athletics, 1993)
Pitcher
Playing Career: Oakland Athletics 1968–76; San Diego Padres 1977–80; Milwaukee Brewers 1981–82, 1984–85

Rollie Fingers, born in Steubenville, Ohio, in 1946, made his major league debut by pitching one game for the Oakland Athletics in 1968. He gave up four hits in only an inning and a third, but that performance would not characterize his career.

Known as much for the handlebar mustache he would sport later as for his talent, Fingers became one of the most dominating relievers in baseball history, although he began his career as a starter. His first full three seasons, in fact, he began as a starter but finished in the bullpen. By 1972 he was a full-time reliever, and he led the American League that year with 11 relief wins, as well as with 9 relief losses. He also recorded 21 saves. He had a 1.69 earned run average in the World Series as the Athletics defeated the Cincinnati Reds in seven games.

He had a minuscule 1.92 ERA the following season as the A's won their second of three consecutive World Championships. In 1974 he led the league with 76 games pitched, and he pitched the final two innings of a no-hitter against the California Angels. It was the only four-pitcher no-hitter in major league history, as Fingers teamed up with Vida Blue, Glenn Abbott, and Paul Lindblad to defeat the California Angels, 5–0. Fingers led the league again the following season with 75 games pitched, and also with 10 wins in relief.

Rollie became a free agent following the 1976 season and signed with the San Diego Padres. In 1977 he led the National League with 78 games pitched, a career high, and with 35 saves en route to winning the league's Rolaids Relief Man Award. The following season he won the award again with a league-leading and career-high 37 saves, although he also paced the circuit with 13 relief losses.

Two years later he won his third award with 23 saves and a league-leading 11 wins in relief.

Despite his success, the Padres believed Fingers was nearing the end of his career, and they traded him to the St. Louis Cardinals in an 11-player deal. Fingers never appeared for St. Louis, as four days later he was dealt again, this time to the Milwaukee Brewers. Rollie responded by going 6–3 with a microscopic, career-low 1.04 ERA and a league-leading 28 saves, walking just 13 batters in 78 innings and winning the Rolaids Relief Man, Cy Young, and Most Valuable Awards in the American League.

He saved another 29 games in 1982, but missed the entire 1983 season because of an injury. He came back to save 23 more in 1984, and although he saved 17 in 1985 his ERA skyrocketed to 5.04 and the Brewers released him.

Fingers retired with 107 wins in relief and 341 saves, as well as with 6 saves in World Series play. The Brewers retired his number in 1992, the year he was inducted into the Hall of Fame, and the Athletics followed suit the following year. He is one of only eight men to have his uniform number retired by more than one team.

Awards/Honors

1977 National League Rolaids Relief Man
1978 National League Rolaids Relief Man
1980 National League Rolaids Relief Man
1981 American League Most Valuable Player
1981 American League Cy Young Award
1981 American League Rolaids Relief Man
1992 Hall of Fame

Carlton Fisk

Retired Number: 72 (Chicago White Sox, 1997)
Retired Number: 27 (Boston Red Sox, 2000)
Catcher/Designated Hitter
Playing Career: Boston Red Sox 1969, 1971–80; Chicago White Sox 1981–93

Carlton Fisk is probably best remembered for the twelfth-inning home run he hit in Game 6 of the 1975 World Series, a shot that went down the left field line and that saw him gesticulating wildly in an attempt to wave it fair by sheer force of will. The ball stayed fair and that home run won the game for the Boston Red Sox. Fisk should be remembered for much more, however, for not only did the Red Sox lose the deciding seventh game of that Series to the Cincinnati Reds, but Carlton himself had a 24-year career containing a multitude of other memorable moments.

Born in Vermont in 1947, "Pudge" was drafted by the Red Sox in 1967 and appeared in two games for them in 1969. In 1971 he was called up for 14 games and hit .313. He became Boston's regular catcher in 1972, hitting .293 in his first full season with 22 home runs and winning the American League Rookie of the Year Award, the first player to win unanimously. He also won a Gold Glove for his work behind the plate, and became the first catcher to lead the league in triples as he tied Joe Rudi with nine.

In 1973 Fisk hit 26 home runs with 99 runs batted in, but in 1974 he broke his collarbone and appeared in only 52 games. The following year he reinjured himself during spring training and was not able to play until June. He played 79 games and hit .331, and then hit .417 in the League Championship Series and hit two home runs in the World Series, including his dramatic Game 6 shot.

In 1977 he batted .315 with 26 home runs, 102 RBIs, and 106 runs scored, and behind the plate he allowed only 4 passed balls all season. He hit another 20 homers in 1978, then suffered another injury in 1979 and was limited to only 91 games. He found himself in the role of designated hitter more than in that of catcher that season. In 1980, however, he was back at his customary position full-time.

Following the 1980 season the Red Sox failed to tender him a contract by the deadline and he was granted free agency. In a move that stunned Boston fans, he signed with the Chicago White Sox, and he would finish his career in Chicago.

Ironically, on Opening Day of the 1981 season, the White Sox played in Boston. Fisk hit a three-run home run in the eighth inning against his former teammates, and the Chisox defeated the Bosox 5–3.

In 1985 he belted a career-high 37 home runs with 107 RBIs. The White Sox tried to convert him to left field in 1986 to make room for youngster Joel Skinner, but by May Fisk was back behind the plate and in July Skinner was traded to the New York Yankees.

Fisk played into the 1993 season, and was released shortly after setting a new major league record for most games caught. His record stands at 2226. He hit .269 for his career, with 376 home runs and 1330 RBIs.

Fisk wore number 27 with the Red Sox, but when he went to the White Sox he reversed it and donned number 72, in part to show that he was going to have a totally fresh start in Chicago and in part to honor his Rookie of the Year season of 1972.

The White Sox retired his number 72 in 1997, the Red Sox his number 27 in 2000, the year he was inducted into the Hall of Fame. The Red Sox have a rule requiring an individual to finish his career with Boston, and although Fisk ended his playing days with the White Sox, he eventually went to work in the Red Sox front office and thus qualified for a number retirement. Fisk is one of only eight men to have his uniform number retired by more than one team, and is one of only two (the other is Nolan Ryan) to have two *different* numbers retired.

Awards/Honors

1972 American League Rookie of the Year
1972 American League Gold Glove Catcher
2000 Hall of Fame

Whitey Ford

Retired Number: 16 (New York Yankees, 1974)
Pitcher/Coach

Playing Career: New York Yankees 1950, 1953–67
Coaching Career: New York Yankees 1968, 1974–75

Edward Charles Ford, better known as "Whitey," was born in New York on October 21, 1926. He joined his hometown Yankees midway through the 1950 season and made an immediate impression by going 9–1 with a 2.81 earned run average. Unfortunately, he would miss the next two seasons because of military service.

Ford came back in 1953 and went 18–6, and followed that up with a 16–8 performance the next season. In 1955 he tied Bob Lemon for the American League lead in victories as he went 18–7 and recorded a 2.63 ERA, and he also topped the loop with 18 complete games.

His 19–6 record in 1956 allowed him to lead the league with a .760 winning percentage, and his 2.47 ERA was also best in the circuit. Two years later his 2.01 ERA led the AL, as did his 7 shutouts.

In 1960 Ford finished in a three-way tie for the league lead with four shutouts, but his best season was 1961. That year he topped all other AL hurlers in victories at 25–4, and his record was good for a league-best .862 winning percentage. He was also best with 283 innings pitched, recorded a career-high 209 strikeouts, and won the Cy Young Award during a time when only a single award was given to the best pitcher in *both* leagues. Furthermore, he won the World Series Most Valuable Player Award as he went 2–0 against the Cincinnati Reds and allowed only 6 hits in 14 innings without allowing an earned run.

He topped the league once again in victories in 1963, going 24–7, and his resulting .774 winning percentage also led the loop, as did his 269⅓ innings pitched.

The next two seasons he won 17 and 16 games, respectively, before being relegated to part-time duty. In 1966 he was only 2–5, although his ERA was a respectable 2.47, and in 1967 he appeared in only 7 games and went 2–4, although his ERA was a sparkling 1.64.

Ford retired with a 236–106 lifetime record; he is, in fact, the winningest pitcher in Yankees history. His lifetime ERA was 2.75, and he struck out 1956 batters.

Like most Yankees, he appeared in multiple World Series, but Whitey set records with 10 Series wins, 22 games pitched, 22 starts, 146 innings pitched, and 94 strikeouts. His eight World Series losses are also a record, although he did not receive much support from the Bronx Bombers in those failings. They averaged only 2.25 runs per game for him in those eight games, and were shut out twice.

Ford retired in 1967, but returned to the Yankees as a coach in 1968 and again from 1974–75. He wore number 19 when he first debuted in 1950, but switched to number 16 when he returned from military service in 1953 and wore that number for the rest of his career. The Yankees retired the number in 1974, the same year he was inducted into the Hall of Fame.

Awards/Honors

1961 Cy Young Award
1974 Hall of Fame

Nellie Fox

Retired Number: 2 (Chicago White Sox, 1976)
Second Baseman/Third Baseman/Coach
Playing Career: Philadelphia Athletics 1947–49; Chicago White Sox 1950–63; Houston Colt .45s 1964; Houston Astros 1965
Coaching Career: Houston Astros 1965–67; Washington Senators 1968–71; Texas Rangers 1972

Jacob Nelson Fox was a Pennsylvania native who was born on Christmas Day of 1927. Second baseman Fox and shortstop Luis Aparicio formed a deadly double play combination for the Chicago White Sox to which very few tandems throughout history can compare.

Fox actually began his career with the Philadelphia Athletics, with whom he played only seven games in 1947 and three the next season. His official rookie season was 1949, when he played 88 games but hit only .255. Unimpressed, the A's traded him to the White Sox shortly after the season, and they regretted the move for a long time thereafter.

Fox had a mediocre first season in Chicago, but then batted .313 in 1951, the first of six times he would top the .300 mark. In 1952 he led the American League with 192 hits, and two seasons later he batted .319 and tied Harvey Kuenn for the league lead in hits, this time with 201.

In 1957 Nellie won the first of three Gold Gloves, and this one was extra special because only one player was chosen to represent a position from *both* leagues. Fox did not slow down at the plate, either, as he batted .317 and led the circuit with 196 hits.

He put together another solid season in 1958, hitting .300 and leading the league with 187 safeties, but the best was yet to come. In 1959 he won not only his second Gold Glove, but the American League Most Valuable Player Award as well. His incredible glove and his .306 batting average helped propel the "Go-Go Sox" to the World Series, where they lost to the Los Angeles Dodgers in six games, but where Fox hit .375 and once again displayed sterling defense.

In 1960 Fox won his third and last Gold Glove, and he also led the league with 10 triples. From August 7, 1956, through September 3, 1960, he played in 798 straight games, a major league record for a second baseman. The streak ended when he was hospitalized with a stomach virus.

He also set a major league record by leading the league in singles every year from 1954 through 1960.

Fox's numbers began to decline at that point, and in December of 1963 the White Sox traded him to the Houston Colt .45s, who would become the Astros in 1965. Nellie played one full season in Houston, then played only 21 games in 1965 and became a coach. In his career, he had struck out only 216 times in 9232 at-bats.

After the 1967 season he continued coaching with the Washington Senators, and would stay with that club when it moved to Arlington, Texas and became the Texas Rangers. He retired after the 1972 season, and died in Baltimore three years later.

An individual must be named on 75 percent of Hall of Fame ballots in order to earn induction, and in 1985 Fox achieved 74.7 percent. The Baseball Writers Association of America and the Hall of Fame committee refused to round the figure up to 75 percent, and it would be another 12 years before Fox finally gained induction through the Veterans Committee.

Nellie wore several different uniform numbers, and with the White Sox he donned number 26 for his first three years but then number 2 thereafter. The White Sox retired that number the year following his death.

Awards/Honors

1957 Gold Glove Second Baseman
1959 American League Most Valuable Player
1959 American League Gold Glove Second Baseman
1960 American League Gold Glove Second Baseman
1997 Hall of Fame

Jim Fregosi

Retired Number: 11 (Anaheim Angels, 1998)
Shortstop/Third Baseman/First Baseman/Manager
Playing Career: Los Angeles Angels 1961–64; California Angels 1965–71; New York Mets 1972–73; Texas Rangers 1973–77; Pittsburgh Pirates 1977–78

Managerial Career: California Angels 1978–81; Chicago White Sox 1986–88; Philadelphia Phillies 1991–96; Toronto Blue Jays 1999–2000

Jim Fregosi was born in San Francisco in 1942, and made his playing debut as a shortstop with the expansion Los Angeles Angels in 1961. In 1962 he hit .291 in 58 games, then became the Angels' regular shortstop the following year. He hit for the cycle in 1964 and would do so again in 1968, when the team was called the California Angels, becoming one of the few players in major league history to accomplish the feat twice.

In 1967 Fregosi batted .290 and won a Gold Glove, and the following year he led the American League with 13 triples. He had hit 18 home runs in 1964, and in 1970 he reached his career high of 22, a rare feat at that time for a shortstop.

His hitting dropped off in 1971, and he became something of a journeyman after that. He spent 1972 and part of 1973 with the New York Mets, to whom he was traded for Nolan Ryan and three other players. He foundered in New York and was dealt to the Texas Rangers in July, and he was relegated to part-time duty at several positions. During the 1977 season the Rangers traded him to the Pittsburgh Pirates, and he hit .286 in Pittsburgh in 36 games.

After 20 games with the Pirates in 1978, he was offered the manager's job with the California Angels. Fregosi accepted the position with his original team and achieved a record of 62–55, guiding the Angels to a second-place finish as they went 87–75 overall, ending up five games behind the Kansas City Royals. In 1979 he went one better, as the Angels were 88–74 and won the American League Western Division title by three games over the Royals. They lost the League Championship Series to the Baltimore Orioles, however, three games to one.

In 1980 the team collapsed and went 65–95, and Fregosi was replaced by Gene Mauch during the 1981 season after a 22–25 start.

In 1986 he became the manager of the Chicago White Sox and finished fifth three straight times. In 1991 he was named manager of the Philadelphia Phillies, and in 1993 he led that squad to the National League Eastern Division Championship. The Phils downed the Braves, four games to two, to capture the NL flag, then dropped the World Series to the Toronto Blue Jays. Fregosi was named Manager of the Year by the Associated Press, who chose only one manager as the best of both leagues.

Jim stayed with the Phillies through the 1996 season, and in 1999 he was named skipper of the Blue Jays. He guided Toronto to two consecutive third-place finishes and a .515 winning percentage. His overall winning percentage as a manager was .484.

The Angels retired his number 11 in 1998.

Awards/Honors

1967 American League Gold Glove Shortstop
1993 Manager of the Year (AP)

Steve Garvey

Retired Number: 6 (San Diego Padres, 1989)
Third Baseman/First Baseman
Playing Career: Los Angeles Dodgers 1969–82; San Diego Padres 1983–87

Tampa native Steve Garvey, born in 1948, spent five part-time seasons at third base and first base with the Los Angeles Dodgers at the beginning of his career before becoming a regular and a perennial All-Star. Between 1969 and 1973 he appeared in only 328 games, an average of 66 per season, although 114 of them came in 1973 when he hit .304.

The Dodgers made him their regular first baseman the following year, and Garvey responded by hitting .312 with 200 hits, 21 home runs, and 111 runs batted in. He won the first of four consecutive Gold Gloves, as well as the National League Most Valuable Player Award. He did not appear on the All-Star ballot that year but received enough write-in votes to make him the starting first baseman, and the choice proved to be a good one as he won the Most Valuable Player Award for the Midsummer Classic as well. He hit .389 in the National League Championship Series as the Dodgers downed the Pittsburgh Pirates, hitting two home runs in the process, and continued his hot hitting with a .381 average in the World Series although the Dodgers fell to the Oakland Athletics.

Beginning in 1973 Garvey hit over .300 for seven out of his next eight seasons, and the only year he failed to do so, 1977, he hit .297. He had 210 hits in 1975 and batted .319, and had 200 more in 1976 with a .317 average.

In 1977 he hit a career-high 33 home runs and drove in a career-high 115 runs. He hit .308 in the LCS as the Dodgers defeated the Philadelphia Phillies, and then .375 with a home run in the World Series in a losing effort against the New York Yankees.

In 1978 Steve hit .316 and led the NL with 202 hits, smashing 21 home runs and driving in 113. For the second time he was the Most Valuable

Player in the All-Star Game, and he went on to hit .308 in the LCS as the postseason was largely a repeat of the preceding year; the Dodgers defeated the Phillies, then lost the World Series to the Yankees.

Garvey hit .315 in 1979 with 204 hits, then .304 the following year as his 200 hits led the league. His numbers fell off somewhat in the strike-shortened year of 1981, but the Dodgers would finally go on to win the World Championship.

After the 1982 season Garvey stunned the Los Angeles baseball world by becoming a free agent and signing with the San Diego Padres. He would play in San Diego from 1983–87, but would never be as productive as he had been as a Dodger. His high average was .294 in 1983, his highest home run count 21 in 1986. He had had over 100 RBIs five times in Los Angeles, but 86 would be his high in San Diego. He did go to the World Series in 1984, but the Padres lost to the Detroit Tigers.

Between September 3, 1975, and July 29, 1983, Garvey played in 1207 consecutive games, a National League record. The streak ended when he dislocated his finger in a collision at home plate.

Oddly, it was the Padres rather than the Dodgers who retired his uniform number 6. The honor was likely bestowed because of his prior accomplishments, considering the fact that only 631 of his 2599 hits, only 61 of his 272 home runs, and only 316 of his 1308 RBIs were as a Padre. Everything else he accomplished was as a Dodger. His lifetime average as a Padre was .275, as a Dodger .301.

When he retired from baseball, Garvey made an unsuccessful attempt to begin a political career.

Awards/Honors

1974 National League Most Valuable Player
1974 National League Gold Glove First Baseman
1975 National League Gold Glove First Baseman
1976 National League Gold Glove First Baseman
1977 National League Gold Glove First Baseman

Lou Gehrig

Retired Number: 4 (New York Yankees, 1939)
First Baseman
Playing Career: New York Yankees 1923–39

Henry Louis Gehrig was a native New Yorker who was born in 1903 and who, because he played in the shadow of the great and far more gregarious Babe Ruth, did not always receive the credit he deserved. He is probably most remembered for his 2130 consecutive games played, a major league record that stood until September 6, 1995, when it was broken by Cal Ripken, Jr.

Gehrig showed incredible talent as a college player, and after being signed by the New York Yankees, made his major league debut at the age of 19. He played mostly in the minor leagues in 1923 and 1924, but played 13 games in New York in 1923, hitting .423, and 10 in 1924, going 6-for-12 for a .500 batting average.

In 1925 with the Yankees he hit 20 home runs in 126 games, and he played his first full season in 1926, batting .313 with 16 homers and 107 runs batted in and leading the American League with 20 triples. The following year, 1927, he won the League Award for the American League, the equivalent of that era's Most Valuable Player Award. He batted .373 with 47 home runs, a league-leading 175 RBIs, 149 runs scored, and a league-leading 52 doubles.

Gehrig hit over .300 all 12 years between 1926 and 1937, topping out at .374 in 1928. He won the Triple Crown in 1934 with a .363 batting average, 49 home runs, and 165 RBIs, while also topping the loop with a .706 slugging average and collecting 210 hits. His RBI totals topped 100 every year between 1926 and 1938, with his *low* being 107 in 1926. He led the AL in 1927 with 175, in 1928 with 142 (tied with his teammate, Babe Ruth), in 1930 with 174, in 1931 with 184, and in 1934 with 165. He failed to hit 20 home runs only once between 1925 and 1938. His career-high for a season was 49, which he accomplished in 1934 and 1936, leading the league both times. He also tied with Babe Ruth in 1931 with 46.

In 1928 he tied with Heinie Manush for the league lead with 47 doubles, and in 1930 he achieved his career high in hits with 220, which was 5 short of the league leader, but he did lead the following season with 211. He led the circuit in runs scored four times, in walks three times, and in slugging percentage twice. In 1936 he won the American League Most Valuable Player Award as he hit .354 with league-leading totals of a .696 slugging percentage, 49 home runs, 167 runs scored, and 130 walks, while also contributing 205 hits, 37 doubles, and 152 RBIs.

In 1939 Gehrig was diagnosed with amyotrophic lateral sclerosis, an incurable disease that is better known today as Lou Gehrig's Disease. The illness cut his career short, as he appeared in only eight games in 1939 and was batting only .143 when he took himself out of the lineup. He retired prematurely with a .340 lifetime batting average, 493 home runs, and 1990 RBIs. He had hit for the cycle twice, one of the few players to accomplish that feat, and had hit four home runs in a game on June 3, 1932, against the Philadelphia Athletics. His 23 career grand slams are still the major league record. Like most Yankees, he had appeared in many World Series — seven — and he had helped win six of them, but his numbers in those games were more impressive than most, as he hit .361 with 10 home runs, 35 RBIs, 30 runs scored, 43 hits, 8 doubles, 3 triples, and 26 bases on balls.

In 1929 the Yankees became the first team to permanently wear uniform numbers, and Gehrig was given number 4 because he batted fourth in the lineup. On July 4, 1939, during a day given in his honor at Yankee Stadium, he also became the first player to have his number retired, and thus also has the unique distinction of being the *only* man to wear a specific number for the Yankees. The Hall of Fame waived its five-year waiting period and inducted him in 1939.

Gehrig died of the disease that would later bear his name on June 2, 1941, only 17 days shy of his thirty-eighth birthday.

Awards/Honors

1927 American League League Award
1936 American League Most Valuable Player
1939 Hall of Fame

Charlie Gehringer

Retired Number: 2 (Detroit Tigers, 1983)
Second Baseman/Coach
Playing Career: Detroit Tigers 1924–42
Coaching Career: Detroit Tigers 1942

Born in 1903 in Fowlerville, Michigan, Charlie Gehringer would put together a 19-year career as one of the most talented second basemen of all time. He spent his entire career with the Detroit Tigers.

Gehringer had a five-game stint with Detroit in 1924 and hit .462, and played only eight games with the big club the following year. He became the team's regular second baseman in 1926, however, and would remain so for a long time thereafter.

Charlie hit .317 in 1927, the first of 13 times in the next 14 years that he would surpass the coveted .300 mark. The one time he failed to do so was 1932, when he hit .298.

Charlie had a spectacular year in 1929, hitting .339 and leading the American League with 19 triples, 131 runs scored, and 28 stolen bases, while also tying teammate Dale Alexander with 215 hits and tying Heinie

Manush and teammate Roy Johnson with 45 doubles. For good measure he hit 13 home runs and had 106 runs batted in.

In 1933 he collected 204 hits, and the following year helped the Tigers to the American League pennant by hitting .356 and pacing the loop with 214 hits and 134 runs scored, while also stroking 50 doubles and driving home 127 runs. The Tigers lost the World Series in seven games to the St. Louis Cardinals, but Charlie hit .379 and belted a home run in the effort.

Detroit was back on top the next year as Gehringer had 201 hits. This time they won the World Championship by besting the Chicago Cubs, four games to two, and Gehringer contributed a .375 average in the Series.

In 1936 he led the American League with an incredible 60 doubles, while also batting .354, driving in 116 runs, and collecting 227 hits, but it was the following year that he was the league's Most Valuable Player as he turned in a .371 average to win the batting title. He added 40 doubles, 133 runs scored, and 96 RBIs.

Gehringer walloped a career-high 20 home runs in 1938, and in 1940 he and the Tigers were back in the World Series, this time losing to the Cincinnati Reds in seven.

Between 1926 and 1940 Gehringer had shown such consistency that he was nicknamed "The Mechanical Man." It was said by teammate Doc Cramer that a person could simply wind Gehringer up on Opening Day and forget about him. He had over 200 hits 7 times, at least 20 doubles 14 times, over 100 RBIs 7 times, and scored over 100 runs 12 times.

In 1941 he slumped to .220, and his playing career was essentially over. He was relegated to part-time duty in 1942, briefly became a Tigers coach that year, and then joined the Navy for three years.

Gehringer retired from playing baseball with a .320 lifetime batting average, 2839 hits, 574 doubles, and 1427 RBIs. Additionally, he hit .321 in three World Series with 26 hits. He was the starting second baseman for the American League in the first six All-Star Games, and hit a record .500 in 20 at-bats all-time. He led the league in assists and fielding percentage at second base seven times each.

Gehringer was inducted into the Hall of Fame in 1949, then he became the Tigers' general manager from 1951 through 1953. He became a club vice president through 1959, and served on the Hall of Fame Veterans Committee.

Gehringer wore number 3 when the Tigers first donned uniform numbers in 1931, but switched to 2 the following year. The Tigers retired his number in 1983. Charlie died in Michigan 10 years later.

Awards/Honors

1937 American League Most Valuable Player
1949 Hall of Fame

Bob Gibson

Retired Number: 45 (St. Louis Cardinals, 1975)
Pitcher/Coach
Playing Career: St. Louis Cardinals 1959–75
Coaching Career: New York Mets 1981; Atlanta Braves 1982–84; St. Louis Cardinals 1995

Bob Gibson was born in Omaha, Nebraska, in 1935. He was diagnosed with a heart murmur as a child, but became an outstanding athlete, excelling in both baseball and basketball. He won a basketball scholarship to Creighton University, and in 1957 was signed to a contract by the St. Louis Cardinals. The Cards assigned him to their minor league club in Omaha, and when the season was over Gibson played the 1957–58 basketball season with the Harlem Globetrotters.

Bob made his major league debut with St. Louis in 1959 and was not particularly impressive his first two seasons. In 1961 he had improved, but led the National League in walks issued. A year later he won 15 games and struck out 208 batters, and in 1963 he truly began to shine.

Between 1962 and 1972 Gibson failed to win 15 games only once, and he was a 20-game winner five times. In 1962 he tied Bob Friend for the league lead with five shutouts, and his 20-win seasons came in five of the six seasons between 1965 and 1970. In 1964 he won 19 games, then won two more in the World Series as the Cardinals defeated the New York Yankees in seven. Gibson was 20–12 in 1965, and 21–12 in 1966 as he finished in a six-way tie for the league lead with five shutouts. His earned run average usually hovered right around or below 3.00, and in the years between 1961 and 1973 the highest it reached was 3.39.

Gibson had a good repertoire of pitches and excellent control of them, and he struck out more than 200 batters nine times, finishing with 3117 in his 17-year career. In the 1967 World Series he went 3–0 with an ERA of 1.00 and 26 strikeouts in 27 innings as the Cardinals bested the Boston Red Sox, four games to three. He won the Series Most Valuable Player Award for his efforts. His best season, however, was 1968, when he went 22–9 with a league-leading 1.12 ERA, the lowest in the major leagues since 1914, while also pacing the loop with 268 strikeouts and 13 shutouts. His performance netted him both the Most Valuable Player Award and the Cy Young Award for the National League. He went 2–1 in the World Series with a 1.67 ERA, striking out 17 Detroit Tigers in the first game and defeating 30-game winner Denny McLain. The Tigers would ultimately take the Series, however.

Gibson won 20 in 1969 and led the league with 28 complete games, then tied Gaylord Perry for victories the following year with a 23–7 record, good for a league-best .767 winning percentage and his second Cy Young Award. He pitched a no-hitter against the Pittsburgh Pirates in 1971, and tied three other pitchers with five shutouts.

As good as Gibson's pitching was, that was not his whole game. He was no slouch at the plate, being sometimes used as a pinch hitter, and even batted .303 in 1970. He also took seriously the admonition that once a pitch is thrown, the pitcher becomes a fielder, as evidenced by the nine consecutive Gold Gloves he won between 1965 and 1973.

Gibson retired as the winningest pitcher in Cardinals history, with a record of 251–174, a 2.91 ERA, and 56 shutouts. He was also 7–2 in World Series play, with an earned run average of 1.89 and 92 strikeouts.

Gibson wore number 58 when he debuted in 1959, then switched to number 31 in 1960 before donning his famous 45 later that year. He retired from active play in 1975, and the Cardinals retired his number the same year.

Joe Torre hired Gibson to be his pitching coach when he was the manager of the New York Mets in 1981, and when Torre went to the Atlanta Braves from 1982–84, he took Gibson with him. Bob then became a baseball radio commentator, but returned to the Cardinals as a coach in 1995, for one season.

Awards/Honors

1965 National League Gold Glove Pitcher
1966 National League Gold Glove Pitcher
1967 National League Gold Glove Pitcher
1968 National League Most Valuable Player
1968 National League Cy Young Award
1968 National League Gold Glove Pitcher
1969 National League Gold Glove Pitcher
1970 National League Cy Young Award
1970 National League Gold Glove Pitcher
1971 National League Gold Glove Pitcher
1972 National League Gold Glove Pitcher
1973 National League Gold Glove Pitcher
1981 Hall of Fame

Jim Gilliam

Retired Number: 19 (Los Angeles Dodgers, 1978)
Second Baseman/Outfielder/Third Baseman/Coach
Playing Career: Brooklyn Dodgers 1953–57; Los Angeles Dodgers 1958–66
Coaching Career: Los Angeles Dodgers 1965–78

A Nashville native who was born in 1928, Jim Gilliam had a successful career in the Negro Leagues before being signed by the Brooklyn Dodgers. He was nicknamed "Junior" when he became the youngest member of the Baltimore Elite Giants of the Negro National League in the 1940s.

A three-time Negro League All-Star, Gilliam was sent to the Montreal Royals, the Dodgers' top farm club, in 1951, and after two successful seasons with them he was called up to Brooklyn. He debuted with the Dodgers in 1953 and won the National League Rookie of the Year Award by batting .278 with 31 doubles, a league-leading 17 triples, and 21 stolen bases.

In a 14-year playing career with the Dodgers that included the team's move to Los Angeles, Gilliam hit .300 only once, in 1956, but he was always a solid performer who was moved around in the field between second base, third base, and the outfield. He had a good eye at the plate, drawing 100 walks in 1953 and receiving at least 90 bases on balls in a season five times. In 1959 he led the league with 96.

He scored at least 100 runs in his first four seasons in Brooklyn, and scored more than 90 on two other occasions. He stole over 20 bases four times, and retired with a career total of 203.

Gilliam played in seven World Series with the Dodgers, the first three in Brooklyn and the last four in Los Angeles. In the 1953 Series he switch-hit two home runs, although the New York Yankees came away with the championship, four games to two. Gilliam hit .292 in the 1955 Series, in which the Dodgers defeated the Yankees in seven games. He did not perform particularly well in the 1963 and 1965 Fall Classics, although the Dodgers won anyway.

Gilliam retired following the 1964 season and served as the Dodgers' third base coach in 1965, but he was called back into service and played 111 games that year, contributing a .280 batting average. He retired again and continued to coach in 1966, but once again was called upon to play and appeared in 88 games. After that he retired for good, and continued to coach the Dodgers through the 1978 regular season. He retired with a

.265 batting average, 1163 runs scored, and 1036 walks, plus 23 bases on balls in World Series play.

The Dodgers were National League Western Division Champions in 1978 and went on to win the pennant by defeating the Philadelphia Phillies, three games to one. They would face the Yankees in the World Series, but just before the start of that Series, Gilliam suffered a brain hemorrhage and died suddenly. The Dodgers retired his uniform number 19 that same year.

Awards/Honors

1953 National League Rookie of the Year

Hank Greenberg

Retired Number: 5 (Detroit Tigers, 1983)
First Baseman/Outfielder
Playing Career: Detroit Tigers 1930, 1933–41, 1945–46; Pittsburgh Pirates 1947

Born in New York on New Year's Day of 1911, Hank Greenberg was the son of Romanian-Jewish immigrants. A large man at almost 6-feet-4 and 210 pounds, he worked hard to overcome his clumsiness and awkwardness and developed into a Hall of Fame player.

Greenberg tried out for the New York Giants but was turned down because manager John McGraw thought he was too uncoordinated. He received offers from other teams, however, and rejected proposals from the New York Yankees and the Washington Nationals before signing with the Detroit Tigers.

Greenberg played in the minor leagues from 1930 through 1932, although his major league debut came in the form of a single, unsuccessful pinch-hit at-bat for the Tigers in 1930. He arrived in Detroit to stay in 1933 and promptly batted .301 at first base.

Hank had a consistent stroke and good power, as he would display many times over the course of his next 12 seasons. He hit over .300 nine times, eight of them consecutively. In 1934 his .339 average was the result of 201 hits, and he led the American League with a whopping 63 doubles while also slamming 26 home runs and driving in 139 runs. He added a .321 average in the World Series, which Detroit lost to the St. Louis Cardinals.

In 1935 Hank won the first of two Most Valuable Player Awards. He hit .328 with 203 hits, while leading the AL with 170 runs batted in and tying Jimmie Foxx with 36 home runs. The Tigers went to the World Series again, but Greenberg broke his wrist in the second game and could only watch from the bench as his squad bested the Chicago Cubs to win the World Championship.

After only a dozen games of the 1936 season, Hank broke the same wrist and was out for the rest of the year. He came back strongly in 1937, however, hitting .337, clubbing 40 home runs, and leading the league with a career-high 183 RBIs.

In 1938 he led the league with 58 home runs and 144 runs scored, and tied Jimmie Foxx with 119 walks. Two years later he switched from first base to left field to make room for Rudy York, and it was obvious that the change did not hamper him as he won his second Most Valuable Player Award. He hit .340 for the season and led the AL with a .670 slugging average, 41 home runs, 150 RBIs, and 50 doubles. He is one of only three players to have won the MVP Award at two different positions. He hit .357 in the World Series, but the Tigers lost in seven games to the Cincinnati Reds.

Greenberg played only 19 games in 1941 before joining the military, and he would not return to the Tigers until 1945. Upon his return he batted .311 in 78 games, and hit two home runs in the World Series as the Tigers once again defeated the Cubs. In 1946 he led the American League with 44 home runs and 127 RBIs.

A salary dispute caused the Tigers to send him to the Pittsburgh Pirates for the 1947 season. Greenberg hit only .249 in Pittsburgh, but he did smack 25 home runs and tied Pee Wee Reese for the National League lead with 104 walks before retiring. In his 13-year career, which actually consisted of only nine full seasons due to injuries and military service, he batted .313 with 331 home runs and 1276 RBIs. He played in four World Series and hit .318.

After his retirement he worked for two years in the Cleveland Indians' farm system, and was promoted to general manager in 1950. In 1956 he was inducted into the Hall of Fame, and two years later he became part-owner and vice president of the Chicago White Sox. He retired from baseball in 1963 and became an investment banker.

When Greenberg played his first game for the Tigers in 1930, the team did not yet wear uniform numbers. When he was called up in 1933 he was given number 7, but switched to his familiar number 5 the following year. The Tigers retired the number in 1983. Greenberg died three years later in Beverly Hills, California.

Awards/Honors

1935 American League Most Valuable Player
1940 American League Most Valuable Player
1956 Hall of Fame

Ron Guidry

Retired Number: 49 (New York Yankees, 2003)
Pitcher
Playing Career: New York Yankees 1975–88

Nicknamed "Louisiana Lightning" because he was a 1950 native of Lafayette, Louisiana, and because he often topped 150 strikeouts per season, Ron Guidry carved out a highly successful 14-year career on the Yankee Stadium mound and never wore a major league uniform other than that made famous by the pinstripes of the Bronx Bombers. Also known as "Gator" and "The Ragin' Cajun," Guidry debuted as a reliever in New York in 1975 and made a single start that year. He would not become a regular in the rotation until 1977, but he was very impressive that season as he put together a 16–7 mark and a 2.82 earned run average. The next season was to be his best. He won 13 consecutive games to start the season, and he never looked back as he eventually led the American League with 25 victories, which he pitted against only 3 losses for a circuit-best .893 winning percentage. He also led the league with a spectacular 1.74 ERA and 9 shutouts, throwing in 248 strikeouts for good measure. On June 17 he struck out 18 California Angels in a single game. As a result of his dominating season he won the AL Cy Young Award unanimously, and finished behind only Jim Rice of the Boston Red Sox in Most Valuable Player voting. In 1979 Guidry followed up his success with a solid 18–8 record and a league-best 2.78 ERA, striking out 201 batters along the way. He continued to be a solid performer for many years, winning the first of five consecutive Gold Gloves in 1982 and becoming a 20-game winner for the second time in 1983 when he went 21–9 and led the AL with 21 complete games. Two years later he was 22–6, leading the circuit once again in victories and with a .786 winning percentage. Because of arm problems, Guidry's career declined after that, and he pitched only three more seasons and never again won more than 9 games in a year. He had elbow surgery following the 1988 season, but had a difficult time as he attempted to recover. He finally retired on July 12, 1989, after pitching mediocre ball at AAA. In his career, however, he had fashioned an impressive 170–91 lifetime record with a 3.29 ERA. He was 2–1 in League Championship Series play, and 3–1 with a 1.69 earned run average in three World Series. He helped the Yanks to the World Championship in both 1977 and 1978, going 1–0 in each Series and fashioning ERAs of 2.00 and 1.00. In the 1981 October Classic he was 1–1, 1.93 in a loss to the Los Angeles Dodgers. In August of 2003 the Yankees held Ron Guidry Day at Yankee Stadium. Their former pithcer was, of course, invited to the event, but he was not aware that the Yankees had planned to retire his number. He wept at the site of the Yankee Stadium monument that was erected in his honor, and that joined those of other incredible Yankee greats who had played throughout the previous century.

Awards/Honors

1978 American League Cy Young Award
1982 American League Gold Glove Pitcher
1983 American League Gold Glove Pitcher
1984 American League Gold Glove Pitcher
1985 American League Gold Glove Pitcher
1986 American League Gold Glove Pitcher

Tony Gwynn

Retired Number: 19 (San Diego Padres, 2004)
Outfielder
Playing Career: San Diego Padres 1982–2001

Born in 1960 in Los Angeles, Tony Gwynn moved slightly south but stayed in California as he spent his entire 20-year career with the San Diego Padres.

He was a third-round draft choice for the Padres in 1981, and was also drafted by the National Basketball Association's San Diego Clippers. Tony chose baseball as his profession, and instantly became the Most Valuable Player of the rookie Northwest League. He was called up to the Padres in 1982 and batted .289. He would then proceed to hit over .300 for the next 19 seasons in a row.

From that point on, the *lowest* average Gwynn put together in a season was .309, in both 1983 and 1990. His high was .394 in 1994, a year that was unfortunately cut short by a players' strike and that had stood a chance of seeing the major leagues' first .400 hitter since 1941.

Gwynn won eight batting titles in his career, and he had over 200 hits five times. In 1984 his 213 safeties led the National League, and in 1986 he paced the circuit with 211 hits and tied Von Hayes with 107 runs scored while, ironically, not winning the batting title. His .329 average was third behind Tim Raines' .334 and Steve Sax's .332. He proved that his game consisted of far more than just his bat, however, as he also won the first of five Gold Gloves for his outfield work, and on September 20 stole five bases in a game against the Houston Astros at the Astrodome, tying a major league record. He swiped 37 for the season.

He went on to win the next three batting championships in a row, hitting .370 in 1987 and leading the league with 218 hits. He also recorded a career-high 56 steals. In 1989 his 203 hits led the loop, and he stole 40 bases.

His second-highest average came in 1997 when he batted .372 to take the batting title, and he also clubbed a career-high 17 home runs. Never known as a power hitter, he would nevertheless hit 16 more the following year. On August 6, 1999, his mother's birthday, Gwynn went 4-for-5 against the Montreal Expos, and his single off Dan Smith in the first inning was the 3000th hit of his career.

Injuries slowed Gwynn in 2000 and 2001, but he never lost his stride with the bat. He played only 36 games in 2000 but hit .323, and managed only 71 in 2001, batting .324. He retired following the 2001 season with a .338 lifetime batting average, 3141 hits, and 319 stolen bases. In six postseason series he batted .306, with a .371 batting average in two World Series.

The Padres retired his number 19 in 2004, three years following his retirement as a player.

Tony's brother, Chris Gwynn, had a 10-year career with the Los Angeles Dodgers, the Kansas City Royals, and the Padres.

Awards/Honors

1986 National League Gold Glove Outfielder
1987 National League Gold Glove Outfielder
1989 National League Gold Glove Outfielder
1990 National League Gold Glove Outfielder
1991 National League Gold Glove Outfielder

Mel Harder

Retired Number: 18 (Cleveland Indians, 1990)
Pitcher/Coach/Manager
Playing Career: Cleveland Indians 1928–47
Coaching Career: Cleveland Indians 1947–63; New York Mets 1964; Chicago Cubs 1965; Cincinnati Reds 1966–68; Kansas City Royals 1969
Managerial Career: Cleveland Indians 1961–62

Mel Harder was born in Nebraska in 1909 and spent 36 years with the Cleveland Indians as a player, coach, and manager. Twenty of those made him one of the winningest pitchers in Indians history.

Mel began his major league career in 1928 and did not put up impressive numbers for several years. However, his 4.21 earned run average in 1930 can be a bit misleading, considering the fact that the composite ERA from among all American League hurlers that year was 4.65. The league batting average was .288, a sign that Harder was truly pitching in the era of the hitter.

In 1932 he threw the first pitch at Cleveland's Municipal Stadium, and he became a 15-game winner for the first time that year. He won 15 again the next year, and his ERA dropped to 2.95. In 1934 he became a 20-game winner, going 20–12 with a 2.61 ERA and tying Lefty Gomez for the league lead with 6 shutouts.

The following year Harder went 22–11 and threw a career-high 17 complete games (the second of three times he would reach that mark) while hurling 4 shutouts in the process. He would never again win 20, but would continue to win consistently for many years to come.

Mel won at least 15 games eight years in a row, from 1932 through 1939. He posted double-digit wins in 13 of his 20 seasons, and in years dominated by hitters kept his ERA below 4.00 eleven times. He pitched nine or more complete games 11 times, 9 of them consecutively.

Harder concluded his pitching career in 1947 with 223 lifetime wins and a misleading all-time ERA of 3.80. He threw 181 complete games and 25 shutouts in 582 games. He became the Indians' pitching coach in 1947, and continued in that role through the 1963 season. On an interim basis he managed one game in 1961 and two games in 1962, winning all three of them. In 1964 he moved to the New York Mets as a coach, then to the Chicago Cubs the following year, to the Cincinnati Reds for the next three years, and to the Kansas City Royals for one final season in 1969.

Harder wore number 18 beginning in 1931, when the Indians first began to wear numbers, and continuing throughout his playing career with Cleveland, although he donned number 43 as a coach and wore number 2 in his final season. The Indians honored him by retiring number 18 in 1990. Mel passed away in 2002.

Gil Hodges

Retired Number: 14 (New York Mets, 1972)
Third Baseman/Catcher/First Baseman/Manager
Playing Career: Brooklyn Dodgers 1943, 1947–57; Los Angeles Dodgers 1958–61; New York Mets 1962–63

Managerial Career: Washington Senators 1963–67; New York Mets 1968–71

A 1924 native of Princeton, Indiana, Gil Hodges was a slugging first baseman who became a successful manager.

He made his major league debut with the Brooklyn Dodgers in a single game at third base in 1943, then joined the Marines and did not return until 1947. When he came back it was as a catcher, but Roy Campanella would join the Dodgers the next year and Hodges would be moved to first base.

Hodges began showing some power in 1949, when he hit 23 home runs with 115 runs batted in, and that was the first of 11 consecutive seasons in which he would smash at least 20 roundtrippers and the first of seven straight that he would drive in at least 100 runs. He hit 32 home runs in 1950 and 40 the following season. His all-time high came in 1954 when he belted 42 and drove in a career-high 130.

Gil hit .302 in 1953 and .304 the next year, the only two times he would top the .300 mark. His strikeout totals were always somewhat high, and he even led the National League in that category in 1951. But he continued to hit home runs and continued to bring runners home, and he seemed to thrive under pressure as evidenced by his 14 career grand slams, a National League record at the time.

He accompanied the Dodgers when they moved to Los Angeles in 1958, and he won the first of two consecutive Gold Gloves that year. He appeared in seven World Series for the Dodgers, helping them to the 1955 championship with a .292 average against the New York Yankees, and to a second title in 1959 as he hit .391 against the Chicago White Sox.

Hodges' power numbers tailed off after the 1959 season, and in 1962 he became one of the original New York Mets as a part-time first baseman. He played 11 games in New York in 1963 when, in May, the expansion Mets traded him to the expansion Washington Senators, who were interested in Gil as a manager. Hodges ended his playing career with 370 lifetime home runs and 1274 RBIs.

Gil could not do much with the Senators, as the team finished last in 1963 out of 10 teams, finished ninth the next year, eighth the following two seasons, and sixth in 1967. Following the 1967 campaign, the Senators traded him back to the Mets, who wanted to make him *their* manager. Gil managed only a ninth-place finish in 1968 in New York, but in 1969 he was dubbed the "Miracle Worker" as he took the "Miracle Mets" to the National League Eastern Division title, to the National League pennant in a three-game sweep of the Atlanta Braves, and to the World Championship in five games over the Baltimore Orioles. The Associated Press named him the National League Manager of the Year.

Gil produced third-place finishes the next two seasons. During spring training of 1972, Hodges died suddenly of a heart attack following a golf game in West Palm Beach, two days before his forty-eighth birthday. The Mets retired his number 14 that same year.

Awards/Honors

1958 National League Gold Glove First Baseman
1959 National League Gold Glove First Baseman
1969 National League Manager of the Year (AP)

Willie Horton

Retired Number: 23 (Detroit Tigers, 2000)
Outfielder/Designated Hitter/Coach
Playing Career: Detroit Tigers 1963–77; Texas Rangers 1977; Cleveland Indians 1978; Oakland Athletics 1978; Toronto Blue Jays 1978; Seattle Mariners 1979–80
Coaching Career: New York Yankees 1985; Chicago White Sox 1986

Willie Horton was born in Virginia in 1942 and made his major league debut 21 years later as an outfielder with the Detroit Tigers. He played only 15 games with the big club that year but hit .326. After another cup of coffee in 1964, he made his mark in 1965 by belting 29 home runs and driving in 104 in Detroit.

Although he struggled with injuries, Horton always had good power, blasting home runs in double digits 15 times in his 18-year career. He hit over 20 seven times. In 1966 his 27 roundtrippers were accompanied with 100 runs batted in, and two years later he smacked a career-high 36 over the fence. The Tigers went to the World Series that year, and Horton hit .304 with a home run in the seven games and even threw out Lou Brock at home plate as Detroit defeated the St. Louis Cardinals to win the championship.

In 1970 Horton's power dropped a bit, as he hit only 17 home runs and appeared in only 96 games, but his average rose to .305. In a game against the Cleveland Indians in 1972, he tied a major league record with 12 putouts. In 1973 he batted .316, the second and last time he would top the .300 mark, and in 1975 he became a full-time designated hitter. Willie took immediate advantage of that situation, crushing 25 home runs with 92 RBIs, but in 1976 his power diminished again as he managed only 14 homers.

Over the next three years Horton bounced around between six different major league teams. He started the 1977 season with Detroit, but appeared in only one game and in April was traded to the Texas Rangers. Prior to the 1978 campaign the Rangers traded him to the Indians, and that season Willie would appear with the Indians, the Oakland Athletics, and the Toronto Blue Jays. He then became a free agent and signed with the Seattle Mariners for 1979.

Horton found new life for one last hurrah with Seattle, as he appeared in all 162 games for the Mariners and hit 29 home runs with a career-high 106 RBIs. The following season he was relegated to part-time duty, and he retired with 325 lifetime home runs and 1163 runs batted in.

Horton became a roving minor league coach for several years, and in 1985 was hired by the New York Yankees to coach at the major league level. He served in a similar role with the Chicago White Sox the following year, and he eventually went back to work for the Tigers in their front office. In 2000, the club retired his number 23.

Elston Howard

Retired Number: 32 (New York Yankees, 1984)
Outfielder/Catcher/First Baseman/Coach
Playing Career: New York Yankees 1955–67; Boston Red Sox 1967–68
Coaching Career: New York Yankees 1969–79

Elston Gene Howard hailed from St. Louis, Missouri, where he was born in 1929 as an only child to very educated and successful parents. He was a star athlete in high school in several sports, and turned down 25 scholarship offers following his graduation.

Signed by the New York Yankees in 1950, Howard spent several years in the minor leagues as a catcher. He joined the Army during the Korean War, then returned to the New York organization in 1953. He was used as both an outfielder and a catcher, and was instructed behind the plate by none other than Bill Dickey. He became the Most Valuable Player in the International League in 1954. When he was called up the next year, he became the Yankees' first black player, and was used primarily in the outfield because Yogi Berra was firmly entrenched at the receiver's position.

Howard hit .314 in 1958, one of three times he would top the .300 mark. He bounced around between the outfield and catching, and in 1959 actually played more games at first base than anywhere else. In 1960 he and Berra shared the catching chores, and the following year he became the regular catcher as Yogi was used primarily in the outfield.

In 1961 Howard hit a career-high .348 and smashed 21 home runs, and he exhibited excellent defensive prowess as evidenced by his .992 fielding percentage. His lifetime percentage behind the plate would be .993.

He hit 21 home runs again in 1962 with 91 runs batted in, and in 1963 he won the American League Most Valuable Player Award when he hit .287 with a career-high 28 home runs, adding 85 RBIs and a .994 fielding percentage. He was the first black player to be so honored, and he also won the first of two consecutive Gold Gloves.

In 1964 Howard hit .313, and he made only two errors all season for a fielding percentage of .998. Both his average and his power tailed off the next two seasons, and he was foundering at the plate in 1967 when he was traded late in the year to the Boston Red Sox. Howard did not improve in Boston, and his cumulative average for the season was .178. He bounced back somewhat to .241 in 1968, then retired with a lifetime average of .274 with 167 home runs.

Between 1955 and 1964 he had appeared in nine World Series for the Yankees, then added one more with the Red Sox in 1967. He helped win four championships. He hit 5 World Series home runs with 42 hits, while scoring 25 runs and driving in 19. He was a nine-time All-Star.

In 1969 Howard returned to the Yankees as a coach, and he remained in that role for 11 seasons. He died in New York in December of 1980, and the Yankees retired his uniform number 32 four years later.

Awards/Honors

1963 American League Most Valuable Player
1963 American League Gold Glove Catcher
1964 American League Gold Glove Catcher

Dick Howser

Retired Number: 10 (Kansas City Royals, 1987)
Shortstop/Second Baseman/Coach/Manager
Playing Career: Kansas City Athletics 1961–63; Cleveland Indians 1963–66; New York Yankees 1967–68
Coaching Career: New York Yankees 1969–78
Managerial Career: New York Yankees 1978, 1980; Kansas City Royals 1981–86

Born in 1936 in Miami, Florida, Dick Howser had an eight-year playing career followed by a successful career as a major league coach and then, most significantly, a manager.

Howser debuted as the regular shortstop for the Kansas City Athletics in 1961 and batted a solid .280 with 108 runs scored and 37 stolen bases. He dropped to .238 the following year and played only 83 games, and was hitting only .195 in 1963 when he was traded to the Cleveland Indians. In 1964 he played all 162 games for Cleveland and hit .256 with 101 runs scored and 20 stolen bases. His average dropped again the next two seasons, and in December of 1966 he was traded to the New York Yankees. He played 63 games for New York in 1967, and retired following the 1968 season. In eight seasons, six of them as a part-time player, he stole 105 bases.

Howser became a coach with the Yankees in 1969, and would coach for the next 10 years. In 1978 he managed a single game on an interim basis when Billy Martin was fired, a game he lost, and Bob Lemon was then named Martin's replacement.

Howser returned as the Yankees' manager in 1980, and he guided the team to the American League Eastern Division title. When the club suffered a three-game sweep to the Kansas City Royals in the League Championship Series, however, he was fired by George Steinbrenner and replaced by Gene Michael.

In late 1981 the Royals hired him to be their skipper to replace Jim Frey, and he took the team to the American League Western Division title for the second half of the strike-shortened season. In the divisional playoffs that were constructed as a result of the players' strike, the Royals were swept by the first-half champion Oakland Athletics in three games.

Howser guided the Royals to consecutive second-place finishes the next two seasons, and in 1984 the club won the West by three games over the California Angels and Minnesota Twins. In the LCS, however, they were eliminated from the postseason when they lost three straight games to the Detroit Tigers.

In 1985 the Royals repeated as division champions by a single game over the Angels, and this time they defeated the Toronto Blue Jays in a seven-game battle for the American League pennant to advance to the World Series. They then won a four-games-to-three decision over the St. Louis Cardinals to bring Kansas City its first World Championship.

In 1986 the Royals were 40–48 when Howser was diagnosed with a brain tumor. He was replaced by Mike Ferraro for the remainder of the season, and in spring training of 1987 he formally retired. His lifetime winning percentage as a manager was .544.

On June 17 in Kansas City, Howser passed away. Sixteen days later, the Royals retired his uniform number 10. Later that year, the Dick Howser Trophy was created, and has been presented to baseball's College Player of the Year ever since.

Kent Hrbek

Retired Number: 14 (Minnesota Twins, 1995)
First Baseman
Playing Career: Minnesota Twins 1981–94

Minneapolis native Kent Hrbek, born in 1960, debuted for his hometown Minnesota Twins in 24 games in 1981. He batted only .239 in that brief stint, but had hit .379 in the California League to win that circuit's batting championship that season.

Hrbek was called up to stay in 1982 and became a local hero to the Minneapolis faithful. He hit .301 in his rookie season with 23 home runs and 92 runs batted in, finishing second in voting for the American League Rookie of the Year Award to Cal Ripken, Jr. The next season he hit .297 with 41 doubles, and in 1984 batted .311 with 27 homers and 107 RBIs. He finished second to Detroit pitcher Willie Hernandez for the Most Valuable Player Award.

Hrbek hit at least 20 home runs 10 times in his 14-year career. His high mark came in 1987 when he smashed 34, third-best in the American League, while driving in 90 runs and helping lead the Twins to the World Championship.

In 1988 he achieved his career-high batting average of .312, while still maintaining excellent power with 25 home runs. Three years later his 20 homers and 89 RBIs once again supported the Twins' drive to baseball's ultimate championship. Hrbek fared poorly at the plate in all of his postseason appearances, averaging only .146 in two League Championship Series and .160 in two World Series. In Game 6 of the 1987 World Series, however, he hit a grand slam, the fourteenth in Series history. He added another homer in the 1991 Fall Classic. In 1987 he made the final putout in the game that clinched the American League Western Division for the Twins, in the game that won the pennant for the Twins, and in the game that won the World Series for Minnesota.

Between 1982 and 1993 Hrbek failed to hit 20 home runs only twice and failed to drive in at least 76 runs only once. He retired in 1994 with a .282 career batting average, 293 lifetime home runs, and 1086 RBIs.

Kent hit the first home run in the Metrodome in an exhibition game against the Philadelphia Phillies on April 3, 1982. He spent his entire career in Minnesota and was a fan favorite.

When Hrbek first made his debut in 1981, he wore uniform number 26, but the following year he switched to number 14 and would wear that number for the rest of his career. In 1995 the Twins retired the number in his honor.

Carl Hubbell

Retired Number: 11 (San Francisco Giants, 1944)
Pitcher
Playing Career: New York Giants 1928–43

Carl Owen Hubbell was born in Missouri in 1903 and had a difficult time in the minor league system of the Detroit Tigers before being obtained by the New York Giants in 1928.

Hubbell threw a screwball that developed quickly when he reached the major leagues, and he went 10–6 for the Giants his rookie season. He threw a no-hitter against the Pittsburgh Pirates in May of 1929, going 18–11 that season and immediately establishing himself as a dominant moundsman in the National League.

"King Carl," as he became known, won 17 more games in 1930, another 14 in 1931, and was 18–11 again in 1932. In 1933 he began a string of five consecutive 20-win seasons, leading the National League in victories that year as he went 23–12 with a league-leading 1.66 earned run average. He pitched 308⅔ innings and threw 10 shutouts, both league bests. His performance earned him the first of two National League Most Valuable Player Awards. The Giants went to the World Series and defeated the Washington Nationals in five games, and Hubbell pitched 20 innings in two games without allowing an earned run and struck out 15 batters.

In 1934 he won 21 games and led the league with a 2.30 ERA. In the All-Star Game, he struck out Babe Ruth, Lou Gehrig, Jimmie Foxx, Al Simmons, and Joe Cronin in succession. After allowing a hit, he struck out Lefty Gomez for good measure, setting an All-Star record with six whiffs.

In 1936 his 26 victories led the league, as did his .813 winning percentage and his 2.31 ERA. He finished the season by winning 16 games in a row, then would begin 1937 by winning 8 more for an incredible 24 consecutive wins. He won his second Most Valuable Player Award, and he also pitched well in the World Series. He was 1–1 in 16 innings with a 2.25 ERA and 10 strikeouts, although the Giants dropped the Series to the crosstown New York Yankees.

Hubbell led the league with 22 wins in 1937, as well as with a .733 winning percentage and 159 strikeouts. He took the Giants to the Series again, but the club once again lost to the Yankees.

Hubbell's numbers would never again approach the level of dominance he achieved in those years, although he would continue to pitch until 1943. In 1939 he posted a strong 2.75 ERA, but in 1943 it skyrocketed to 4.91.

Hubbell retired with a lifetime record of 253–154 and a sterling 2.97 ERA. He pitched 258 complete games and struck out 1678 batters. In three World Series he was 4–2 with a 1.79 ERA and 32 strikeouts.

Carl went to work in the Giants' farm system following his retirement, and he would spend 30 years in that role.

Hubbell was a member of the Giants when they first donned uniform numbers in 1932, and for that first season he was given number 10. He would wear number 11 from 1933 on, and the Giants retired that number in 1944. He was elected to the Hall of Fame in 1947.

Carl died in Arizona in 1988.

Awards/Honors

1933 National League Most Valuable Player
1936 National League Most Valuable Player
1947 Hall of Fame

Jim Hunter

Retired Number: 27 (Oakland Athletics, 1990)
Pitcher
Playing Career: Kansas City Athletics 1965–67; Oakland Athletics 1968–74; New York Yankees 1975–79

Jim "Catfish" Hunter, a North Carolina native born in 1946, received his nickname from Kansas City Athletics owner Charlie Finley for publicity reasons. Finley believed the public would respond better to players with colorful histories or personality traits, and he created stories about Hunter catching fish in North Carolina creeks and the nickname stuck.

In reality Hunter injured his foot in a hunting accident as a teenager, and that accident badly diminished the velocity of his fastball. He adjusted, however, and became a crafty pitcher who was overlooked by most scouts but signed by Finley.

Jim missed the 1964 season with an injury but made his major league debut with Kansas City the following year. In 1967 he won 13 games and his earned run average was an excellent 2.81.

He was a member of the Athletics when the team moved from Kansas City to Oakland in 1968, and on May 8 he wowed the team's new fans by pitching a perfect game against the Minnesota Twins.

From 1965 through 1976, Hunter did not miss a single start. In 1970 he began to truly establish his dominance as he won 18 games, and the following season he became a 20-game winner for the first of five consecutive times, going 21–11 with a 2.96 ERA and helping the A's to the American League Western Division title. In 1972 he was 21–7 for a league-leading winning percentage of .750, and his ERA was a sparkling 2.04. He helped lead Oakland to the first of three straight World Championships, posting a 1.17 ERA in the League Championship Series against the Detroit Tigers and then winning two in the World Series as the A's defeated the Cincinnati Reds in seven games.

His 1973 season was similar, as he posted a 21–5 record for a league-best winning percentage of .808. He was 2–0 in the playoffs as Oakland defeated the Baltimore Orioles, and 1–0 against the New York Mets in the World Series.

His best year was 1974, when he led the league with a 2.49 ERA and tied Ferguson Jenkins with 25 victories, then went on to help the A's win the pennant against the Orioles and the World Championship against the Los Angeles Dodgers. For his efforts he won the American League's Cy Young Award.

When Charlie Finley failed to pay part of Hunter's salary to a life insurance fund, as stipulated in his contract, Jim was made a free agent by arbitrator Peter Seitz following the season. He then signed with the New York Yankees, and he continued his dominance by tying Jim Palmer for the league lead with 23 victories in 1975, as well as by leading with 30 complete games and 328 innings pitched. He won 17 games the next year, but then diabetes and arm strain began to take their toll and his numbers dropped dramatically. He was a contributing factor to the Yankees' back-to-back World Championships in 1977 and 1978, but was not the same pitcher. After going 2–9 in 1979, he retired at the age of 33.

Hunter was inducted into the Hall of Fame in 1987, and in 1990 the Athletics retired his uniform number 27.

In 1999, at the age of 53, Hunter died of amyotrophic lateral sclerosis (Lou Gehrig's Disease).

Awards/Honors

1974 American League Cy Young Award
1987 Hall of Fame

Fred Hutchinson

Retired Number: 1 (Cincinnati Reds, 1965)
Pitcher/Manager
Playing Career: Detroit Tigers 1939–41, 1946–53
Managerial Career: Detroit Tigers 1952–54; St. Louis Cardinals 1956–58; Cincinnati Reds 1959–64

Fred Hutchinson, born in 1919 in Seattle, Washington, put together a solid career as a major league pitcher but made his real mark as a manager.

"Hutch" debuted with the Detroit Tigers in 1939 and struggled somewhat; in 13 games his earned run average was 5.21. He fared even worse the next year, pitching 17 times and posting an ERA of 5.68. He did not pitch at the major league level in 1941 but did make two pinch-hitting appearances with the Tigers, then he spent four years in the Navy during World War II. The right-hander returned to Detroit in 1946 and was suddenly a success. He went 14–11 in his first full season with an ERA of 3.09, 138 strikeouts, and 16 complete games.

In 1947 he posted a career-high 18 wins, and two years later he won 15 and his ERA dipped to a career-best 2.96. He won 17 more games in 1950.

In 1952 Detroit was mired in last place when they named Hutchinson player/manager to replace Red Rolfe. Fred went 2–1 as a pitcher that year and 27–55 as a manager. In 1953 he pitched only three games, although his ERA in those three was an outstanding 2.79. As a manager he brought the Tigers up two notches to sixth place, and they finished with a record of 60–94.

Hutchinson wanted a multi-year contract to continue managing, and the Tigers would not give him more than a one-year deal. He left the team following the 1954 season, and two years later was hired to manage the St. Louis Cardinals. He spent nearly three seasons in St. Louis, and in 1957 guided them to a second-place finish behind the Milwaukee Braves. The Cardinals replaced him with Stan Hack toward the end of the 1958 campaign, and midway through 1959 he was signed to manage the Cincinnati Reds.

The Reds were in seventh place when Fred took over the reins, and he brought them in fifth, then managed only a sixth-place finish the following year. In 1961, however, he guided the team to the National League pennant, as the Reds achieved a record of 93–61 and finished four games ahead of the Los Angeles Dodgers. They would go on to lose the World

Series to the New York Yankees, but the Associated Press named Hutchinson the National League Manager of the Year.

The Reds came in third in 1962 and fifth the following year. In December of 1963 Hutchinson was diagnosed with throat cancer, and he kept his illness a secret and struggled through much of the 1964 season before finally being forced by his faltering health to step down in August. The Reds finished in a tie for second place with the Philadelphia Phillies, both teams only a single game behind the pennant-winning Cardinals.

Hutchinson died on November 12 at the age of 45, and the Reds retired his uniform number 1 the following year. Also in 1965, the Hutch Award was created to honor the major league player who best exemplifies the competitive spirit of Fred Hutchinson.

Awards/Honors

1961 National League Manager of the Year (AP)

Reggie Jackson

Retired Number: 44 (New York Yankees, 1993)
Outfielder/Designated Hitter/Coach
Playing Career: Kansas City Athletics 1967; Oakland Athletics 1968–75, 1987; Baltimore Orioles 1976; New York Yankees 1977–81; California Angels 1982–86
Coaching Career: Oakland Athletics 1992

Pennsylvania native Reggie Jackson was born in 1946 and made his major league debut in Kansas City 21 years later.

He was rather disappointing in 35 games with the Athletics in 1967, but was with the team as a regular the next season when it moved to Oakland and showed some power by connecting for 29 home runs. The following season was perhaps his best, as he clubbed 47 home runs with 118 runs batted in while leading the American League with a .608 slugging average and 123 runs scored.

Jackson always had good power, and would hit over 20 home runs 16 times in his 21-year career. He topped the 100-RBI mark six times, and hit at least 20 doubles on 12 occasions. He also had a penchant for striking out, however, leading the league five times in that category, striking out more than 100 times in 18 seasons, and retiring as the all-time leader with 2597 whiffs. In his debut 1967 season, he struck out 46 times in 35 games.

But he was always a threat with the bat, and in 1973 he won the

American League Most Valuable Player Award by hitting .293 and leading the league with 32 home runs, 117 RBIs, 99 runs scored, and a .531 slugging percentage. Two years later he tied George Scott atop the circuit with 36 roundtrippers and drove in 104.

Jackson never got along well with Athletics owner Charlie Finley, and following the 1975 season Finley traded him in a package deal to the Baltimore Orioles. Jackson spent only one season in Baltimore, and while his .502 slugging percentage led the league, he craved the spotlight and signed as a free agent with the New York Yankees the following year.

Reggie spent five seasons in New York and had some fine moments there, although he caused some controversy when he first arrived by calling himself "the straw that stirs the drink." His comment angered several fellow Yankees, chief among them catcher Thurman Munson and manager Billy Martin. Jackson did produce, however, hitting 32 home runs in 1977 and knocking in 110 runs. In the World Series he hit a home run in Game 4 and another in Game 5, then connected for *three* in Game 6 to become the first player since Babe Ruth to hit a trifecta in a Series game and the first player ever to hit five in a single Series.

In 1980 Jackson tied Ben Oglivie for the AL lead with 41 homers and hit .300 for the only time in his career, but following the 1981 season he left as a free agent and signed with the California Angels. He immediately paced the league in 1982 with 39 home runs (tied with Gorman Thomas), but also led the circuit in strikeouts for the fifth time. In 1985 he hit 27 homers, then his numbers began to drop.

Jackson left the Angels as a free agent following the 1986 campaign, and he returned to the Athletics for 1987. He put together a mediocre season and then retired with 563 lifetime home runs and 1702 RBIs. He became the first player to hit at least 100 home runs for three different teams, accomplishing the feat with the A's, the Yankees, and the Angels. He returned to Oakland in 1992 as a coach.

Jackson earned the moniker "Mr. October" by playing in 11 postseasons with those three clubs, and he played for five World Champions: the A's in 1972, 1973, and 1974, and the Yankees in 1977 and 1978. With the 1972 A's he was injured in the League Championship Series against the Detroit Tigers and was unable to play in the World Series. In 27 World Series games lifetime, he crushed 10 home runs with 24 RBIs and a .755 slugging percentage.

When Jackson first joined the Kansas City Athletics in 1967 he wore number 31, but he switched to number 9 when the team went to Oakland. He continued to wear 9 for his one season in Baltimore, but switched to 44 with the Yankees and would wear that number for the remainder of his career, including during his return to the A's. He was inducted into the Hall of Fame in 1993, and the Yankees retired his number the same year. It may seem just a little puzzling that the Yankees would retire a number for a player that spent only 5 years with the club, especially considering the fact that he had played 10 pretty good ones with the A's, but he had apparently made quite an impression in New York ... especially in October.

Awards/Honors

1973 American League Most Valuable Player
1993 Hall of Fame

Randy Jones

Retired Number: 35 (San Diego Padres, 1997)
Pitcher
Playing Career: San Diego Padres 1973–80; New York Mets 1981–82

Randy Jones was born in Fullerton, California, in 1950, and at the age of 23 made his big league debut with the nearby San Diego Padres as a starting pitcher.

Jones did not have a long career — it consisted of but 10 seasons — but he had some good ones along the way. He started off in solid enough fashion, compiling a 7–6 record in 1973 with a 3.16 earned run average in 19 starts. The following year was a disaster, as he tied for the National League lead in losses with his 8–22 record and put up a 4.46 ERA. In fairness, the Padres as a whole could not have been much worse, losing 102 games and boasting a league-worst team batting average of .229.

Jones rebounded incredibly the next year, putting together a 20–12 season and leading the league with a 2.24 ERA. He finished second to Tom Seaver in voting for the National League's Cy Young Award.

He did not remain a runner-up for long. In 1976 he led the league in victories as he posted a 22–14 record and fashioned a 2.74 ERA. He also paced the circuit with 25 complete games and 315⅓ innings pitched, all of which earned him the Cy Young Award. He was the starting and winning pitcher in the All-Star Game, and he did not make an error all season.

Randy fell off to a 6–12 record and a 4.59 ERA in 1977 for a Padres team that lost 93 games. He improved to 13–14 in 1978 with an excellent 2.88 ERA and 7 complete games, but he would never win that many games in a season again. He won but 11 in 1979 and went 5–13 in 1980, although he did pitch three consecutive shutouts that season.

In December of 1980 the Padres traded Jones to the New York Mets, but Randy was not the same pitcher. He suffered through frequent injuries and put together two unspectacular seasons in New York. He retired with a 100–123 lifetime mark and an earned run average of 3.42.

Jones wore number 35 throughout his career with the Padres, but when he first went to the Mets he was given 25 because Ed Lynch was wearing 35. Lynch switched to 34 later in the season, however, and Jones donned 35 for the remainder of his short career. The Padres retired his number in 1997.

Awards/Honors

1976 National League Cy Young Award

Al Kaline

Retired Number: 6 (Detroit Tigers, 1980)
Outfielder/Designated Hitter
Playing Career: Detroit Tigers 1953–74

"Mr. Tiger" was actually a native of Baltimore, Maryland, born in 1934, but he never played a single game for any professional team — major *or* minor league — other than the Detroit Tigers.

The Tigers signed Al Kaline in 1953, and their new outfielder hit modestly in 30 games. In 1954, his first full season, he batted .276 and connected for his second career home run, a grand slam. He hit only one home run in 1953 and four in 1954, but in 1955 he belted 27 and became the youngest player ever to win a batting title by hitting .340 and leading the American League with 200 hits. He drove in 102 runs and scored 121, and he finished second to Yogi Berra of the New York Yankees in voting for the Most Valuable Player Award. He hit 27 home runs again in 1956, knocking in a career-high 128 and hitting .314.

In 1957 he won the first of 10 Gold Gloves. This one came before the award was given separately to the National and American Leagues, and when outfielders were considered individually for their work in left, center, or right field. Kaline won it as a right fielder, and in 1958, when a Gold Glove was awarded to each position in *each league*, he won again as a right fielder for the AL. He also hit .313 that year.

In 1959 Al was shifted to center field, and he won another Gold Glove at that position. He would go on to win seven more when no distinction was made between the three outfield positions.

Kaline led the league with a .530 slugging percentage in 1959, and two years later he paced the circuit with 41 doubles. He belted 29 home runs in only 100 games in 1962, missing part of the season due to a fractured right collarbone.

In 1963 Al batted .312 and swatted 27 homers with 101 RBIs. He finished second in MVP voting once again, this time losing out to Elston Howard of the Yankees.

In 1966 Kaline matched his career high by once again hitting 29 home runs. In 1968 he suffered a broken arm and was able to play only 102 games, but he recovered in time for the World Series as the Tigers squared off against the St. Louis Cardinals. Kaline hit .379 in the postseason and bashed two home runs as the Tigers defeated the Redbirds in seven games.

In 1972 he split time between the outfield and a pinch-hitting role. His last season was 1974, and on September 24 of that year he collected his 3000th hit, somewhat poetically against the Orioles in his hometown of Baltimore.

Kaline retired with a .297 lifetime batting average, 3007 hits, 399 home runs, and 1583 RBIs. After leaving the playing field, he went to work as a Tigers broadcaster and later as a Tigers board member.

Kaline first wore number 25 in 1953 and part of 1954, then he switched to number 6 and kept that number for the rest of his career. The Tigers retired it in 1980, the same year he was inducted into the Hall of Fame.

Awards/Honors

1957 Gold Glove Right Fielder
1958 American League Gold Glove Right Fielder
1959 American League Gold Glove Center Fielder
1961 American League Gold Glove Outfielder
1962 American League Gold Glove Outfielder
1963 American League Gold Glove Outfielder
1964 American League Gold Glove Outfielder
1965 American League Gold Glove Outfielder
1966 American League Gold Glove Outfielder
1967 American League Gold Glove Outfielder
1980 Hall of Fame

Harmon Killebrew

Retired Number: 3 (Minnesota Twins, 1975)
Second Baseman/Third Baseman/First Baseman/Outfielder/Designated Hitter

Playing Career: Washington Nationals 1954–56; Washington Senators 1957–60; Minnesota Twins 1961–74; Kansas City Royals 1975

Born in Payette, Idaho, in 1936, Harmon Killebrew was signed by the Washington Nationals on the recommendation of a U.S. Senator from his own home state. He signed in 1954, and would bounce around between the major and minor leagues until 1959, when he made the big leagues for good.

The Nationals — who were originally called the Senators from 1901 until 1904, who were often commonly called the Senators while they were officially the Nationals, and who became the Senators again in 1957 — used Killebrew at a variety of different positions. Between 1954 and 1958 he played second and third base and appeared in only 113 major league games in that five-year span, but he would later also be used at first base, in the outfield, and as a designated hitter.

Killebrew had enormous power, and he would lead the American League six times in home runs and hit at least 40 eight times in his 22-year career. The first time was 1959, his first full season, when he bashed 42 to tie Rocky Colavito for the league lead and also knocked in 105 runs.

He hit 31 in 1960, and was with the Senators when they moved to Minnesota and became the Twins. He hit 46 roundtrippers the first year there with 122 runs batted in, and would lead the league the next two years with 48 and 45, respectively. His 126 RBIs were also best in the league in 1962, but so were his 142 strikeouts.

In 1964 he led the league in home runs for a third straight year, swatting a career-high 49, and he also drove in 111 runs. He would tie Carl Yastrzemski in 1967 with 44.

Killebrew also had a good eye at the plate. Like a true power hitter, he accumulated a lot of strikeouts, but that was mainly due to his swinging from the heels. He led the league in walks on four occasions, and drew more than 100 seven times.

In 1969 Harmon won the American League Most Valuable Player Award, leading the league with 49 home runs, matching his career high, and with 140 RBIs and 145 bases on balls.

He hit 41 home runs in 1970, and in 1971 topped the league with 119 RBIs, the ninth and final time he would accumulate at least 100. He managed 28 home runs that year and 26 the next, and his power numbers practically disappeared after that. He battled injuries in 1973 and appeared in only 69 games, and hit only 13 homers in 1974.

He spent a final season in 1975 with the Kansas City Royals, then became a broadcaster for the Twins. He retired with 573 lifetime home runs, 1584 RBIs, and 1559 walks. He appeared in one World Series, in 1965 when the Twins lost in seven games to the Los Angeles Dodgers.

Killebrew first wore number 25 with the Nationals in 1954, then switched to number 12 the next two seasons. From 1957 on he donned number 3, and that was the number the Twins retired for Harmon in 1975. Killebrew was inducted into the Hall of Fame in 1984.

Awards/Honors

1969 American League Most Valuable Player
1984 Hall of Fame

Ralph Kiner

Retired Number: 4 (Pittsburgh Pirates, 1987)
Outfielder
Playing Career: Pittsburgh Pirates 1946–53; Chicago Cubs 1953–54; Cleveland Indians 1955

Ralph Kiner had a relatively brief major league career — it consisted of only 10 seasons — but during that time he generated power at a rate surpassed only by Babe Ruth and Mark McGwire in baseball history and brought fans to the ballpark in droves.

Kiner was born in New Mexico in 1922, and he was signed by the Pittsburgh Pirates for $8000. He spent two years in the minor leagues and hit only 27 home runs total, then he went into the military from 1943 until 1945. When he returned to baseball in 1946, he became the Pirates' starting left fielder.

Beginning with that rookie season, Kiner would lead the National League in home runs for seven consecutive seasons. He hit 23 that year, which is not an impressive total on the surface — it was, in fact, the lowest total to lead the NL since 1921 — but it *was* the best in the circuit. The following year he batted .313 and led the league with a whopping 51 roundtrippers (tying Johnny Mize), as well as with a .639 slugging percentage. He drove in 127 runs, the first of six times he would top the 100-RBI mark.

In 1948 he blasted 40 homers (again tying Mize), then in 1949 belted 54 to become the first National League player in history to hit at least 50 homers in a season twice. He also led the league that year with 127 RBIs, 117 bases on balls, and a .658 slugging percentage, all while batting .310.

Kiner's 47 home runs were best in the loop the following year, and in 1951 he led not only with 42 home runs but also with 124 runs scored (tying

Stan Musial), 137 walks, and a .627 slugging percentage. He batted .309 in the process, the third and final time he would reach the .300 plateau. He topped the loop for the last time in home runs in 1952 when he hit 37, tying him with Hank Sauer of the Chicago Cubs, and he also led with 110 walks.

Between 1946 and 1952 the Pirates finished in the bottom three in the National League — several times coming in dead last — every year except 1948, when they finished fourth. Kiner was a huge draw, and fans would endure numerous Pittsburgh losses just to see him hit. During the 1953 season, however, Pirates management included him in a multi-player deal that sent him to the Cubs.

Between Pittsburgh and Chicago Kiner hit 35 home runs on the year, but back problems had been plaguing him throughout his career and were getting worse with time. In 1954 he managed only 22 home runs with the Cubs despite playing a full season. In November the Cubs dealt him to the Cleveland Indians for two players and cash.

Kiner played his last season in 1955, appearing in only 113 games with the Indians and hitting just 18 home runs. He was only 33 years of age when his back problems then forced him into retirement. He came away with 369 career home runs in only 10 years and a ratio of 7.1 home runs for every 100 at-bats. The only players more prolific in baseball history were Ruth and McGwire.

After his retirement from the playing field, Kiner became general manager of the Pacific Coast League's San Diego Padres, then he became a broadcaster. He was inducted into the Hall of Fame in 1975.

When Kiner debuted with the Pirates in 1946 he wore number 43, but he switched to number 4 the following season and wore that number for the rest of his career with the Pirates and Cubs, although he donned number 9 with the Indians in 1955 because Jim Hegan was wearing number 4. The Pirates retired number 4 in his honor in 1987.

Awards/Honors

1975 Hall of Fame

Chuck Klein

Retired Number: None (Philadelphia Phillies, 2001)
Outfielder/Coach
Playing Career: Philadelphia Phillies 1928–33, 1936–39, 1940–44; Chicago Cubs 1934–36; Pittsburgh Pirates 1939
Coaching Career: Philadelphia Phillies 1942–45

Chuck Klein was an Indianapolis native who was born in 1904. He made his major league debut in July of 1928 with the Philadelphia Phillies and put together an outstanding career in the outfield.

In 64 games that first year Klein batted .360, and that was the first of nine times that he would top the .300 mark. In 1929 he hit .356 and led the National League with 43 home runs while also driving home 145, quickly establishing himself as a rare high-average hitter who could also generate prodigious power. That was the first of five consecutive seasons in which he would collect at least 200 hits, as he finished with 219.

In 1930 he batted .386, but incredibly, that average was good for only third place behind Bill Terry's .401 and Babe Herman's .393. His 250 hits were second behind Terry's 254. His 59 doubles and 158 runs scored were both best in the league, however, and he also connected for 40 home runs and drove in 170.

The following season his .584 slugging percentage paced the National League, as did his 31 home runs, 121 runs batted in, and 121 runs scored (which tied him with Terry). His 1932 campaign was even better, as he hit .348 and led the league with a .646 slugging percentage, 226 hits, 38 home runs (tying him with Mel Ott), 152 runs scored, and 20 stolen bases, becoming only the third player in major league history to lead the league in both home runs and stolen bases. As a result of his performance he won the National League Most Valuable Player Award.

Almost unbelievably, 1933 was better still, as Klein won the National League Triple Crown with a .368 batting average, 28 home runs, and 120 RBIs. He was also the league's best with a .602 slugging percentage, 223 hits, and 44 doubles, but he lost in the MVP voting to Carl Hubbell, who went 23–12 for the New York Giants.

In November the Phillies traded Klein to the Chicago Cubs for three players and cash. Klein found Wrigley Field a bit more difficult than Philadelphia's Baker Bowl for a hitter, and his numbers came down in all categories. He still managed to hit .301 in 1934 along with 20 home runs, but he batted .293 the following season, although he hit .333 in the World Series. In spite of that performance, the Cubs lost to the Detroit Tigers, four games to two. In May of 1936 the Cubs sent him back to the Phillies as part of a four-player deal. On July 10 of that year, Klein connected for four home runs in a 10-inning game.

Chuck hit .325 in 1937 but only .247 the following year. He played only 25 games for the Phillies in 1939 and then went to the Pittsburgh Pirates. In 1940 he returned to the Phillies once again, and that was to be his last full season.

From 1942–44 he served as a player/coach for Philadelphia, and in 1945 he became a coach full-time and then retired. His lifetime average was .320, and he hit 300 home runs with 1202 RBIs.

Several players in the major leagues never wore uniform numbers but have been honored by their teams in the same way as those who did. In 2001, when the Phillies retired Jim Bunning's number 14, they also placed on the outfield wall two block-like *P*'s that had adorned Phillies uniforms in the early part of the twentieth century. One was for Klein, the other for Grover Cleveland Alexander.

The Phillies' decision to honor Klein in this manner is a bit puzzling, however. While it is true that the Phillies did not adopt uniform numbers until 1932, and that Klein thus played his first four seasons without a number, he did eventually wear several numbers with Philadelphia. He wore number 3 in 1932 and '33, and later wore numbers 32, 36, 1, 26, 29, and 8. The Phillies might have retired any one of these numbers in his honor, but for some reason chose not to do so.

Klein died in his hometown of Indianapolis in 1958, and was inducted into the Hall of Fame in 1980.

Awards/Honors

1932 National League Most Valuable Player
1980 Hall of Fame

Bill Klem

Retired Number: 1 (National League Umpires)
Umpire
Umpiring Career: National League 1905–40

Bill Klem was one of six major league umpires to have his uniform number retired.

Born Bill Klimm in Rochester, New York, in 1874, Bill became a ticket-taker at a local ballpark at the age of 16. He was a catcher with Hamilton of the Canadian League in 1896, but suffered an arm injury and later became a painter and construction worker. He tried playing baseball again, and for a time worked occasional construction jobs and played baseball on the side. In 1902 he saw a newspaper article about a friend, Silk O'Loughlin, who was umpiring in the National League, and he decided to give that profession a try.

He received $5 for umpiring his first game, a contest between a local Rochester team and the Negro Leagues' Cuban Giants. He was soon hired by the Connecticut State League and received $7.50 per game and $10.50 for doubleheaders, with nothing for expenses.

In 1903 he moved up to the New York State League, then to the American Association in 1904. His work was so outstanding that he was courted by both the National and American Leagues, and Klem chose the NL and went to work in 1905 for a yearly salary of $2100.

Klem would eventually be considered by many the greatest umpire in the history of the game. He was particularly noted for his accuracy in calling balls and strikes, and for the first 16 years of his major league career he worked exclusively behind the plate. He eventually pioneered the use of the inside chest protector, claiming that he was thus able to move closer behind the catcher and get a better look at pitches. He also created arm signals to go along with verbal calls so that spectators could recognize the calls from a distance.

Klem umpired 18 World Series totaling 104 games, and also officiated the first All-Star Game in 1933. He was the home plate umpire for five no-hitters.

Bill earned the nickname "The Old Arbitrator" because of his fairness and impartiality. He claimed at one point that he had never missed a call, but later modified that statement to say he had never missed a call in his heart. He retired when he made a particular call and realized he was not entirely certain that he had called the play correctly.

Klem then became chief of National League umpires. On September 2, 1949, he received a rare honor for an umpire when he was given "Bill Klem Night" at the Polo Grounds in New York, where he was presented with gifts.

Klem died in Miami in 1951, and he was inducted into the Hall of Fame two years later.

His number 1 was eventually retired by the National League office along with the numbers of Al Barlick and Jocko Conlan. The number came back into use, however, when the National League and American League offices were shut down and the umpires from those leagues came under the joint aegis of Major League Baseball in 2000.

Awards/Honors

1953 Hall of Fame

Ted Kluszewski

Retired Number: 18 (Cincinnati Reds, 1998)
First Baseman/Coach

Playing Career: Cincinnati Reds 1947–52; Cincinnati Redlegs 1953–57; Pittsburgh Pirates 1958–59; Chicago White Sox 1959–60; Los Angeles Angels 1961
Coaching Career: Cincinnati Reds 1970–78

Ted Kluszewski came upon the Cincinnati scene from Argo, Illinois, where he was born in 1924, and joined the Reds in 1947 as a solid, power-hitting first baseman. "Big Klu," as he would soon be known, had massive arms and tore the sleeves off his uniform jerseys to allow himself greater freedom of movement.

Ted appeared in 9 games for the Reds in 1947, then 113 in 1948. He batted .309 in 1949 but had not yet begun to show his true power, connecting for only 20 home runs in the last two seasons combined. That changed in 1950, as he bashed 25 with 111 runs batted in while hitting .307.

Beginning in 1952 he would hit over .300 for five consecutive seasons, reaching his career high of .326 in 1954. He crushed 40 home runs in 1953 with 108 RBIs while the Reds changed their name to Redlegs. In 1954 his 49 home runs topped the National League, as did his 141 RBIs.

Kluszewski continued his torrid hitting in 1955 as he batted .314, leading the NL with 192 hits, and he also connected for 47 roundtrippers and 113 RBIs. He was a vital part of the powerful 1956 Redlegs who finished only two games behind the Brooklyn Dodgers, batting .302 with 35 homers and 102 knocked in.

Ted soon became hampered by injuries, and he would never again play a full season as a regular. He played only 69 games in 1957, and in December the Redlegs traded him to the Pittsburgh Pirates for Dee Fondy.

Kluszewski batted .292 for the Pirates in 1958, but his power was almost completely gone. From 1957 through 1960, he hit only 19 home runs total.

During the 1959 season the Pirates traded him to the Chicago White Sox, and although Big Klu hit only 4 home runs all season, he hit another 3 in the World Series and drove in 10 runs in a six-game losing effort against the Los Angeles Dodgers. Ted was largely a pinch hitter for the White Sox in 1960, and he finished his career as one of the original Los Angeles Angels in 1961, where he hit 15 home runs.

Kluszewski retired with a .298 lifetime batting average and 279 home runs. In 1970 he returned to Cincinnati and became a coach with his original team, which was once again called the Reds. He coached through the 1978 season, then became an instructor and served in that capacity through 1983.

Ted died in Cincinnati in 1988. He had worn number 20 when he first joined the Reds in 1947 and during part of 1948, but switched to number 18 in '48 and wore that number during the rest of his Cincinnati career. The Reds retired the number in 1998.

Sandy Koufax

Retired Number: 32 (Los Angeles Dodgers, 1972)
Pitcher
Playing Career: Brooklyn Dodgers 1955–57; Los Angeles Dodgers 1958–66

Born December 30, 1935, in Brooklyn, New York, Sanford Koufax played both baseball and basketball in high school and attended the University of Cincinnati on a basketball scholarship. He continued to play both sports in college, and was signed by his hometown Brooklyn Dodgers at the age of 19.

Koufax was used somewhat sparingly during the first 6 years of his 12-season career, and the best earned run average he achieved during that period was the 3.02 he posted in his rookie year of 1955 in only 12 games. In 1958, the Dodgers' first season in Los Angeles, he won 11 games, but he also lost 11 and his ERA was 4.48. Sandy struggled with his control during those early years, but in 1961 he found his form and put together an outstanding — if all too brief — Hall of Fame career.

Koufax went 18–13 that year and led the National League with 269 strikeouts. The following year he was 14–7, and his 2.54 ERA paced the circuit, the first of five consecutive seasons in which he would lead the league in that category. He also struck out 216 batters in just over 184 innings and pitched the first of four no-hitters. On April 24 he tied a modern major league record by striking out 18 Chicago Cubs in a nine-inning game.

In 1963 he won the pitching Triple Crown with a 25–5 record (Juan Marichal also won 25), a 1.88 ERA, and 306 strikeouts, while he also led the league with 11 shutouts and recorded his second no-hitter. He was 2–0 with a 1.50 ERA and 23 strikeouts in the World Series as the Dodgers swept the New York Yankees. He won not only the National League Most Valuable Player Award, but also the Cy Young Award, which at that time was given to only one pitcher representing *both* leagues.

Koufax went 19–5 in 1964 for a league-best winning percentage of .792. His 1.74 ERA and 7 shutouts led the National League, and he struck out 223 batters in the same number of innings. He also pitched his third no-hitter. In 1965 he won the pitching Triple Crown for the second time with a 26–8 record, a 2.04 ERA, and 382 strikeouts — a league record — in a league-leading 335⅔ innings. His 27 complete games were also the NL's best, and he went 2–1 in the World Series with 29 strikeouts and a microscopic 0.38 ERA as the Dodgers bested the Minnesota Twins in seven games. On September 9, he pitched his fourth and last no-hitter, a perfect game against the Chicago Cubs which the Dodgers won by a score of 1–0. His performance netted him his second Cy Young Award.

Because of a circulatory condition in his arm, 1966 would be Koufax's last season, but it was every bit as good as the previous five, if not better. He won the pitching Triple Crown for the third time, going 27–9 with a 1.73 ERA and 317 strikeouts, while also leading the league with 27 complete games, 323 innings pitched, and, with five other pitchers, 5 shutouts. He was 0–1 in the World Series although his ERA was an excellent 1.50, but the Dodgers were swept by the Baltimore Orioles. He won his third Cy Young Award for his efforts.

Koufax retired at the age of 31 rather than risk a severe injury to his arm, and his lifetime record in 12 seasons was 165–87 for a .655 winning percentage. He struck out 2396 batters, posted an ERA of 2.76, and pitched 40 shutouts. His World Series ERA was 0.95, and he recorded 61 strikeouts in 57 innings.

In 1972 Koufax became the youngest man elected to the Hall of Fame, and the Dodgers retired his number the same year.

Awards/Honors

1963 National League Most Valuable Player
1963 Cy Young Award
1965 Cy Young Award
1966 Cy Young Award
1972 Hall of Fame

Bill Kunkel

Retired Number: 9 (American League Umpires)
Pitcher/Umpire
Playing Career: Kansas City Athletics 1961–62; New York Yankees 1963
Umpiring Career: American League 1968–84

Bill Kunkel was a rare player-turned-umpire, and following an outstanding career as an American League crew chief became one of six umpires to have his uniform number retired.

Kunkel was born in Hoboken, New Jersey, in 1936, and he emerged as a right-handed relief pitcher with the Kansas City Athletics in 1961. He pitched 58 games that year, compiling a 3–4 record and an unimpressive 5.18 earned run average. He did strike out 46 batters in 88⅔ innings, however.

In 1962 he appeared in only 9 games, and his ERA improved to a respectable 3.52 although his work consisted of a mere 7⅔ innings. He struck out six batters in those innings, but also allowed eight hits and walked four.

He signed with the New York Yankees for 1963 and had his best — and last — season as a major league player. He appeared in 22 games and went 3–2 with a 2.72 ERA, striking out 31 hitters in 46⅓ innings. His lifetime record was 6–6, his ERA 4.29.

Kunkel became an umpire after retiring as a player, and he reached the American League in that capacity in 1968. He eventually became a crew chief because of his excellence, and he also served as a basketball referee for 20 years.

Bill's son, Jeff Kunkel, played for the Texas Rangers from 1984 through 1992. In 1984, during a spring training game, Bill was the home plate umpire during a Rangers game, and Jeff brought the lineup card to home plate before the contest. It marked the only time a father and son have participated in a major league game as umpire and player.

Bill had a long battle with cancer, and he died of the disease in 1985 in New Jersey.

The American League office eventually retired Kunkel's number 9, but the number came back into use when the National League and American League offices were shut down and the umpires from those leagues came under the joint aegis of Major League Baseball in 2000.

Tom Lasorda

Retired Number: 2 (Los Angeles Dodgers, 1997)
Pitcher/Coach/Manager
Playing Career: Brooklyn Dodgers 1954–55; Kansas City Athletics 1956
Coaching Career: Los Angeles Dodgers 1973–76
Managerial Career: Los Angeles Dodgers 1976–96

Tom Lasorda, born in 1927 in Norristown, Pennsylvania, was an outstanding minor league pitcher who struggled in short stints as a major leaguer, and eventually became one of the most successful major league managers of all time.

In a minor league game for the Schenectady Blue Jays in 1948, Lasorda struck out 25 batters against the Amsterdam Rugmakers. He struck out 28 in his next two starts combined, and was soon signed by the Brooklyn Dodgers. He was assigned to Brooklyn's Montreal Royals farm club, where he would eventually spend nine seasons and compile an excellent 98–49 record.

In the midst of those years he was called up to the Dodgers twice. The first time was in 1954, when he got into four games but gave up eight hits in nine innings and put up an earned run average of 5.00. In 1955 he pitched four more for the big club, and this time his ERA was 13.50. He was sold to the Kansas City Athletics for 1956, and he pitched 18 games for the A's and went 0–4 with a 6.15 ERA.

Lasorda then pitched for the minor league Los Angeles Angels before returning to the Montreal Royals from 1958 through 1960. He turned to scouting in 1961 for the Dodgers, who were now based in Los Angeles, and in 1965 he became a minor league manager. From his first season at the helm through 1972, he won five pennants.

In 1973 Tom was named a major league coach under Walter Alston. In 1976, when Alston retired with four games left in the season, Lasorda was named manager and went 2–2.

Lasorda instantly won the National League pennant in both 1977 and 1978, becoming the first NL manager to accomplish that feat in his first two seasons, but the club lost the World Series to the New York Yankees both years. In 1977, however, Lasorda was named the National League's Manager of the Year by the Associated Press.

After finishing third and second the next two seasons, Lasorda guided the Dodgers to the World Championship in 1981 in a rather bizarre split season caused by a players' strike. The team finished half a game ahead of the Cincinnati Reds in the National League Western Division in the first half of the season, which, it was decided in a later owners' meeting, qualified it for the postseason. The Dodgers ended up six games behind the Houston Astros in the second half, but then defeated Houston three games to two in a divisional playoff series. They went on to defeat the Montreal Expos for the National League pennant, and the Yankees for the World Championship. The Reds and the St. Louis Cardinals both had better records than the Dodgers overall in 1981, but because of the split-season format, neither team qualified for postseason play. Nevertheless, the AP once again named Lasorda the league's Manager of the Year.

After a second-place finish in 1982, Lasorda was back on top in 1983 as the Dodgers bested the Atlanta Braves by three games in the Western

Division. They lost the League Championship Series to the Philadelphia Phillies, but Lasorda was named Manager of the Year by both the AP and the Baseball Writers Association of America.

The following season the Dodgers finished under .500, but in 1985 they came back to once again win the West. They lost the pennant to the Cardinals, however.

The club won its division again in 1988, this time topping the Reds by seven games for the division title, then squeaking by the New York Mets in a seven-game League Championship Series and defeating the Oakland Athletics, four games to one, in a dramatic World Series. Lasorda tied for NL Manager of the Year honors by the BBWAA with Jim Leyland of the Pittsburgh Pirates, and was named Manager of the Year by the AP, which had begun to present only a single award to the best manager from both leagues.

The Dodgers were in first place in 1994 when a players' strike halted the season, and there was no postseason. They won their division for the last time under Lasorda's reign in 1995, although they lost baseball's first official Division Series to the Reds.

Lasorda stepped down during the 1996 season due to heart problems. His lifetime record was 1599 wins against 1439 losses for a career winning percentage of .526. His clubs finished under .500 only 6 times in 21 seasons. In 1997 he was inducted into the Hall of Fame, and in 1998 was named the Dodgers' general manager. In 2000 in Sidney, Australia, he managed the United States Olympic baseball team to the gold medal.

Lasorda first wore number 29 with the Dodgers as a pitcher, then number 27. With the Athletics he donned number 23, then, upon becoming a Dodgers' coach in 1973, wore number 52. He finally switched to his famous number 2 in 1977 when he became LA's manager for his first full season. The Dodgers retired that number in his honor in 1997, the same year he was inducted into the Hall of Fame.

Awards/Honors

1977 National League Manager of the Year (AP)
1981 National League Manager of the Year (AP)
1983 National League Manager of the Year (AP)
1983 National League Manager of the Year (BBWAA)
1988 Manager of the Year (AP)
1988 National League Manager of the Year (BBWAA)
1997 Hall of Fame

Bob Lemon

Retired Number: 21 (Cleveland Indians, 1998)
Third Baseman/Pitcher/Coach/Manager
Playing Career: Cleveland Indians 1941–42, 1946–58
Coaching Career: Cleveland Indians 1960; Philadelphia Phillies 1961; California Angels 1967–68; Kansas City Royals 1970; New York Yankees 1976
Managerial Career: Kansas City Royals 1970–72; Chicago White Sox 1977–78; New York Yankees 1978–79, 1981–82

Bob Lemon hailed from San Bernardino, California. Born in 1920, he made his major league debut with the Cleveland Indians in 1941 as a third baseman. He appeared in only five games with Cleveland that year, four of them as a pinch hitter, and batted only .250. The following season he repeated those numbers, except that he did not manage a hit in five at-bats and therefore batted .000.

He spent World War II in the Navy, then returned to the major leagues in 1946 as a pitcher, although he played 14 games in the outfield between 1946 and '47. It was on the mound that he came into his own.

Lemon finished 4–5 in 1946 in 32 games, but had an excellent 2.49 earned run average. He went 11–5 the next season, then won 20 games in 1948, the first of seven times that he would reach that mark. He went 20–14 with a 2.82 ERA that season and led the American League with 293⅔ innings pitched, 20 complete games, and 10 shutouts. On June 30 he pitched a no-hitter against the Detroit Tigers, a game he won by a 2–0 score. In the World Series he continued his mastery, posting a 2–0 record and a 1.65 ERA as the Tribe defeated the Boston Braves, four games to two.

After winning 22 in 1949, Lemon led the league with 23 victories in 1950. He also topped the circuit with 288 innings pitched and 170 strikeouts, and he tied Ned Garver with 22 complete games. He went 22–11 in 1952, leading all hurlers with 28 completions and 309⅔ innings pitched.

He won 21 in 1953, then tied Early Wynn for the league lead in victories in 1954 as he went 23–7. His 21 complete games tied Bob Porterfield for best in the loop, but he took two losses in the World Series as the Indians fell to the New York Giants in four straight. Although he pitched well in the first game until the tenth inning, he was brought back on only two days' rest and was ineffective in Game 4.

His 18 wins tied two other pitchers for best in the AL in 1955, and he won 20 games for the last time in 1956, when he also tied Billy Pierce for the league lead with 21 complete games. He pitched two more seasons before retiring with 207 lifetime victories, a 3.23 ERA, and 188 complete games.

He pitched in the Pacific Coast League briefly after leaving the major leagues, then became a scout and a coach. He coached the Indians in 1960, and the Philadelphia Phillies in 1961. In 1966 he managed the Seattle Angels to the Pacific Coast League championship and was named Minor League Manager of the Year by *The Sporting News*.

Lemon reemerged in the American League as a coach with the California Angels in 1967, and in 1970 he became a coach with the Kansas City Royals and was named to replace Charlie Metro as manager partway through the season when the club was struggling. He brought the team in second in 1971, but they fell to fourth the following year and Bob was himself replaced.

In 1976 he coached the league champion New York Yankees under Billy Martin, and was also inducted into the Hall of Fame because of his outstanding pitching career. The next year he became skipper of the Chicago White Sox, and he brought that club in third as the team won 90 games, but he was 34–40 in 1978 when he was replaced by Larry Doby. The Yankees, in third place with a 52–43 record, hired him to replace Martin, and the team finished in a tie with the Boston Red Sox and then won a one-game playoff to advance to the League Championship Series. The Yanks bested the Royals, three games to two, to win the American League pennant, then overpowered the Los Angeles Dodgers in six games to win the World Championship. The Associated Press named Lemon the American League's Manager of the Year.

About a third of the way through the 1979 season, George Steinbrenner replaced him with none other than Billy Martin. He brought him back toward the end of the 1981 season to replace Gene Michael, however, and the club went on to win the American League pennant although it dropped the World Series to the Dodgers. In 1982, when the Yankees came out of the gate with a 6–8 record, the merry-go-round continued as Lemon was fired and replaced with Michael.

Lemon had worn several different numbers during his first few years with the Indians, but the 21 he settled on was the number he wore for the majority of his playing career. The Tribe retired the number in 1998. In 2000 Lemon died in Long Beach, California.

Awards/Honors

1976 Hall of Fame
1978 American League Manager of the Year (AP)

Ted Lyons

Retired Number: 16 (Chicago White Sox, 1987)
Pitcher/Manager/Coach
Playing Career: Chicago White Sox 1923–42, 1946
Managerial Career: Chicago White Sox 1946–48
Coaching Career: Detroit Tigers 1949–53; Brooklyn Dodgers 1954

Ted Lyons was a Louisiana native who spent his entire 21-year playing career with the Chicago White Sox. He debuted with Chicago in 1923 at the age of 22, having been signed by the White Sox based on his college performance. He had attended Baylor University, where he was studying law, but was coaxed away from that goal by the Sox after Lyons had previously turned down the Philadelphia Athletics.

Lyons never pitched in the minor leagues, and in fact had never even witnessed a major league game until he made his first appearance on the mound against the St. Louis Browns on July 2, 1923. He pitched only 9 games that year — 8 in relief— then spent his first full professional season with Chicago in 1924 and posted a 12–11 record. In 1925 he became a 20-game winner, the first of three times he would attain that height, as he tied Eddie Rommel for the American League lead in victories with a record of 21–11 and also paced the circuit with 5 shutouts.

Lyons won 18 the next year, and on August 21 pitched a no-hitter against the Boston Red Sox in a 6–0 victory. The game lasted only an hour and seven minutes.

In 1927 Lyons tied Waite Hoyt for the league lead in wins as he went 22–14 and posted a 2.84 earned run average. His career-high 30 complete games were also best in the AL, and his 307$\frac{2}{3}$ innings pitched tied teammate Tommy Thomas.

In 1930 he went 22–15, the last time he would win 20 games, and he led the league with 297$\frac{2}{3}$ innings pitched and with 29 complete games.

The following season Lyons suffered an arm injury, and he would never again be the same pitcher. The injury effectively destroyed his fastball, and in 1933 he led the league with 21 losses. But he worked to develop a knuckleball to compensate, and was soon able to pitch respectably once again, even if he was not as dominating as he had once been. In truth it took such domination to put up the numbers he had previously posted, because the White Sox teams for which he played regularly finished in the bottom half of the American League standings.

By 1935 Lyons had righted himself and went 15–8. He would not win that many games in a season again, although he won 12 in 1937 and 14 in both 1939 and 1942. In 1940, his four shutouts were part of a three-way tie for best in the league, and in 1942 his ERA of 2.10 topped the circuit.

Ted joined the Marines during World War II, and returned to the White Sox in 1946 for one final season as a pitcher. He pitched only five games, winning but one, and finished his playing career with a record of 260 wins against 230 losses. Thirty games into the season, he was named to replace Jimmy Dykes as the White Sox manager.

Chicago had been 10–20 under Dykes to that point, and went 64–60 under Lyons to finish at 74–80. They finished sixth in 1947 and dead last in 1948, and Lyons was then replaced by Jack Onslow.

In 1949 he began the first of five years as a coach for the Detroit Tigers, and coached a final season in 1954 with the Brooklyn Dodgers. He was inducted into the Hall of Fame the following year.

Lyons died in Louisiana in 1986. He had worn number 14 when the White Sox first adopted uniform numbers in 1931, but donned his familiar 16 in 1932. The White Sox retired the number in his honor the year following his death.

Awards/Honors

1955 Hall of Fame

Mickey Mantle

Retired Number: 7 (New York Yankees, 1969)
Outfielder/First Baseman/Coach
Playing Career: New York Yankees 1951–68
Coaching Career: New York Yankees 1970

Named after Hall of Fame catcher Mickey Cochrane of the Philadelphia Athletics and Detroit Tigers, Mickey Mantle had tremendous power, hitting some of the longest home runs ever recorded, and became something of a hero not only in New York but throughout the United States. He once hit a home run in Washington that was estimated to have traveled 565 feet.

Mantle emerged from Oklahoma to begin his own Hall of Fame career with the New York Yankees in 1951 at the age of 19. He struggled at first and was sent to the minor leagues, but a visit from his father put him back on track and he would soon begin to shine like few players before him.

Mantle became a regular in 1952, and from that point through 1968 he hit at least .300 ten times, led the American League in home runs four times, and led in runs scored six times. He would play in 12 World Series, contributing to 7 championships.

Mickey had a truly outstanding season in 1955, when he batted .306 and led the league with 37 home runs, 113 walks, and a .611 slugging percentage, and tied teammate Andy Carey with 11 triples. His 1956 season was even better, however. He won the Triple Crown with a .353 batting average, 52 home runs, and 130 runs batted in, the only time he would ever top the league in RBIs. He was also the league leader with 132 runs scored and a .705 slugging percentage, and his numbers earned him the American League Most Valuable Player Award.

Mantle's batting average rose to .365 the next season, although Ted Williams won the crown with a .388 mark. Mickey led the league with 121 runs scored and 146 walks, while slugging 34 home runs and knocking in 94, good for his second consecutive American League MVP Award.

He led the league with 42 home runs in 1958, and with 40 in 1960. In 1961 he crushed a career-high 54 and spent most of the season beside Roger Maris in a chase of Babe Ruth's single-season record of 60. Injuries hampered Mantle during the final month of the season, and Maris eventually broke the record by hitting 61.

Mantle hit .321 in 1962 along with 30 home runs and 89 RBIs, and his 122 walks led the league. He won his only American League Gold Glove for his work in center field, and his performance netted him his third and last MVP Award.

Mantle continued to hit home runs — and battle injuries — through 1968, and he retired with a .298 lifetime batting average, 536 home runs, 1509 RBIs, and 2415 hits. He hit 18 home runs in World Series play along with 40 RBIs, 59 hits, 42 runs scored, and 43 bases on balls.

When Mantle first joined the Yankees, he was immediately projected to be the next New York superstar. As he was following in the wake of Babe Ruth, who wore number 3, Lou Gehrig, who wore number 4, and Joe DiMaggio, who wore number 5, he was first given number 6 in the belief that he would continue the procession. But he struggled and was sent to the minor leagues, and when he returned in 1952 number 6 was taken, so he was instead given number 7. That number was retired for him in 1969, the year following his retirement. In 1970 he came back to the Yankees as a coach, and in 1974, his first year of eligibility, he was inducted into the Hall of Fame.

Mantle died in Dallas in 1995.

Awards/Honors

1956 American League Most Valuable Player
1957 American League Most Valuable Player
1962 American League Most Valuable Player

1962 American League Gold Glove Outfielder
1974 Hall of Fame

Juan Marichal

Retired Number: 27 (San Francisco Giants, 1975)
Pitcher
Playing Career: San Francisco Giants 1960–73; Boston Red Sox 1974; Los Angeles Dodgers 1975

A native of the Dominican Republic, Juan Marichal made his major league debut with the San Francisco Giants in 1960 at the age of 22. He had just come off of two minor league seasons in which he had led his respective leagues in both wins and earned run average.

Marichal's trademark was a high leg kick, and he had excellent control that made him a dominant hurler throughout his 16-year major league career. In his first game with the Giants, on July 19, 1960, he pitched a one-hitter against the Philadelphia Phillies, having carried a no-hitter into the eighth inning. He went 6–2 that season with an excellent ERA of 2.66.

During his first 12 major league seasons, in fact, his ERA would top the 3.00 mark only three times. Two of those seasons were 1961 and 1962, but in '62 he also posted 18 wins. In 1963 he tied Sandy Koufax for the National League lead in victories as he went 25–8 with a 2.41 ERA, also leading the circuit with 321⅓ innings pitched and striking out a career-high 248 batters. It was the first of six times he would win over 20 games and the first of six times he would record over 200 strikeouts in a season. On June 15 he pitched a no-hitter against the Houston Colt .45s, a game he won by a score of 2–0.

Marichal went 21–8 in 1964 and led the league with 22 complete games. The following season he was 22–13 and his ERA was a minuscule 2.13 while his 10 shutouts were best in the NL. He was involved in a serious altercation in August with Los Angeles Dodgers catcher John Roseboro, a confrontation that led to Marichal's hitting Roseboro over the head with a bat and giving the Dodger a concussion. An onfield brawl ensued between the two teams, and Marichal ended up with a $1750 fine and a one-week suspension. The Giants finished two games behind the Dodgers that season, so the two starts that Marichal missed may have made all the difference.

In 1966 he was 25–6 for a league-leading winning percentage of .806. He won a career-high 26 games in 1968, once again the best mark in the NL, and he topped the league with 30 complete games and 325⅔ innings pitched.

Marichal won 20 for the last time in 1969, posting a 21–11 record and a league-leading ERA of 2.10. His eight shutouts also paced the loop.

Juan was affected by a reaction to penicillin in the spring of 1970, a reaction that resulted in chronic arthritis and, when he tried to come back too soon, a back injury. He won only 12 games that year, but bounced back in 1971 with an 18–11 record. His numbers declined thereafter, and in December of 1973 the Giants sold him to the Boston Red Sox.

Marichal started only nine games for the Red Sox in 1974 and struggled somewhat. He was signed by the Dodgers for 1975, but after starting only two games and going 0–1 with an ERA of 13.50, he decided to retire. His lifetime record was 243–142, his ERA 2.89 with 2303 lifetime strikeouts.

The Giants retired his number 27 in 1975, the year of his own retirement. In 1983, Marichal was inducted into the Hall of Fame.

Awards/Honors

1983 Hall of Fame

Roger Maris

Retired Number: 9 (New York Yankees, 1984)
Outfielder
Playing Career: Cleveland Indians 1957–58; Kansas City Athletics 1958–59; New York Yankees 1960–66; St. Louis Cardinals 1967–68

Born on September 10, 1934, in Hibbing, Minnesota, Roger Maris was signed out of high school in 1953 by the Cleveland Indians for a $5000 bonus. He spent his first four seasons in the minor leagues, and began to show some real power in 1954 with the Keokuk Kernels.

He made his major league debut with the Indians in Chicago on Opening Day of 1957 and went 3-for-5, then the next day hit a grand slam in the top of the eleventh inning to win the game against the White Sox. He hit 14 home runs in all that season, but in mid–1958 the Indians included him in a five-player deal with the Kansas City Athletics. Between the Indians and A's Maris clubbed 28 home runs his second year, then hit 16 the next season in Kansas City.

In December of 1959 the Athletics packaged him in a seven-player trade with the New York Yankees, a deal that saw Don Larsen going to Kansas City. Maris responded in a big way in his first season in New York, hitting 39 home runs and leading the American League with 112 runs batted in and with a .581 slugging percentage. He won the American League

Most Valuable Player Award, as well as a Gold Glove for his defensive prowess in right field.

The season for which Maris is most noted is 1961, the year he broke Babe Ruth's single-season record of 60 home runs. Maris and Mickey Mantle chased the record all season long, but Mantle suffered an injury with a month to go and finished with 54. Maris kept hitting them out, and finally connected for number 61 in the final game of the season against the Boston Red Sox. That swing produced the game's only run, as the Yankees won by a score of 1–0. Roger also led the American League with 142 RBIs that year, a career high, and with 132 runs scored, also a personal best, although he tied in that category with Mantle. His feats resulted in his second consecutive MVP Award.

Maris would not approach those heights again, but he still had power. He hit 33 home runs in 1962 with 100 RBIs, then hit 23 in only 90 games the following season. After hitting 26 in 1964, he suffered a hand injury that would affect him for the final four years of his career. He played only 46 games in 1965, and in 1966 managed only 13 home runs. In December of that year, the Yankees traded him to the St. Louis Cardinals.

Maris played two seasons in St. Louis, but hit only 14 home runs in those two seasons combined. He retired with 275 lifetime homers, and he had also appeared in seven World Series. He helped the Yankees to victories in 1961 and 1962, and did the same for the Cardinals in 1967.

Maris wore several different numbers throughout his career, but in his seven years with the Yankees he wore only number 9. The Yankees retired the number in 1984. The following year, Maris died of cancer in Houston, Texas.

Awards/Honors

1960 American League Most Valuable Player
1960 American League Gold Glove Right Fielder
1961 American League Most Valuable Player

Billy Martin

Retired Number: 1 (New York Yankees, 1986)
Second Baseman/Coach/Manager
Playing Career: New York Yankees 1950–53, 1955–57; Kansas City Athletics 1957; Detroit Tigers 1958; Cleveland Indians 1959; Cincinnati Reds 1960; Milwaukee Braves 1961; Minnesota Twins 1961

Coaching Career: Minnesota Twins 1965–68
Managerial Career: Minnesota Twins 1969; Detroit Tigers 1971–73; Texas Rangers 1973–75; New York Yankees 1975–78, 1979, 1983, 1985, 1988; Oakland Athletics 1980–82

Billy Martin was known for his aggressive play, for his managerial ability, and, probably most of all, for his fiery temper. A native of Berkeley, California, he was born in 1928 and began his professional career in the minor leagues in 1946.

A second baseman, he played for the Oakland Oaks under Casey Stengel in 1948, and when Stengel went to the New York Yankees, he had the club acquire Martin. Billy made his Yankee debut in 1950, and although he never hit for a high average, his aggressive style of play and excellent defense were much admired. In the 1952 World Series, his diving catch of a bases-loaded Jackie Robinson popup may have saved the Series for New York in a seven-game win over the Brooklyn Dodgers. In 1953 he was the World Series Most Valuable Player, as he batted .500 with 12 hits and 2 home runs. In the bottom of the ninth inning of Game 6, his single knocked in the winning run for the Yankees as the club once again bested Brooklyn for the title.

Martin spent 1954 in the Army, and came back in 1955 for only 20 games, but batted .300. In June of 1957 he was involved in a nightclub fight that also included several other Yankees stars, most notably Mickey Mantle, and Martin was held responsible. Seeing him as a bad influence in the clubhouse, especially on Mantle, the Yankees traded him to the Kansas City Athletics.

Martin moved to the Detroit Tigers in 1958, to the Cleveland Indians in 1959, to the Cincinnati Reds in 1960, and to the Milwaukee Braves in 1961. After appearing in only six games for the Braves, he went to the Minnesota Twins and retired following the 1961 season. His lifetime batting average was .257, but he had hit .333 in five World Series.

Martin became a coach for the Twins in 1965, and was named manager in 1969. He brought the Twins in nine games ahead of the A's to win the American League Western Division title, but they were swept by the Baltimore Orioles in the playoffs. Because he attacked one of his pitchers, Dave Boswell, and generally refused to heed the wishes of Twins owner Calvin Griffith, he was fired in spite of his onfield success.

In 1971 he was hired to manage the Detroit Tigers, and the following year led that club to the AL Eastern Division title. They were defeated by the A's in a five-game League Championship Series, however. In late 1973 he was fired and replaced by Joe Schultz, but was immediately hired to finish out the season with the last-place Texas Rangers.

In 1974 he brought the Rangers in second, only five games behind the A's. Their record improved from 57–105 the previous season to 84–76, and the Associated Press named Martin the American League Manager of the Year. He was fired midway through the 1975 season, again because of problems with upper management, and he then began his tumultuous relationship with George Steinbrenner and the Yankees.

Martin finished out 1975 with the Yankees, who finished third, then he took the team to the American League Eastern Division Championship in 1976. They defeated the Kansas City Royals in five games to go to the World Series, and although they fell to the Reds in a four-game sweep, the AP once again named Martin the AL's Manager of the Year.

In 1977 the Yankees were back on top, and they once again defeated the Royals in a five-game playoff and then bested the Dodgers, four games to two, to win the World Championship. In 1978 Martin had words in the press with Reggie Jackson and Steinbrenner, and he was forced to resign midway through the season. The Yankees repeated as World Champions without him.

In July of 1979 New York was 34–31 when Martin was hired back to replace Bob Lemon. The team finished in fourth place, and Billy was fired in October when he got into a fight with a marshmallow salesman.

He was hired to manage the Athletics in 1980, a club that had gone 54–108 the previous season. With his usual flair, Martin brought them in second, improving their record to 83–79 and once again being named the league's Manager of the Year by the AP. The following year, the split season of 1981, the team won the first-half Western Division title by a game and a half over the Rangers, and finished only a game behind the Royals in the second half. They swept Kansas City in a three-game divisional playoff, but were in turn swept by the Yankees in three games for the pennant. Nevertheless, Martin was named the AP's Manager of the Year for the AL for the fourth time.

The A's fell to fifth in 1982, and Martin was fired. He was hired back by Steinbrenner to manage the Yankees for a third term for the 1983 season, finished third, and was fired for the third time. Early in 1985 he was hired for a fourth time to replace Yogi Berra, finished second — only two games behind the Toronto Blue Jays — and was fired for the fourth time. He was hired for a fifth time in 1988, and after getting into another nightclub fight, was fired for the fifth time in midseason. On Christmas Day of 1989, he was killed in a car accident.

Martin wore number 12 in 1950, his first season with the Yankees, but would wear number 1 the rest of the time he was in a New York uniform. The Yankees retired the number in 1986, between his fourth and fifth terms as manager.

Awards/Honors

1974 American League Manager of the Year (AP)
1976 American League Manager of the Year (AP)
1980 American League Manager of the Year (AP)
1981 American League Manager of the Year (AP)

Eddie Mathews

Retired Number: 41 (Atlanta Braves, 1969)
Third Baseman/First Baseman/Coach/Manager
Playing Career: Boston Braves 1952; Milwaukee Braves 1953–65; Atlanta Braves 1966; Houston Astros 1967; Detroit Tigers 1967–68
Coaching Career: Atlanta Braves 1971–72
Managerial Career: Atlanta Braves 1972–74

Texas native Eddie Mathews was the only man to have played for the Braves in Boston, Milwaukee, and Atlanta. In fact, no other player has played for *any* franchise in three different cities.

Eddie was born in 1931 and signed with the Boston Braves in 1949 on the night of his high school graduation. By 1952 he had risen through the minor leagues and was a regular in the Boston lineup, and although he led the National League in strikeouts, he also belted 25 home runs.

The Braves moved to Milwaukee the following year, and Mathews improved there as he batted .302 and led the league with 47 home runs, which would be his career high. He drove in 135 runs, also a career high, and scored 110.

He hit 40 home runs in 1954 and 41 in 1955, driving in over 100 runs both years. In 1957 batted .292 with 32 homers and 94 RBIs as the Braves won the National League pennant. Mathews struggled against New York Yankees' pitching in the World Series, but he hit a tenth-inning home run in Game 4 off Bob Grim and the Braves won the World Championship in seven games.

The following year Eddie clubbed 31 home runs, and the Braves once again went to the World Series. Mathews once again floundered against the Yankees, hitting only .160; his four hits in the seven games included two singles and two doubles, and New York took the Series.

Mathews hit .306 in 1959 and led the National League with 46 home runs while driving in 114 and scoring 118, a career best. In 1961 he batted .306 again with 32 home runs and 91 RBIs, while leading the league by drawing 93 bases on balls.

He would lead the league in walks the next three years, in fact, receiving a career-high 124 free passes in 1963. Following the 1965 season, his numbers began to decline.

The Braves moved to Atlanta in 1966, and Mathews hit only .250 that season with 16 home runs. In December the Braves included him in a five-player deal with the Houston Astros.

Mathews moved from third base to first base, but he hit only .238 in Houston. Late in the season the Astros traded him to the Detroit Tigers. In 1968 he batted but .212 in 31 games as a pinch hitter for the Tigers, but he went 1-for-3 with a walk in the World Series as Detroit defeated the St. Louis Cardinals in seven games.

Mathews retired with 512 career home runs and 1453 RBIs. In 1971 he returned to the Braves as a coach, and partway through the 1972 season he was named to replace Lum Harris as manager. The Braves finished fourth that year, fifth in 1973, and were 50–49 in 1974 when Mathews was replaced by Clyde King.

The Braves retired his number 41 in 1969, the year following his retirement from the playing field. Eddie died in California in 2001.

Awards/Honors

1978 Hall of Fame

Christy Mathewson

Retired Number: None (San Francisco Giants, 1988)
Pitcher/Coach/Manager
Playing Career: New York Giants 1900–16; Cincinnati Reds 1916
Managerial Career: Cincinnati Reds 1916–18
Coaching Career: New York Giants 1919–20

Christy Mathewson was born on a farm in Pennsylvania in 1880, and was an outstanding multi-sport athlete by the time he got to college. In 1900 he won 20 games as a pitcher for the Norfolk Mary Janes of the Virginia League, and his contract was bought by the New York Giants for $1500.

Mathewson went 0–3 for the Giants at the end of that season, and the club returned him to Norfolk. He was then picked up by the Cincinnati Reds, who traded him back to the Giants for Amos Rusie because Reds owner John T. Brush was preparing to buy the Giants and wanted Mathewson to be there for him.

Christy responded admirably, going 20–17 in 1901 with a 2.41 earned run average. The following season he finished in a three-way tie for the National League lead with eight shutouts and had a sparkling ERA of 2.11.

From that point on, Mathewson became one of the most dominating pitchers in major league history. In the next 12 consecutive seasons, he never won fewer than 22 games, and he led the league in victories four times and in shutouts four times. He was the ERA leader five times, won at least 30 games four times, and won the pitching Triple Crown twice.

He first became a 30-game winner in 1903, going 30–13 and leading the league with 267 strikeouts. He was 33–12 in 1904, and won his first pitching Triple Crown in 1905 with a 31–8 record, a 1.27 ERA, and 206 strikeouts. In the World Series he was 3–0 as he shut out the Philadelphia Athletics in Games 1, 3, and 5, allowing only 14 hits in those three games combined and striking out 18 batters.

He won the Triple Crown again in 1908, going 37–11 with a 1.43 ERA and 259 strikeouts, while also leading the league with 12 shutouts and 34 complete games. His league-best ERA the following season was a remarkable 1.14, and his 25–6 record was good for a league-leading winning percentage of .806. Howie Camnitz of the Pittsburgh Pirates shared leadership with an identical record.

Mathewson led the league in victories for the last time in 1910 when he was 27–9, but he would continue to be a 20-game winner for four more years. He led the league in ERA again in 1911 at 1.99, and in 1913 at 2.06.

Christy's numbers fell dramatically in 1915, and after pitching 12 games in 1916 he was included in a five-player trade to the Reds. Cincinnati was primarily interested in him as a manager, however, and after pitching only one game for the Reds — which he won — he settled in as a full-time skipper. He ended his playing career with 373 wins, a 2.13 lifetime ERA, 2502 strikeouts, and 80 shutouts. He pitched 10 complete games and 4 shutouts in 4 World Series.

The Reds finished in a tie for last place in 1916, but they improved to fourth place the following season. In 1918 they were 61–57 when Mathewson was commissioned as a captain in the Army and was replaced by Heinie Groh, and the Reds finished third in a season shortened by World War I. Mathewson was accidentally gassed in a training exercise and contracted tuberculosis. In 1919 he returned to the Giants as a coach for two years, then worked in the Boston Braves organization. He died in 1925 at the age of 45.

Mathewson is one of several players who never wore a uniform number, but who have been honored by their teams in the same way as those who did. The Giants did not adopt numbers until 1932, twelve years after Mathewson had last worn a uniform. In 1988, however, the team, now in

San Francisco, placed an old-style "NY" logo on the outfield wall with Mathewson's name, next to the other players' retired numbers. They added another for John McGraw.

Mathewson's brother, Henry, also pitched three games for the Giants — two in 1906, and one in 1907.

Christy was one of the first five Hall of Fame inductees in 1936.

Awards/Honors

1936 Hall of Fame

Don Mattingly

Retired Number: 23 (New York Yankees, 1997)
Outfielder/First Baseman
Playing Career: New York Yankees 1982–95

A 1961 native of Evansville, Indiana, Don Mattingly was drafted by the New York Yankees as an outfielder. He hit .349 in 53 games in his first professional season with the Oneonta Yankees of the New York–Penn League in 1979, then won the South Atlantic League batting title with the Greensboro Hornets in 1980 with a .358 average. He continued to hit over .300 on his way up until he debuted in New York in 1982 in seven games.

Seven games was not a fair trial for Mattingly, as he batted .167, and neither were the 91 he played in 1983 as he hit .283. But in 1984 he was moved to first base and played regularly, and he responded immediately by winning the American League batting title with a .343 average, while also leading the league with 207 hits and 44 doubles.

In 1985 he had a spectacular season, batting .324 with a career-high 35 home runs and leading the league with 145 runs batted in and 48 doubles. He also established himself as an excellent defensive specialist at first base and won the first of nine Gold Gloves. Better yet, he was named the American League Most Valuable Player.

Mattingly led the league in 1986 with 238 hits and 53 doubles, while also hammering 31 home runs and driving in 113. In all he would hit over .300 seven times in his major league career, would hit at least 30 home runs three times, and would drive in at least 100 runs on five occasions. In 1987 he hit his first grand slam, then proceeded to hit five more that year, setting a new single-season record.

Don was plagued by nagging injuries toward the end of his career, spending time on the disabled list five times between 1987 and 1994. He missed more than a month and a half in 1990 with lower back pain and managed only a .256 average.

Mattingly retired in 1995 with a .307 lifetime batting average, 2153 hits, and 442 doubles.

Don had worn number 46 during his first two seasons in New York, but he switched to his familiar 23 in 1984 and wore that number for the rest of his career. The Yankees retired it in 1997.

Awards/Honors

1985 American League Most Valuable Player
1985 American League Gold Glove First Baseman
1986 American League Gold Glove First Baseman
1987 American League Gold Glove First Baseman
1988 American League Gold Glove First Baseman
1989 American League Gold Glove First Baseman
1991 American League Gold Glove First Baseman
1992 American League Gold Glove First Baseman
1993 American League Gold Glove First Baseman
1994 American League Gold Glove First Baseman

Willie Mays

Retired Number: 24 (San Francisco Giants, 1972)
Outfielder/Coach
Playing Career: New York Giants 1951–52, 1954–57; San Francisco Giants 1958–72; New York Mets 1972–73
Coaching Career: New York Mets 1974–79

He hit for average. He hit for power. He stole bases. He made miraculous plays in the outfield. On anyone's list of the greatest players of all time, Willie Mays is always somewhere near the top.

He was an Alabama native, born in 1931, and at the age of 17 he was playing for the Birmingham Black Barons of the Negro National League. In 1950 his contract was purchased by the New York Giants, and after a year with the Trenton Giants he moved up to the Minneapolis Millers in 1951. After hitting .477 in 35 games, he was summoned to New York.

Mays struggled a bit in his early days in the major leagues, going hitless in his first 12 at-bats, but then he belted a home run for his first major league hit and great things began to happen. He hit .274 for the season with 20 home runs and 68 runs batted in and was named the National League Rookie of the Year.

Mays put together a sensational 22-year career during which he hit over .300 ten times, hit at least 20 home runs 17 times, had at least 100 RBIs 10 times, and stole at least 20 bases 7 times.

After 34 games in 1952 he left to serve in the Army, and he missed the entire 1953 season. He came back with a vengeance in 1954, winning the National League batting title with a .345 average and leading the league with 13 triples and a .667 slugging percentage. He also cracked 41 home runs and drove in 110. In the World Series against the Cleveland Indians, he made one of the most famous defensive plays of all time; Vic Wertz hit a fly ball to deep center field, and Mays raced back toward the wall and, with his back to the infield, gloved the ball and spun to fire it back to the infield. The Giants ended up sweeping the Series, and Mays was named the National League's Most Valuable Player for the season.

Willie led the league with 51 home runs in 1955 and tied Dale Long with 13 triples while also batting .319, and the following year he led with 40 stolen bases. It was the first of four times he would top the circuit in home runs, and the first of four consecutive times he would lead in stolen bases.

He led the league in triples again in 1957 with 20, and in steals with 38. The Giants moved to San Francisco the next season, breaking the hearts of many New Yorkers, but Mays continued to flourish on the West Coast. He hit .347 his first year in California, leading the league with 121 runs scored and 31 stolen bases. He also won the first of 11 consecutive Gold Gloves for his defense.

In 1962 he hit 49 home runs to pace the loop, but he hit only .250 in the World Series as the Giants fell to the New York Yankees in seven games. His 47 homers were best in the NL in 1964, and his career-high 52 led the following year. He hit .317 that season with 112 RBIs and 118 runs scored, also leading the league with a .645 slugging percentage, the fifth and last time he would set the pace in that category. He also won his second MVP Award.

Mays' numbers gradually began to taper off, although they were more than sufficient for most players. On July 18, 1970, he hit a second-inning single off Mike Wegener of the Montreal Expos for his 3000th hit in a 10–1 Giants win, becoming the first player to reach that milestone on the West Coast. In May of 1972 he was traded to the New York Mets in a deal that returned him to a city where his feats had not been forgotten. He was relegated to part-time duty and hit only eight home runs, however, and after one final season in New York he retired from the playing field. He stepped down with a .302 lifetime average, 660 home runs, 1903 RBIs, 3283 hits, and 338 stolen bases.

Mays became a coach with the Mets the following season, and he served in that capacity until 1979, the year he was inducted into the Hall of Fame.

Willie wore number 24 throughout his career, and the Giants retired the number the year he was traded to the Mets.

Awards/Honors

1951 National League Rookie of the Year
1954 National League Most Valuable Player
1958 National League Gold Glove Center Fielder
1959 National League Gold Glove Center Fielder
1960 National League Gold Glove Center Fielder
1961 National League Gold Glove Outfielder
1962 National League Gold Glove Outfielder
1963 National League Gold Glove Outfielder
1964 National League Gold Glove Outfielder
1965 National League Most Valuable Player
1965 National League Gold Glove Outfielder
1966 National League Gold Glove Outfielder
1967 National League Gold Glove Outfielder
1968 National League Gold Glove Outfielder
1979 Hall of Fame

Bill Mazeroski

Retired Number: 9 (Pittsburgh Pirates, 1987)
Second Baseman/Coach
Playing Career: Pittsburgh Pirates 1956–72
Coaching Career: Pittsburgh Pirates 1973; Seattle Mariners 1979–80

Bill Mazeroski was an average hitter; his lifetime batting average was .260. He hit only 138 home runs in his career, although he is probably most famous for a home run he hit in the 1960 World Series. The strongest facet of Mazeroski's game, and undoubtedly that for which he was enshrined in the Hall of Fame, was his defense.

Mazeroski was born in Wheeling, West Virginia, in 1936, and in 1954, at the age of 17, he was signed by the Pittsburgh Pirates as a shortstop. The Pirates moved him to second base and called him up to the big club in 1956. He became a regular the following season, and batted his career-high of .283.

In 1958 he batted .275 and hit a more-than-respectable 19 home runs, the most he would ever hit. He also won the first of eight Gold Gloves for his work at second base. Two years later he and the Pirates were in the World Series against the New York Yankees, and in the first game Mazeroski connected for a two-run homer. The Series went to seven games, and in that seventh contest, in the bottom of the ninth inning, Bill drove a Ralph Terry pitch into the left field stands for a 10–9 victory and the Pirates first World Championship in 35 years.

Bill won his second Gold Glove that year, and he eventually led the National League in assists nine times, in fielding percentage three times, and in double plays eight times.

His best season was probably 1966, when he batted .262 but connected for 16 home runs and 82 RBIs, while committing just 8 errors in the field for an outstanding .992 fielding percentage. He led all NL second basemen in chances, putouts, and assists.

A 9-time All-Star, Mazeroski played his entire 17-year career with the Pirates. When he retired in 1972 he had a respectable 2016 hits at the plate, but his real strength lay in his .983 fielding percentage, as well as in his 4976 putouts, his 6694 assists, and his 1706 double plays. He committed a mere 204 errors in those 17 years at one of the most demanding positions on the diamond.

Bill continued with the Pirates as a coach in 1973, then went to the Seattle Mariners in that role from 1979–80.

Mazeroski wore number 9 throughout his career, and the Pirates retired the number in 1987. He was inducted into the Hall of Fame by the Veterans Committee in 2001.

Awards/Honors

1958 National League Gold Glove Second Baseman
1960 National League Gold Glove Second Baseman
1961 National League Gold Glove Second Baseman
1963 National League Gold Glove Second Baseman
1964 National League Gold Glove Second Baseman
1965 National League Gold Glove Second Baseman
1966 National League Gold Glove Second Baseman
1967 National League Gold Glove Second Baseman
2001 Hall of Fame

Willie McCovey

Retired Number: 44 (San Francisco Giants, 1975)
First Baseman/Outfielder

Playing Career: San Francisco Giants 1959–73, 1977–80; San Diego Padres 1974–76; Oakland Athletics 1976

Willie McCovey was a native of Mobile, Alabama, who was born in 1938. He made his major league debut in 1959, after hitting 29 home runs in a mere three months in the Pacific Coast League. With the San Francisco Giants for the rest of the season — and going 4-for-4 in his first big league contest — Willie batted .354 with 13 home runs in 52 games. Despite the low number of games — he had only 192 official at-bats — he was named the National League's Rookie of the Year.

McCovey had a rougher time in 1960; when he went into a bad slump, the Giants demoted him to the Tacoma Giants, but he was back in the majors after a very short stay in AAA and got into 101 major league games that year. He batted only .238 with 13 home runs, but was back the next year with an improved .271 mark and 18 roundtrippers.

In 1962 he improved to .293 and 20 homers in only 91 games, although he struggled in the World Series in a losing effort against the New York Yankees. He really broke out the following season, however, tying Hank Aaron for the league lead with 44 home runs while driving in 102 and scoring 103.

Beginning in 1965, McCovey would not hit fewer than 31 home runs during the next six consecutive seasons. In 1968 he led the league with 36, as well as with 105 runs batted in and a .545 slugging percentage. Still, the best was yet to come, as Willie experienced a Most Valuable Player season in 1969 by leading the National League with a career-high 45 home runs, as well as with 126 RBIs and a .656 slugging mark while batting .320. On April 27, he hit three home runs in both games of a doubleheader.

McCovey had become one of the most feared hitters in the NL, as evidenced by his record 45 intentional walks in 1969. He scarcely missed a beat in 1970 as he topped the loop with 137 bases on balls, as well as with a .612 slugging percentage while belting 39 home runs.

His numbers began to tail off after that, however, although he did hit 29 homers in 1973. It nevertheless came as something of a shock to Giants' fans when, in October, San Francisco traded McCovey and Bernie Williams to the San Diego Padres for Mike Caldwell.

With his new team Willie hit 22 and 23 home runs in the next two seasons, respectively, but he was struggling with a .203 average in 1976 when the Padres sold him to the Oakland Athletics. McCovey batted only .208 in Oakland in 11 games, and was released at the end of the season.

In January, the Giants brought him back as a free agent, and McCovey responded admirably as he batted .280 and slugged 28 home runs with 86 RBIs. He hit only 27 homers during the next two seasons combined, however, and after hitting only one in 48 games in 1980, Willie retired from the playing field and took another position within the organization. At the time of his retirement McCovey had amassed 521 lifetime home runs and 1555 RBIs, plus 1345 walks and 18 career grand slams.

Willie wore number 44 throughout his career because he admired Hank Aaron, another Mobile native who bore the same number with the Milwaukee Braves at the start of McCovey's career. The Giants retired the number in 1975, during McCovey's second season with the Padres, but they gave it back to him when he returned in 1977.

In 1986, McCovey was inducted into the Hall of Fame.

Awards/Honors

1959 National League Rookie of the Year
1969 National League Most Valuable Player
1986 Hall of Fame

John McGraw

Retired Number: None (San Francisco Giants, 1988)
Shortstop/Second Baseman/Outfielder/Third Baseman/Manager
Playing Career: Baltimore Orioles (first) 1891–99; St. Louis Cardinals 1900; Baltimore Orioles (second) 1901–02; New York Giants 1902–06
Managerial Career: Baltimore Orioles (first) 1899; Baltimore Orioles (second) 1901–02; New York Giants 1902–32

There have been three teams called the Baltimore Orioles in major league baseball history. John McGraw played for — and managed — two of them. The first was an American Association team, part of a league that rivaled the National League in the nineteenth century, until it joined the NL in 1892. That team was absorbed by the Brooklyn Superbas — later the Dodgers — following the 1899 season. The second was the team that played in the American League and that, after two seasons, became the New York Highlanders and later the Yankees. (The third, the current team, was originally the Milwaukee Brewers and later the St. Louis Browns).

McGraw was born in Truxton, New York, in 1873, and he was a fiercely competitive player as well as a fiery manager. Debuting as a shortstop with the Orioles of the AA in 1891, he batted .270 in 33 games. With the demise of the AA at the conclusion of that campaign, the Orioles joined the NL the following season and would stay there for the remaining eight years of their history. McGraw became a regular in 1893 and responded by hitting .321 with 38 stolen bases. He switched to third base the following season and hit .340 with a career-high 78 steals. He also scored 156 runs.

In 1895 he batted .369 while recording 61 steals. He would continue to bat over .300 through the 1901 campaign, totaling nine consecutive seasons achieving that coveted mark. In 1896 and 1897, the Orioles won the National League championship, which at that time was determined by the winner of a series between the first- and second-place finishers in the league standings and which was called the Temple Cup.

In 1898 McGraw hit .342 and led the NL with 143 runs scored and 112 bases on balls. He hit a career-high .391 in 1899, nearly repeating his previous year's performance by topping the loop with 140 runs scored (tying Wee Willie Keeler) and 124 walks, while stealing 73 bases to top it all off. He was the Orioles' player/manager that year.

The National League reduced itself to eight teams in 1900, and the Orioles were one of the fatalities. The Orioles' owners also owned the Brooklyn Superbas, however, and absorbed their Baltimore team into their Brooklyn one. McGraw was sold to the St. Louis Cardinals, where he hit .344 in one season before signing with the new Baltimore Orioles of the new American League in 1901. He was named player/manager, but he did not get along with league president Ban Johnson and, in the midst of the 1902 season, he left for the New York Giants of the National League. The Giants also named him player/manager, and McGraw's playing time shrank to almost nothing over the next four seasons. He quit playing after the 1906 season, retiring with a .333 lifetime batting average and 436 stolen bases.

McGraw made a huge impression as a manager, even more so than as a player. He had finished no better than fourth at the helm of his Baltimore teams, but after finishing second with the Giants as player/manager in 1903, he took the league championship in 1904 by 13 games over the Chicago Cubs. The National and American Leagues had devised the World Series the previous season, but in 1904 McGraw refused to allow his Giants to face the American League champion Boston Americans, unilaterally — and more than questionably — declaring his team World Champions.

He relented in 1905, however. The Giants finished nine games ahead of the Pittsburgh Pirates to capture the National League pennant, and in the World Series McGraw claimed to have established the NL's superiority over the AL when his squad bested the Philadelphia Athletics, four games to one.

Over the next five seasons McGraw's team finished second three times. They won the pennant once again in 1911 and would do so for three consecutive seasons. They lost the World Series all three years, however, falling to the Athletics in 1911 and 1913 and to the Boston Red Sox in 1912 in a Series consisting of eight games. (One was a tie.)

The Giants were back on top in 1917, finishing 10 games ahead of the Philadelphia Phillies. They fell in the World Series once again, this time to the Chicago White Sox.

After three consecutive second-place finishes, the Giants then won four consecutive pennants. By then the World Series had become a best-of-nine affair, and the Giants defeated the New York Yankees in 1921, five games to three. The Series returned to its previous best-of-seven format in 1922, and the Giants once again topped the Yankees, this time four games to none in a postseason that also featured one tie. The Yankees finally got revenge in 1923, taking the Series four games to two. In 1924 the Giants fell to the Washington Nationals in a seven-game contest.

McGraw continued to manage into 1932, and although he never won another pennant, the Giants did manage three more second-place showings. McGraw retired with 2784 victories against 1959 defeats, good for a winning percentage of .587. In 9 World Series he won 26 games while losing 28, taking 3 ultimate championships. In the process, John had managed more future Hall of Fame players than any other manager in baseball history. He came out of retirement in 1933 to manage the National League in the first All-Star Game.

McGraw is one of several men who never wore a uniform number, but who have been honored by their teams in the same way as those who did. The Giants adopted numbers in June of 1932, but McGraw had retired 40 games into the season and was already gone by that time. In 1988, the team, now in San Francisco, placed an old-style "NY" logo on the outfield wall with McGraw's name, next to the other players' retired numbers. They added another for Christy Mathewson.

McGraw died in 1934. He was inducted into the Hall of Fame posthumously in 1937, in the Hall's second year of existence.

Awards/Honors

1937 Hall of Fame

Billy Meyer

Retired Number: 1 (Pittsburgh Pirates, 1954)
Catcher/Manager

Playing Career: Chicago White Sox 1913; Philadelphia Athletics 1916–17

Managerial Career: Pittsburgh Pirates 1948–52

Billy Meyer was a native of Knoxville, Tennessee, who was born in 1892 and who had a very brief career as a major league player before managing a rather poor Pittsburgh Pirates team for five years.

A catcher by trade, Meyer made his professional debut with the Knoxville Appalachians of the Southeastern League in 1910. He played one game for the Chicago White Sox in 1913 which consisted of several innings behind the plate and a single at-bat. He singled his only time up, giving him a perfect 1.000 major league batting average for that season.

In 1916 he played 50 games for the Philadelphia Athletics, hitting only .232, and played 62 more for the A's in 1917 but recorded only a .235 batting average.

After a lengthy minor league career, Meyer went into managing, and he found great success there at the minor league level. He won pennants in the International League, the New York-Penn League, the Eastern League, and the American Association, and was named the Manager of the Year in 1939 with the Kansas City Blues of the AA.

In 1946 the New York Yankees tried to hire him to fill their managerial vacancy, but Meyer had suffered a heart attack a short time before that and did not feel that he could handle the pressure of the job. Two years later, he accepted the same position with the Pirates, a club that had finished in last place in 1947 with a 62–92 record, 32 games behind the Brooklyn Dodgers. In 1948, Meyer brought the team in fourth, improving their record to 83–71 and prompting *The Sporting News* to name him its Manager of the Year.

Meyer would not enjoy that kind of success again, however. The Pirates finished a disappointing sixth in 1949, then fell to eighth and last place again the following season. They finished in the bottom two in 1951 and last once again in 1952, and Meyer stepped down with a record of 317 wins and 452 losses. He continued to work in the Pirates organization, however, being given the title Managerial Consultant and also doing some scouting.

The Pirates retired his uniform number in 1954. Billy's health soon began to fail, and he died in Knoxville three years later.

Minnie Minoso

Retired Number: 9 (Chicago White Sox, 1983)
Outfielder/Designated Hitter/Coach

Playing Career: Cleveland Indians 1949, 1951, 1958–59; Chicago White Sox 1951–57, 1960–61, 1964, 1976, 1980; St. Louis Cardinals 1962; Washington Senators 1963
Coaching Career: Chicago White Sox 1976–78, 1980–81

A native of Havana, Cuba, speedy Minnie Minoso played for the aptly named New York Cubans of the Negro National League beginning in 1946 at the age of 23. He was 26 years old when he debuted for the Cleveland Indians in 1949. He played only nine games that debut season and hit but .188, and he returned for only eight more games in 1951. He was hitting .429 that time around, however, when the Indians traded him to the Chicago White Sox in a three-team deal that also involved the Philadelphia Athletics.

Minoso became the first black player to wear a White Sox uniform. He finished that season, officially his rookie year, hitting .326, and he led the American League with 31 stolen bases and with 14 triples.

He led the league in steals the next two years as well, swiping 22 in 1952 and 25 in 1953 while batting .313. His stolen base numbers declined somewhat after that, although they were frequently between 17 and 19 and he continued to chase down fly balls with amazing speed in the outfield. In 1954 he led the AL with 18 triples while batting .320 and driving in a career-high 116 runs. Two years later his 11 triples put him in a four-way tie for best in the league, and he hit .316 while also belting 21 home runs.

Gold Gloves were first awarded in 1957, and for that first year only one player was selected from each position to represent both leagues. Minoso was the choice for left field, and when individual awards were given to each league, he won again in 1959 and 1960.

Minnie hit .310 in 1957 and tied Billy Gardner of the Baltimore Orioles for the league lead with 36 doubles while driving in 103 runs. In December, despite his successes, he was traded back to the Indians in a four-player deal.

Minnie kept right on hitting in Cleveland. He hit .302 both seasons in his Indians' return, as well as contributing a career-high 24 homers in 1958 and 21 more the following season.

Nevertheless, in December the Tribe and the Chisox conducted a seven-player transaction, and Minoso found himself back in Chicago for a second term. He had an impressive homecoming in 1960, batting .311 with 20 home runs and 105 runs batted in while leading the league with 184 hits and winning his third Gold Glove. After the 1961 season, he was traded to the St. Louis Cardinals for Joe Cunningham.

On May 11, 1962, Minoso ran into the outfield wall while chasing a triple off the bat of the Los Angeles Dodgers' Duke Snider, and he suffered a fractured skull and a broken wrist. He did not return to the lineup until July 19, but on August 18 he was hit with a pitch that broke his left forearm. Those injuries limited him to only 39 games in St. Louis — not to mention to a .196 batting average — and in April of 1963 the Cardinals dealt him to the Washington Senators for cash and a minor league player to be named. Minnie had a disappointing season with Washington, hitting only .229 and stealing but eight bases, and his career as a regular was over. The White Sox signed him as a pinch hitter for 1964, but he went only 4-for-22 in that role and batted only .226 for the season. He retired that year ... for the first time. He did, however, continue to play with the minor league Indianapolis Indians and then in the Mexican League before retiring in 1973 at age 50.

In 1976 he was brought back to the Sox as a coach, but he was activated for three games as a designated hitter, making him a rare four-decade player. In eight at-bats he managed one single.

He retired for the second time but continued to coach through 1978, then he returned in the same role in 1980. He was activated to pinch hit on two occasions, mainly as a publicity stunt that made him, along with Nick Altrock, one of the only two five-decade players in major league history. He did not get a hit, but he was 57 years old.

He "retired" for the third time with a .298 lifetime batting average, but he continued as a coach for one more season. Two years later, the White Sox retired his number 9.

In 1993, at the age of 70, he batted for the St. Paul Saints of the independent Northern League and thus became professional baseball's first six-decade player. In 2003, now 80 years of age, he became the only seven-decade player in history when he was named the Saints' designated hitter in a game in which the team wore Negro League uniforms as a tribute to those leagues. He came to bat in the first inning and drew a walk.

Awards/Honors

1957 Gold Glove Left Fielder
1959 American League Gold Glove Left Fielder
1960 American League Gold Glove Left Fielder

Paul Molitor

Retired Number: 4 (Milwaukee Brewers, 1999)
Second Baseman/Outfielder/Third Baseman/Designated Hitter/ Coach

Playing Career: Milwaukee Brewers 1978–92; Toronto Blue Jays 1993–95; Minnesota Twins 1996–98
Coaching Career: Minnesota Twins 2000–01

Paul Molitor was born on August 22, 1956, in St. Paul, Minnesota. He started his 21-year major league career in 1978 with the Milwaukee Brewers when that team was a member of the American League. Paul put together a decent .273 batting average as a second baseman in his first year with the club, but improved to .322 the following season. It would be the first of 12 times that he would bat over .300.

After hitting .304 in 1980, he played only 64 games in strike-shortened 1981, most of them in the outfield. He shifted to third base in 1982, and he hit .302 while leading the American League with 136 runs scored. He also clubbed 19 home runs, a mark he would top only once. The Brewers went to the World Series that year, and in Game 1 Molitor went 5-for-6 to become the first player with five hits in a World Series game. He batted .355 in the Series, but the Brewers lost to the St. Louis Cardinals in seven games.

In 1984 an elbow injury limited him to only 13 games, but he hit .297 in 1985 and the Brewers named him their Comeback Player of the Year. In 1987 injuries forced him to the disabled list twice and limited him to 118 games, but between July 16 and August 25 he hit in 39 consecutive games, the highest total since Pete Rose achieved 44 in 1978 and the highest in the American League since Joe DiMaggio's record 56 in 1941. The streak ended on August 26 when he went 0-for-4 against the Cleveland Indians, and he was on deck in the bottom of the tenth inning when teammate Rick Manning ended the game with an RBI pinch-hit single. Molitor batted .353 for the season, and despite his limited playing time he led the league with 41 doubles and 114 runs scored.

He hit over .300 for three years in a row beginning that season, then in 1991 he batted .325 and led the AL with 216 hits, 13 triples (tied with Lance Johnson), and 133 runs scored.

In 1993 Paul went to the Toronto Blue Jays, and he immediately put together a big season as he batted .332 with a career-high 22 home runs while knocking in 111 and leading the league with 211 hits. He then proceeded to hit .391 in the League Championship Series as the Blue Jays bested the Chicago White Sox, and an incredible .500 in the World Series with two home runs as Toronto captured the ultimate championship in six games over the Philadelphia Phillies. Molitor was named the Series' Most Valuable Player.

In 1996 the St. Paul native went home, joining the Minnesota Twins and immediately making his presence felt with a .341 batting average and leading the AL with a career-high 225 hits. On September 16 against the Kansas City Royals, he collected the 3000th hit of his career, a triple off Jose Rosado. He was the twenty-first player to reach 3000 hits, the first to triple for his 3000th hit, and the first to collect 200 hits in the same season that he reached that career milestone.

Molitor put together two more solid seasons with the Twins before retiring. His career batting average was .306, and he had accumulated 3319 hits. In World Series play he had batted an incredible .418 in 13 games.

The Brewers retired his number in 1999, and in 2000 Molitor returned to the Twins as a coach for two seasons.

Joe Morgan

Retired Number: 8 (Cincinnati Reds, 1998)
Second Baseman
Playing Career: Houston Colt .45s 1963–64; Houston Astros 1965–71, 1980; Cincinnati Reds 1972–79; San Francisco Giants 1981–82; Philadelphia Phillies 1983; Oakland Athletics 1984

Joe Morgan is probably best known for being one of the vital cogs in the Big Red Machine of the 1970s. A native of Bonham, Texas, who was born in 1943, "Little Joe" made his major league debut in 1963 in only eight games for the Houston Colt .45s — later the Astros — and became the team's full-time second baseman in 1965.

Morgan stood only 5-feet-7-inches in height, and as a result drew a great many bases on balls. In his first full season, in fact, he led the National League with 97, and he made many a pitcher regret the free pass as his speed also allowed him to steal bases at a prodigious rate. He stole 20 in 1965.

He played with Houston through 1971, and although he never hit over .300 he drew over 100 walks twice, scored over 100 runs twice, and stole at least 40 bases three times. He swiped 49 in 1968, 42 the following year, and 40 in 1971 while tying teammate Roger Metzger for the National League lead with 11 triples.

On November 29, 1971, Morgan was part of the one of the biggest trades in baseball history. The Astros sent him, along with Denis Menke, Jack Billingham, Ed Armbrister, and Cesar Geronimo, to the Cincinnati Reds for Lee May, Tommy Helms, and Jimmy Stewart. The Big Red Machine was about to become a true powerhouse.

In 1972 Morgan hit .292 for the Reds and led the league with 115 walks and 122 runs scored. He also stole 58 bases, his career high to that point. In the All-Star Game, he singled in the winning run in the bottom of the tenth inning and was named the game's Most Valuable Player. He drew six walks in the World Series, although the Reds lost in seven games to the Oakland Athletics. In 1973 he batted .290 with 26 home runs, 111 walks, 116 runs scored, and a career-high 67 stolen bases as the Reds won the NL Western Division title. He also won the first of five consecutive Gold Gloves for his work at second base, where, along with Dave Concepcion, he formed one of the most deadly up-the-middle defensive combinations in major league history.

Morgan batted .327 in 1975, and along with 17 home runs, he drove in 94 runs while leading the league with 132 walks, scoring 107 runs, and matching his career high of 67 stolen bases. The Reds won the World Championship in an exciting seven-game contest over the Boston Red Sox, and Morgan won the league's Most Valuable Player Award.

In 1976 Joe hit .320 and led the NL with a .576 slugging percentage. He boasted career highs of 27 home runs and 111 runs batted in while drawing 114 walks, scoring 113 runs, hitting 30 doubles, and stealing 60 bases. He hit .333 in the World Series as the Reds swept the New York Yankees for their second consecutive championship, and Morgan won his second consecutive MVP Award.

In 1980 the Big Red Machine was effectively dismantled, and Morgan returned to the Astros as a free agent. Although he hit only .243, he tied Dan Driessen of the Reds with 93 walks, then he signed with the San Francisco Giants in 1981. He spent two mediocre seasons there, and the Giants traded him to the Philadelphia Phillies in December, where he joined former teammates Pete Rose and Tony Perez. The Phillies went to the World Series but lost in five games to the Baltimore Orioles.

Morgan signed as a free agent with the Athletics for 1984, and after hitting only .244, he retired. His lifetime batting average was .271, and he had accumulated 2517 hits, 268 home runs, 1865 bases on balls, and 689 stolen bases. He then started a career in broadcasting, and was inducted into the Hall of Fame in 1990. The Reds retired his number 8 in 1998.

Awards/Honors

1973 National League Gold Glove Second Baseman
1974 National League Gold Glove Second Baseman
1975 National League Most Valuable Player
1975 National League Gold Glove Second Baseman
1976 National League Most Valuable Player
1976 National League Gold Glove Second Baseman

1977 National League Gold Glove Second Baseman
1990 Hall of Fame

Thurman Munson

Retired Number: 15 (New York Yankees, 1979)
Catcher
Playing Career: New York Yankees 1969–79

Thurman Munson emerged from Akron, Ohio, where he was born in 1947, to become a star catcher with the New York Yankees. He played fewer than 100 games in the minor leagues before being called up to New York in 1969, and while he struggled in only 26 games that year, he was back in 1970 with a vengeance.

Still qualifying as a rookie, Munson hit .302 in '70 with 25 doubles and won the American League Rookie of the Year Award. He was somewhat mediocre in 1971, but hit .280 the following year while showing great aptitude at handling pitchers and displaying a quick release that allowed him to nail many a baserunner attempting to steal. In 1973 he hit .301 and belted career highs of 20 home runs and 29 doubles, while winning the first of three consecutive Gold Gloves behind the plate.

Two years later he batted .318, the highest mark he would achieve, and also drove in 102 runs. In 1976 he was named the league's Most Valuable Player as he contributed a .302 average, 17 home runs, 105 runs batted in, and 27 doubles — not to mention 14 stolen bases, an unusually high number for a catcher — to the Yankees' division championship. He hit .435 in a five-game victory over the Kansas City Royals for the pennant, and .529 in a losing World Series effort against the Cincinnati Reds.

The Yankees were back in 1977, however, thanks in part to Munson's .308 average, 18 homers, and 100 RBIs. It was the fifth and last time the catcher would top the .300 mark, but he did hit .320 in the World Series as New York emerged victorious in six games over the Los Angeles Dodgers. They would repeat in 1978, and Munson did his part by hitting .297 and once again batting .320 in a Series that was a virtual repeat of the previous year's — the Yankees won in six over the Dodgers.

Munson had begun to slow in 1979, and he was batting .288 through 97 games when, on August 2, tragedy struck. Thurman was flying a twin-engine jet in Canton, Ohio, practicing takeoffs and landings, when his plane fell short of the runway and burst into flames. Only 32 years of age, Munson did not survive.

He hit .292 in his 11-year career, while batting .339 in three League

Championship Series and .373 in three World Series. He hit over 20 doubles on six occasions, accumulating 229 lifetime. The year he died, the Yankees retired his uniform number 15.

Awards/Honors

1970 American League Rookie of the Year
1973 American League Gold Glove Catcher
1974 American League Gold Glove Catcher
1975 American League Gold Glove Catcher
1976 American League Most Valuable Player

Dale Murphy

Retired Number: 3 (Atlanta Braves, 1994)
Catcher/First Baseman/Outfielder
Playing Career: Atlanta Braves 1976–90; Philadelphia Phillies 1990–92; Colorado Rockies 1993

Dale Bryan Murphy was born on March 12, 1956, in Portland, Oregon. It was in Atlanta with the Braves, however, that he would achieve notoriety.

Murphy debuted as a catcher with Atlanta in 1976, playing 19 games with the big club and 18 the following year as he batted .316. He had problems throwing from behind the plate, however, sometimes nearly hitting his own pitcher with the ball when he attempted to throw out would-be basestealers at second base. He was moved to first base in 1978, although he occasionally found himself at his former position, and he led the National League in strikeouts for the first of three times. In 1980 he was shifted to the outfield, and it was there that he began to blossom.

While he led the league in strikeouts once again, his power was developing; he had hit 23 and 21 home runs the previous two seasons, respectively, and hit 33 in 1980. In 1982 he batted .281 with 36 homers, tying Al Oliver with a league-leading 109 runs batted in, and he scored 113 runs en route to the league's Most Valuable Player Award. He also won the first of five consecutive Gold Gloves for his defense.

In 1983 he batted .302 and repeated with 36 home runs. This time he led the NL with 121 RBIs and a .540 slugging percentage, scoring a career-high 131 runs and winning his second consecutive MVP Award.

In 1984 he hit 36 home runs for the third year in a row, but this time that total was the league high, although it was matched by Mike Schmidt. He also drove in 100 runs and led the league with a .547 slugging percentage.

Murphy batted an even .300 in 1985, and his 37 home runs once again paced the circuit, as did his 118 runs scored and his 90 bases on balls. He knocked in 111 runs.

Between 1981 and 1986 Dale played in 740 consecutive games; he was in the Opening Day lineup every year from 1978 through 1988.

In 1987 he experienced another outstanding season, hitting .295 with a career-high 44 home runs. He drove in 105 and scored 115.

His numbers began to slip after that, and in August of 1990 the Braves traded him to the Philadelphia Phillies. Dale hit only .245 that year, although he did slug 24 homers, but in 1991 he managed only 18 home runs. Knee injuries limited him to only 18 games in 1992, and he then signed with the expansion Colorado Rockies for 1993. He played only 26 games for Colorado, however, and retired with 398 lifetime home runs and 1266 RBIs.

Murphy wore number 3 throughout his career, and the year following his retirement, the Braves retired the number.

Awards/Honors

1982 National League Most Valuable Player
1982 National League Gold Glove Outfielder
1983 National League Most Valuable Player
1983 National League Gold Glove Outfielder
1984 National League Gold Glove Outfielder
1985 National League Gold Glove Outfielder
1986 National League Gold Glove Outfielder

Eddie Murray

Retired Number: 33 (Baltimore Orioles, 1998)
Designated Hitter/First Baseman/Coach
Playing Career: Baltimore Orioles 1977–88, 1996; Los Angeles Dodgers 1989–91, 1997; New York Mets 1992–93; Cleveland Indians 1994–96; Anaheim Angels 1997
Coaching Career: Baltimore Orioles 1998–2001; Cleveland Indians 2002–

One of the greatest switch hitters of all time, Eddie Murray was a Los Angeles native who was born on February 24, 1956, and who won the American League's Rookie of the Year Award in 1977 as a designated hitter with the Baltimore Orioles. He was the first DH to be so honored.

Murray hit .283 that season and served notice with 27 home runs and

88 runs batted in. He was moved to first base in 1978 and was a model of consistency, in his first three seasons batting .283, .285, and .295, and belting 27, 27, and 25 home runs, respectively. On August 15, 1979, in an extra-inning game against the Chicago White Sox, Murray stole home in the twelfth inning to give Baltimore a 2–1 victory.

In 1980 he hit an even .300, the first of seven times he would reach that benchmark. He also hit 32 home runs, his highest total to that point, and drove in 116 runs.

In strike-shortened 1981 he finished in a four-way tie for the AL lead with 22 homers while also leading with 78 RBIs. Between 1982 and 1984 he hit .316, .306, and .306, and he also won a Gold Glove all three years. He hit 33 home runs in 1983, his career high, and in 1984 he led the league with 107 bases on balls. For four years in a row he drove in over 100 runs, a feat he would accomplish six times in his career, peaking in 1985 with 124. In May of 1987, he became the first player to homer from both sides of the plate in two consecutive games.

Following the 1988 season, the Orioles traded Eddie to the Los Angeles Dodgers for three players. Murray did not perform particularly well for the Dodgers in 1989, but he rebounded in 1990 and contributed a career-high .330 average with 26 home runs and 95 RBIs. He spent three years in Los Angeles before signing as a free agent with the New York Mets for the 1992 season. He spent two years with that club, in 1993 belting 27 homers and driving in 100. He then joined the Cleveland Indians, and with the Tribe he batted .323 in 1995. On June 30 of that year, he collected his 3000th hit in a game against the Minnesota Twins.

In the midst of the 1996 season, Murray rejoined the Orioles, and on September 6 he hit his 500th home run against the Detroit Tigers, joining Willie Mays and Hank Aaron as one of the only three players to collect 3000 hits and 500 home runs in a career.

In 1997 Murray signed with the Anaheim Angels, but after 46 games he returned to the Dodgers, where he was used in a pinch-hitting role. He went 2-for-7 before deciding to call it quits. He retired with a .287 lifetime batting average, 3255 hits, and 504 home runs. He was second to Mickey Mantle for most career home runs by a switch hitter, and first all-time for RBIs by a switch hitter.

In 1998 Murray returned to the Orioles as a coach, and the O's retired his number in June. He coached in Baltimore for four seasons before returning to Cleveland in 2002 and continuing as a coach there. Eddie was inducted into the Hall of Fame in 2003.

Murray's brother Rich had a brief career with the San Francisco Giants.

Awards/Honors

1977 American League Rookie of the Year
1982 American League Gold Glove First Baseman
1983 American League Gold Glove First Baseman
1984 American League Gold Glove First Baseman
2003 Hall of Fame

Danny Murtaugh

Retired Number: 40 (Pittsburgh Pirates, 1977)
Second Baseman/Shortstop/Coach/Manager
Playing Career: Philadelphia Phillies 1941–43, 1946; Boston Braves 1947; Pittsburgh Pirates 1948–51
Coaching Career: Pittsburgh Pirates 1956–57
Managerial Career: Pittsburgh Pirates 1957–64, 1967, 1970–71, 1973–76

Not usually a strong hitter, Danny Murtaugh was a solid-fielding second baseman who made his true mark on the game at the helm of the Pittsburgh Pirates.

Murtaugh was a Pennsylvania native who was born in 1917, and he debuted in 1941 with the Philadelphia Phillies. Although he hit only .219, he led the National League in stolen bases with 18. His average improved over the next two seasons, then he served in the military and returned in 1946. He played three games with the Boston Braves in 1947, and in November he was traded to the Pirates, with whom he would spend the rest of his career.

Murtaugh hit a solid .290 in 1948 with Pittsburgh, and he would hit .294 two years later. In between he batted only .203, and in his final season of 1951 he hit .199. His lifetime average was only .254 and he had only eight major league home runs lifetime, but he then turned his attention to managing in the Pirates' minor league system in 1952.

In 1956 he was brought back to the big club as a coach, and late in 1957 he was named manager to replace Bobby Bragan. The Pirates came in tied for last place that year, but in 1958 they improved to second, only eight games behind the Milwaukee Braves. Their record improved from 62–92 to 84–70.

After a fourth-place finish in 1959, the Pirates won the National League pennant in 1960, outdistancing the Braves by seven games. In a thrilling World Series, they came away with an improbable seven-game win over the powerful New York Yankees.

The club won 93 games in 1962, but nevertheless finished in fourth place, eight games behind the San Francisco Giants. Their fortunes continued to fade, and Murtaugh stepped down following the 1964 season due to poor health.

In 1967 Danny returned to manage the Pirates on an interim basis as a fill-in for the departed Harry Walker. The club finished sixth with an even .500 record, and Murtaugh turned the reins over to Larry Shepard.

He was back for a third go of it in 1970, and this time his Pirates took the National League Eastern Division title by five games over the Chicago Cubs. They dropped the League Championship Series to the Cincinnati Reds, but the Associated Press named Danny its National League Manager of the Year.

The Bucs were back on top the following season, finishing seven games ahead of the St. Louis Cardinals, and this time they won the pennant in a four-game playoff over the Giants. They followed this success with a World Championship in seven games over the Baltimore Orioles.

Murtaugh retired again, missing out on another Pirates' division title in 1972, but near the end of the 1973 season he returned for a fourth term to replace Bill Virdon. The team finished third, but in 1974 they won the division by a game and a half over St. Louis, although they fell to the Los Angeles Dodgers in the playoffs. The following season they came in six and a half games ahead of the Phillies, and this time dropped the pennant to the Reds. The club finished second in 1976, and Murtaugh passed away in December of that year in his hometown of Chester, Pennsylvania. He had won 1115 games in his managerial career, and his lifetime winning percentage was .540.

Murtaugh wore many numbers throughout his career, but wore only two with the Pirates. As a player he bore number 7, but as a coach and manager he always wore number 40, and that was the number the Pirates retired in his honor in 1977, the year following his death.

Awards/Honors

1970 National League Manager of the Year (AP)

Stan Musial

Retired Number: 6 (St. Louis Cardinals, 1963)
Outfielder/First Baseman
Playing Career: St. Louis Cardinals 1941–44, 1946–63

One of the greatest hitters of all time, Stan "The Man" Musial was a 1920 native of Donora, Pennsylvania, who spent his entire 22-year career with the St. Louis Cardinals.

Musial debuted in 1941 and in only 12 games hit .426. He would eventually win seven batting titles, and, including that debut year, would hit over .300 for his first 17 seasons in a row and for 18 total.

The Cardinals shifted him between the outfield and first base frequently, but his position changes never affected his hitting. He batted .315 in his sophomore season and won his first batting title in 1943, only his second *full* season in the big leagues. He batted .357 that year and topped the National League with 220 hits, 48 doubles, 20 triples, and a .562 slugging percentage. As a result he was named the league's Most Valuable Player, the first of three times he would win that coveted award. He batted .347 in 1944, and then hit .304 in the World Series as the Cardinals defeated their intracity foes, the St. Louis Browns, in six games.

In addition to his seven batting championships, Musial would lead the league in hits six times, in doubles eight times, in triples five times, in runs batted in twice, in runs scored five times, in bases on balls once, and in slugging percentage six times.

He spent the entire 1945 season in the military, but came back in 1946 to win his second batting championship with a .365 average. He also won his second MVP Award as he topped the loop with 228 hits, 50 doubles, 20 triples, 124 runs scored, and a .587 slugging percentage.

Incredibly, he improved on most of those numbers two years later in the process of winning his third MVP Award. His .376 average not only won him his third batting title, but was also his career high, and he led the league with 230 hits, 46 doubles, 18 triples, 131 RBIs, 135 runs scored, and a .702 slugging percentage.

Musial also had some power, as he slugged 475 home runs in his career. He never led the league in that department, but his career high was the 39 he hit in 1948, and he hit over 20 for 10 years in a row. He had over 100 RBIs on 10 occasions as well, with 131 being his high.

In 1953 Stan achieved a personal high for doubles with 53, while he was in the midst of leading the NL for three consecutive years in that category. On May 2, 1954, he hit five home runs in a doubleheader against the New York Giants.

In 1957 Musial batted .351 to win his seventh and last batting title. On May 13, 1958, he was inserted as a pinch hitter for pitcher Sam Jones during a game at Wrigley Field against the Chicago Cubs. Stan doubled to left field off Moe Drabowsky for his 3000th career hit, becoming the only player to reach that milestone with a pinch hit. He hit .337 for the season, but then his numbers began to diminish. His lifetime average to that point was .340, but it would eventually fall to .331.

Over the next three seasons he hit between .255 and .288, although he rebounded in 1962 to hit .330. After one final season in 1963, he retired with 3630 hits, along with 725 doubles, 177 triples, and 1951 RBIs.

The Cardinals retired his number 6 the year of his own retirement, and in 1969 Musial was inducted into the Hall of Fame.

Awards/Honors

1943 National League Most Valuable Player
1946 National League Most Valuable Player
1948 National League Most Valuable Player
1969 Hall of Fame

Hal Newhouser

Retired Number: 16 (Detroit Tigers, 1997)
Pitcher
Playing Career: Detroit Tigers 1939–53; Cleveland Indians 1954–55

Hal Newhouser debuted with his hometown Detroit Tigers in 1939 at the age of 18. He appeared in only one game that year and gave up three hits while walking four in five innings, but nevertheless he was back the following year and made 28 appearances. His earned run average was high and improved only slightly during his first three seasons, but in 1942 it was an excellent 2.45, although his record was a mere 8–14. Still, he struggled with his control, walking 114 batters that year and leading the American League in that category in 1943 with 111 while going 8–17.

Hal was not happy with his early performances and was noted for throwing temper tantrums. A heart ailment kept him out of military service during World War II, and for the next three years he became one of the most dominant pitchers in major league baseball.

In 1944 Newhouser led the league with 29 victories and 187 strikeouts, posting a sparkling 2.22 ERA and winning the league's Most Valuable Player Award. The following year he went 25–9, once again topping the circuit in victories and also, this time, with a .735 winning percentage. He topped all other AL hurlers with a 1.81 ERA and 212 strikeouts to win the pitching Triple Crown, while also posting league bests of 313⅓ innings pitched, 29 complete games, and 8 shutouts. His performance made him the only pitcher to win back-to-back MVP Awards in major league history.

The Tigers won the AL pennant by a game and a half over the Washington Nationals, and Newhouser won the game that clinched the title. He won two of the three games he pitched in a seven-game World Series victory over the Chicago Cubs, striking out 22 batters in 20⅔ innings, although he struggled a bit and put up a 6.10 ERA.

In 1946 Hal continued his dominance, tying Bob Feller for the league lead with 26 victories and also leading with a 1.94 ERA. The following season he went only 17–17, and those 17 losses were tops in the league. He did lead the league with 24 complete games, however, and his ERA was a more-than-respectable 2.87.

Hal won 21 games in 1948, the league high, but that was the last time he would be a 20-game winner. Shoulder problems began to limit his effectiveness, and while he won 18 and 15 the next two seasons, respectively, he would not win in double digits again from 1951 on.

In 1954 Newhouser joined the Cleveland Indians and went 7–2. He pitched only two games in 1955, however, and walked four batters in only two and a third innings before retiring with a career mark of 207–150, a lifetime ERA of 3.06, and 1796 career strikeouts.

Hal was inducted into the Hall of Fame by the Veterans Committee in 1992. The Tigers retired his number in 1997, and Newhouser died a year later.

Awards/Honors

1944 American League Most Valuable Player
1945 American League Most Valuable Player
1992 Hall of Fame

Phil Niekro

Retired Number: 35 (Atlanta Braves, 1984)
Pitcher
Playing Career: Milwaukee Braves 1964–65; Atlanta Braves 1966–83, 1987; New York Yankees 1984–85; Cleveland Indians 1986–87; Toronto Blue Jays 1987

Phil Niekro was born on April 1, 1939, in Blaine, Ohio. He pitched until he was 48 years old, putting together a 24-year career based on his trademark pitch, the knuckleball.

Niekro debuted in 1964 when the Braves were still playing in Milwaukee. He pitched two seasons, fashioning a 2.89 earned run average in 1965 while pitching almost exclusively in relief, and he accompanied the team when it moved to Atlanta. In 1967, nearly half of his 46 appearances were starts, and he led the National League with a 1.87 ERA. Two years later he became a 20-game winner for the first of three times, going 23–13 while posting a 2.57 ERA and striking out 193 batters.

Between 1967 and 1980 Phil won in double digits every year, and he did so 19 times in 24 years. He won at least 15 games 13 of those times, and his ERA was under 3.00 on seven occasions.

On August 5, 1973, Phil pitched a no-hitter against the San Diego Padres. In 1974 he became a 20-game winner again, going 20–13, and his 20 victories (tying him with Andy Messersmith), 18 complete games, and 302 innings pitched were best in the league. Although he lost 20 games in 1977, leading the league in that dubious category, he also did so with 20 complete games, 262 strikeouts, and 330 innings pitched. It marked the first of three consecutive seasons in which he would strike out over 200 batters.

Unfortunately, it was also the first of four consecutive years in which he would lead the league in losses, although he was posting decent ERAs — 4.04 was the highest, 2.88 the lowest — and was pitching for Braves' teams that were consistently finishing in the cellar, except for 1980 when they came in third-last. Additionally, his own winning percentage was over .500 for two of those seasons, and in 1979 he not only led with 20 losses but also with 21 victories, which tied him with his brother Joe, who was pitching for the Houston Astros. He topped the circuit in complete games and innings pitched three years in a row, but also in hits allowed three years in a row and in bases on balls two out of three years.

Niekro fielded his position well, and in 1978 he won his first Gold Glove. He would win that award five times in the next six years.

In 1982 he went 17–4, leading the NL with an .810 winning percentage. Following the 1983 season, he became a free agent and signed with the New York Yankees, and the Braves retired his number 35 upon his departure. Niekro went 16–8 and 16–12 in two seasons in New York, leaving there at the age of 46. On the final day of the 1985 season, he won his 300th career game.

He signed with the Cleveland Indians for 1986, and after making 22 appearances for the Tribe in 1987 he was traded to the Toronto Blue Jays. He pitched only three games for Toronto, then returned to the Braves for one final game before retiring. His lifetime record was 318–274, and he and his brother Joe, who had won 221 in a 22-year career, had fashioned 539 victories together, the most by any brother combination. Phil had an ERA of 3.35 and had struck out 3342 batters, but he never got to pitch in a World Series.

In 1994, Niekro became the manager of the Colorado Silver Bullets, an independent professional women's team, and he served in that capacity through 1996, then became the team's general manager in 1997. He was also inducted into the Hall of Fame that year.

Awards/Honors

1978 National League Gold Glove Pitcher
1979 National League Gold Glove Pitcher
1980 National League Gold Glove Pitcher
1982 National League Gold Glove Pitcher
1983 National League Gold Glove Pitcher
1997 Hall of Fame

Tony Oliva

Retired Number: 6 (Minnesota Twins, 1991)
Outfielder/Designated Hitter/Coach
Playing Career: Minnesota Twins 1962–76
Coaching Career: Minnesota Twins 1976–78, 1985–91

Pedro Oliva was born in Pinar del Rio, Cuba, in 1940, and used his brother Tony's passport to get into the United States and play professional baseball in 1961. Thus, the man who would put together a 15-year career with — and would eventually have his uniform number retired by — the Minnesota Twins became known as Tony Oliva.

In 1962 Oliva appeared in nine games for the Twins and batted .444, and he nearly repeated that performance in 1963 when he played seven games — all of them in a pinch-hitting role — and hit .429. In the meantime, he was hitting .410 with the Wytheville Twins of the Appalachian League.

In 1964 he made the Minnesota roster for good, and he responded by winning the American League batting title with a .323 average and missing only a single game. He also led the league with 217 hits, setting the league record for a rookie, as well as with 43 doubles and 109 runs scored. Along the way he also displayed impressive power, belting 32 home runs, which would remain his career high. As a result of all these achievements he was named the league's Rookie of the Year.

The following season he again won the batting title with a .321 average, becoming the first player to win two titles in his first two full seasons. He led the league in hits with 185, and would do so for a third consecutive time in 1966 with 191. He also hit .307 that year with 25 home runs, and he won his only Gold Glove for his outfield defense.

In 1967 he led the AL with 34 doubles, and two years later he hit .309 and topped the circuit with 197 hits and 39 doubles, while belting 24 home runs. The Twins won the American League Western Division title, and although they were swept by the Baltimore Orioles in the League

Championship Series in a three-game set, Oliva did his part by hitting .385 with a home run.

He had an even better year in 1970 as he batted .325 and led the league in hits for the fifth and last time with 204, as well as in doubles for the fourth and last time with 36, tying him with two other hitters that year. He hit .500 in the League Championship Series, although the Twins were once again swept by the Orioles. Tony won his third and last batting title in 1971, hitting .337 and also topping the loop with a .546 slugging percentage.

Oliva had a troublesome right knee and would eventually undergo seven operations because of it. In 1972 he was limited to only 10 games all season, and his .321 average marked the last time he would top the .300 mark. He continued to play into 1976, becoming solely a designated hitter in 1973. On April 6 of that year, he hit the first home run ever by a DH in Oakland against the Athletics. In '76 he retired as a player but continued as a coach with Minnesota. He had a .304 lifetime batting average along with 1917 hits, 329 doubles, and 220 home runs.

He coached through 1978, and again from 1985 through 1991. Oliva had worn number 38 with the Twins before switching to number 6, and the Twins retired 6 in his honor in 1991.

Awards/Honors

1964 American League Rookie of the Year
1966 American League Gold Glove Outfielder

Mel Ott

Retired Number: 4 (San Francisco Giants, 1949)
Outfielder/Third Baseman/Manager
Playing Career: New York Giants 1926–47
Managerial Career: New York Giants 1942–48

Mel Ott played his entire 22-year career with the New York Giants, and spent his entire seven-year managerial career with the same club, six of them as the Giants' player/manager.

A Louisiana native who was born in 1909, Ott was playing semipro ball when he was offered a tryout with the Giants at the Polo Grounds. He made his major league debut in 1926 but was used sparingly his first two seasons. He became a regular outfielder in 1928 and responded by hitting .322 and belting 18 home runs.

It did not take long for Ott to become a sensation in New York. He hit over .300 eleven times in his career, and led or tied for the league lead in home runs six times. He had a keen eye, never striking out much, especially for a power hitter, and leading the circuit in bases on balls on six occasions.

He hit his career high of 42 home runs in 1929, although, ironically, that total was second to Chuck Klein's 43 with the Philadelphia Phillies. In the season's final game, which found the Giants facing the Phillies, Philadelphia pitchers walked Ott intentionally five times to prevent him from tying the mark.

In 1932 Ott swatted 38 home runs, good for a tie for National League leadership with Klein. In 1934 he hit 35, tying Ripper Collins of the St. Louis Cardinals. He finally got the title to himself in 1936 when he hit 33, then tied with Ducky Medwick of the Cardinals the following year with 31. Ott gained the title for himself again in 1938 when he slugged 36.

Mel had led the National League in slugging percentage in 1936 with a .588 mark, and he would also lead in runs scored twice. He won only one RBI title, knocking in 135 runs in 1934, although he would match that number two years later. His career high, however, was 152 in 1929, but that total was four shy of Rogers Hornsby's 156 with the Chicago Cubs.

In 1942 Ott was named the Giants' player/manager. He had a typical season on the field, leading the league with 30 home runs, 118 runs scored, and 109 walks, and in the process became the first player/manager ever to lead his league in home runs. The Giants' third-place finish that year was the best Ott would achieve at New York's helm. He was somewhat ill-tempered as a manager, often blasting his own team in the press and, in 1946, becoming the first manager to be thrown out of both games of a doubleheader.

He continued as player/manager into the 1947 season, although he played only 31 games in 1946 and made only 4 pinch-hitting appearances in 1947. He turned strictly to managing in 1948, but with only a .467 lifetime winning percentage, he was replaced at midseason by Leo Durocher.

Ott had retired from playing with a .304 lifetime batting average, and with 511 home runs he was the first National Leaguer to reach the 500 mark. In three World Series, he had hit .295 and slugged four homers.

Ott had begun his career before the Giants wore uniform numbers. When the club donned them in 1932, Ott wore number 5 and Bill Terry wore 4, but Ott switched to 4 in 1933. The team retired number 4 for Ott in 1949, when they were still the New York Giants.

Mel became a minor league manager for the Oakland Oaks of the Pacific Coast League in 1951, and he was inducted into the Hall of Fame that same year. He managed for two seasons in the minor leagues, and eventually became a broadcaster for the Detroit Tigers. In New Orleans in November of 1958, he and his wife were hit head-on by a drunk driver while returning home from dinner, and Mel died of his injuries a few days later.

Awards/Honors

1951 Hall of Fame

Jim Palmer

Retired Number: 22 (Baltimore Orioles, 1985)
Pitcher
Playing Career: Baltimore Orioles 1965–67, 1969–84

New York native Jim Palmer made his debut with the Baltimore Orioles in 1965, at the age of 19, and he would spend his entire 19-year career with that club.

Palmer experienced arm problems early on, and although he won 23 games and lost only 15 in his first three partial seasons in Baltimore — splitting time between the major and minor leagues — he did not become truly effective until he had surgery in 1968. Coming back in 1969, he went 16–4 and led the American League with an .800 winning percentage. He spent some additional time on the disabled list that year, but on August 13 he came back and pitched a no-hitter against the Oakland Athletics, winning the game by an 8–0 score.

In 1970 Palmer became a 20-game winner for the first of four consecutive times and eight times total. He was 20–10 with a 2.71 earned run average and tied Sam McDowell for the league lead with 305 innings pitched and tied Chuck Dobson with 5 shutouts.

He went 20–9 the next year, 21–10 in 1972, and 22–9 in 1973 with a league-leading 2.40 ERA en route to winning the first of three American League Cy Young Awards.

Elbow problems limited him to only 26 games in 1974 — many of them less than satisfactory — but the following season he tied Jim Hunter for the AL lead in victories with a 23–11 record, and in also leading with a 2.09 ERA and 10 shutouts, he won his second Cy Young Award.

He repeated in 1976, leading the AL in wins with a 22–13 record and in innings pitched with 315 while posting a 2.51 ERA. Palmer was an excellent athlete all around, and he fielded his position well enough to win the first of four consecutive Gold Gloves that season.

In 1977 Jim finished in a three-way tie for the league lead in wins — the third straight time he led in that category — by going 20–11. He had overcome his arm woes to also become one of the league's most durable pitchers, as evidenced by the fact that he led the league for the second of three straight years — and four years overall — in innings pitched with 319. He also tied Nolan Ryan with 22 complete games.

Palmer was a 20-game winner for the last time in 1978 when he went 21–12. He continued to pitch effectively for some time, however, winning 16 games in 1980 and 15 in 1982, when his 15–5 record was good for a league-best .750 winning percentage (tying him with Pete Vuckovich). Until 1983, he had never posted an ERA above 3.98, and 10 times it was below 3.00. His best came in 1972, when it was 2.07.

Palmer struggled badly in 1984, and in May, when he refused to retire at the Orioles' behest, he was released. He had won 268 games in his career and put up a lifetime ERA of 2.86. He had pitched in six League Championship Series, going 4–1, and in six World Series, going 4–2. Having won one game in the 1966 Series, one each in 1970 and 1971, and one in 1983, he was the only pitcher to win World Series games in three different decades.

Jim went into broadcasting following his retirement, and the Orioles retired his number 22 in 1985. He made several comeback attempts, none of them successful. In 1990 he was inducted into the Hall of Fame, and in the spring of 1991 he attempted a comeback with the Orioles that was unprecedented because he was already a Hall-of-Famer. After a miserable spring, however, he retired for good.

Awards/Honors

1973 American League Cy Young Award
1975 American League Cy Young Award
1976 American League Cy Young Award
1976 American League Gold Glove Pitcher
1977 American League Gold Glove Pitcher
1978 American League Gold Glove Pitcher
1979 American League Gold Glove Pitcher
1990 Hall of Fame

Tony Perez

Retired Number: 24 (Cincinnati Reds, 2000)
First Baseman/Third Baseman/Designated Hitter/Coach/Manager
Playing Career: Cincinnati Reds 1964–76, 1984–86; Montreal Expos 1977–79; Boston Red Sox 1980–82; Philadelphia Phillies 1983

Coaching Career: Cincinnati Reds 1987–92
Managerial Career: Cincinnati Reds 1993; Florida Marlins 2001

Tony Perez was a native of Cuba who was born in 1942, and who became a critical part of the Big Red Machine of the 1970s.

Perez made his major league debut in 1964 in 12 games for the Cincinnati Reds. For his first three years he shared time at first base, then switched to third in 1967 to make room for Lee May. He hit .290 that year and began to display some power by hitting 26 home runs and driving in 102. Over the course of his 23-year career, it was runs batted in that would become his true trademark; he would top the 100-RBI mark seven times, and would reach at least 90 twelve times.

On July 11, 1967, Tony hit a home run in the fifteenth inning of the All-Star Game off Jim Hunter of the Oakland Athletics to give the National League the victory. It was the longest All-Star Game in history.

Perez hit 37 home runs in 1969 with 122 RBIs, but he did even better in 1970. His .317 average that year, along with career highs of 40 home runs, 129 RBIs, and 107 runs scored, helped propel the Reds to the National League Western Division title. Perez hit .333 in a League Championship Series victory over the Pittsburgh Pirates, but a dismal .056 in a World Series loss to the Baltimore Orioles.

Beginning in 1969, Perez hit at least 20 home runs seven consecutive times, and did so nine times total. On three other occasions he hit at least 18. In 1975 he batted .282 with 20 homers and 109 RBIs, hit .417 in an LCS win over the Pirates, and then, despite hitting only .179 in the World Series, contributed three home runs that helped seal the championship over the Boston Red Sox, including a crucial two-run shot in Game 7. The following year he hit 19 homers and drove in 91 runs, then batted .313 in a World Series sweep over the New York Yankees.

Perez was playing first base again, and in December of 1976 the Reds traded Tony to the Montreal Expos to make room for young first baseman Dan Driessen. Even more than Cincinnati would come to miss Perez's power and ability to drive in runs, however, they would miss his clubhouse leadership. The Reds won another division title in 1979, but the days of the Big Red Machine were effectively over.

Perez played three years with the Expos, then became a free agent at the conclusion of the 1979 campaign and signed with the Red Sox. He experienced a comeback season in 1980, batting .275 with 25 home runs and 105 knocked in, but he became a part-time player after that and would never again hit more than 9 home runs in a season. He signed with the Philadelphia Phillies in 1983, a team that won the NL pennant but lost the

World Series to the Orioles, then returned to the Reds in 1984. He hit .328 in a part-time role with Cincinnati in 1985 while playing under former teammate Pete Rose, and after the 1986 season he retired with a .279 lifetime batting average, 379 home runs, and 1652 RBIs.

He became a coach with the Reds in 1987 and served in that capacity until 1993, when he was named Cincinnati's manager. After only 44 games, however, having posted a record of 20–24, he was fired. He went to work for the Florida Marlins organization, and became their manager on an interim basis in 2001. He went 54–60, then returned to the front office.

Tony was inducted into the Hall of Fame in 2000, and the Reds retired his number the same year.

Awards/Honors

2000 Hall of Fame

Billy Pierce

Retired Number: 19 (Chicago White Sox, 1987)
Pitcher
Playing Career: Detroit Tigers 1945, 1948; Chicago White Sox 1949–61; San Francisco Giants 1962–64

Left-hander Billy Pierce debuted with his hometown Detroit Tigers in 1945 at the age of 18. He pitched only 10 innings in 5 games, and although he posted a 1.80 earned run average, he would not reemerge in the major leagues until 1948.

He struggled in 22 appearances with the Tigers that year, but the Chicago White Sox recognized his value and acquired him from Detroit in November. Pierce pitched 13 years for the White Sox, and during that period he won 20 games twice and an ERA title once.

During Pierce's first few years with Chicago, the Sox were either last in the American League in runs produced, or were close to last. In 1951, Billy's 14 losses led the American League, but he had also won 15 games and his ERA was a solid 3.03.

He won 15 games in 1952 and posted a 2.57 ERA, and the following year he won 18 with a 2.72 ERA while leading the league with 186 strikeouts. Two years later he won the ERA crown by posting a glittering mark of 1.97, while going 15–10.

Pierce became a 20-game winner in 1956 as he went 20–9. He led the league for the first of three consecutive times with 21 complete games, a mark matched by Bob Lemon, and he also struck out 192 batters, a career high.

His 20 victories in 1957 tied for the league lead with Jim Bunning of the Tigers, and his 16 complete games were best in the circuit, tying him with teammate Dick Donovan. In 1958 he was 17–11, 2.68, leading the loop with two other pitchers with 19 complete games, and on June 27 came within one out of pitching a perfect game against the Washington Senators. The effort was ruined with two outs in the ninth inning when pinch hitter Ed Fitz Gerald hit a Pierce pitch fair down the right-field line.

Pierce went 14–15 in 1959, but he also pitched 4 innings in the World Series without allowing an earned run in a losing effort against the Los Angeles Dodgers.

Billy posted 14 and 10 victories the next two seasons, respectively, then was traded to the San Francisco Giants. He experienced a resurgence in 1962 when he went 16–6, and he pitched two games in the World Series and went 1–1 with a 2.40 ERA overall, winning Game 6 in a 2–0, three-hit effort. Nevertheless, the Giants lost in seven games to the New York Yankees.

Pierce pitched mainly in relief in 1963 and started only a single game in 1964 in 34 appearances. He retired with 211 lifetime victories and a 3.27 earned run average. His World Series ERA was 1.89.

The White Sox retired his number in 1987.

Kirby Puckett

Retired Number: 34 (Minnesota Twins, 1997)
Outfielder
Playing Career: Minnesota Twins 1984–95

Chicago native Kirby Puckett spent his entire 12-year career with the Minnesota Twins. Born in 1960, he worked for the Ford Motor Company and later as a census taker while playing recreational baseball. He visited a tryout camp for the Kansas City Royals, and while failing to impress the Royals, he was recruited by the coach from Bradley University.

Puckett played a year at Bradley and then transferred to Triton College. He hit .472 with 16 home runs in his last year at Triton, and he was selected by the Twins in the 1982 draft and signed a minor league contract.

After becoming the Appalachian League Player of the Year in 1982 and the California League Rookie of the Year in 1983, Puckett debuted with the Twins in 1984 and collected four hits in his very first game. He batted .296 for the season and hit .288 the following year. In 1986, under the tutelage of Twins hitting coach Tony Oliva, Kirby finally found his power stroke and belted 31 home runs after hitting only 4 in the previous two seasons combined. He also established himself as an excellent defensive outfielder, winning the first of six Gold Gloves.

Puckett would hit over .300 eight times in the next 10 seasons. The two times he failed to do so he hit .298 and .296. In 1987 he batted .332, and his 207 hits led the American League, a mark tied by Kevin Seitzer. He would lead in that category for the next three seasons, and would collect over 200 hits five times. He also hit 28 home runs that year, and batted .357 in a seven-game World Series victory over the St. Louis Cardinals.

Kirby led the league the following year with a career-high 234 hits, and led with 215 in 1989 as he won his only batting title with a .339 average.

In 1991 he hit .319 to help the Twins to the postseason once again. He became the Most Valuable Player of the League Championship Series against the Toronto Blue Jays when he batted .429 with two home runs and six runs batted in, and the Twins came out on top, four games to one. In a seven-game World Series win over the Atlanta Braves, he hit two more roundtrippers, and he had a sensational Game 6 with an RBI triple in the first inning, a leaping outfield catch in the third, a sacrifice fly to drive in the go-ahead run in the fifth, a single and a stolen base in the eighth, and a game-winning home run in the eleventh.

His 210 hits led the league once again in 1992 as he hit .329. The next year he hit a double and a home run in the All-Star Game while driving in two, and was named the game's MVP. In 1994, a season cut short by a players' strike, he led the AL with 112 RBIs in only 108 games, becoming one of the few players to record more RBIs than games played in a season.

Kirby hit .314 in 1995, but his season was cut short on September 28 when he was hit in the face by a fastball from Dennis Martinez, shattering his jaw. No one realized at the time that his entire career had just been cut short, but not because of the jaw. During spring training of 1996 he was batting .360 when, on March 28, he woke unable to see out of his right eye. He was diagnosed with glaucoma, and although he underwent four surgical procedures over the next four months in an effort to correct the condition, his sight did not improve. He announced his retirement on July 12 at the age of 36.

Puckett's lifetime batting average was .318. He had accumulated 2304 hits and 207 home runs, as well as a .308 average in two World Series. The Twins retired his number in 1997, and he was inducted into the Hall of Fame in 2001.

Awards/Honors

1986 American League Gold Glove Outfielder
1987 American League Gold Glove Outfielder
1988 American League Gold Glove Outfielder
1989 American League Gold Glove Outfielder
1991 American League Gold Glove Outfielder
1992 American League Gold Glove Outfielder
2001 Hall of Fame

Jimmie Reese

Retired Number: 50 (Anaheim Angels, 1995)
Second Baseman/Coach
Playing Career: New York Yankees 1930–31; St. Louis Cardinals 1932
Coaching Career: California Angels 1972–94

Jimmie Reese spent a 78-year career in organized baseball before his death in 1994.

Born in New York in October of 1901, Reese was 15 years old when he became a bat boy for the Los Angeles Angels of the Pacific Coast League. In 1924 he began to play professionally with the PCL's Oakland Oaks, and he spent six years in the minor leagues before making his major league debut with the New York Yankees in 1930.

Primarily a second baseman, although he played a few games at third that year, Reese appeared in 77 games for the Yankees that season and batted an impressive .346. He hit 3 home runs and committed only 5 errors in the field, good for a .975 fielding percentage, while also contributing 14 doubles. His spring training roommate was none other than Babe Ruth.

In 1931 Reese appeared in 65 games for the Yanks, although his average dropped to .241. He still managed 3 more home runs, however, as well as 10 doubles, and his fielding percentage was a solid .972.

In January of 1932 the Yankees placed Jimmie on waivers, and he was claimed by the St. Louis Cardinals. He appeared in 90 games for St. Louis and batted .265, contributing 2 homers along with 15 doubles, and his fielding percentage was a career-best .979. That would also be his final season playing in the major leagues, however, although he continued to play in the PCL, totaling 13 seasons altogether.

Reese filled a number of different roles after he retired from playing. He had played for a time for the San Diego Padres of the PCL, and became a coach for that club from 1948–60. He also managed the team on an interim basis in 1948 and in 1960 and '61. He later became a scout, and was named a coach for the California Angels in 1972. Jimmie then wore an Angels' uniform for the next 23 years, and he had worn one in 1994, the year he died at the age of 92.

Jimmie wore number 23 during his first two years as an Angels' coach, but he switched to number 50 in 1974. Because of his longevity and the dedication he had shown to the organization, the Angels retired the number in 1995.

Pee Wee Reese

Retired Number: 1 (Los Angeles Dodgers, 1984)
Shortstop/Third Baseman/Coach
Playing Career: Brooklyn Dodgers 1940–42, 1946–57; Los Angeles Dodgers 1958
Coaching Career: Los Angeles Dodgers 1959

Kentucky native Pee Wee Reese — who was a champion marble shooter as a child and was nicknamed for a "pee wee," or type of marble — was born in 1918 and became a fleet-footed shortstop with the Louisville Colonels of the American Association before reaching the major leagues with the Brooklyn Dodgers in 1940.

He was originally signed by the Boston Red Sox, but was sold to Brooklyn for $75,000 and spent his entire career with the Dodgers. He hit .272 in 1940, but appeared in only 84 games because of a fractured heel. He was back in 1941 as the Dodgers' regular shortstop, but he struggled at the plate the next two seasons before joining the Navy during World War II.

Reese did not return until 1946, missing three full seasons because of the war. He batted .284 when he returned, and he duplicated that average in 1947 while also tying Hank Greenberg for the National League lead with 104 bases on balls. That was the year Jackie Robinson broke the color barrier and joined the Dodgers, and amid tumult and threats to Robinson from some fans — and even from a few teammates — Reese went out of his way to make Jackie feel welcome. On one occasion he publicly put his arm around Robinson on the field to show everyone that he was in full support of the Dodgers' first black player.

Pee Wee began stealing bases at an increasing rate in 1948, swiping 25. The following year he stole 26 and led the league with 132 runs scored while also drawing a career-high 116 walks. He stole a career-best 30 bases in 1952, and that total was the NL's high for the year.

Reese experienced his only .300 season in 1954, batting .309 with a career-high 35 doubles and scoring 98 runs. His numbers began to decline following the 1956 campaign, and he was moved primarily to third base in 1957 but appeared in only 103 games. He remained with the Dodgers when they moved to Los Angeles in 1958, but was used sparingly and batted only .224. He retired from the playing field that year with a .269 lifetime average and 232 stolen bases.

Reese had always been outstanding defensively, and he led the National League in putouts four times, in double plays twice, in assists once, and in fielding percentage once. He had appeared in seven World Series with the Dodgers, and in those Series batted .304 in 1947, .316 in 1949, and .345 in 1952. The Dodgers lost to the Yankees in six of those Series, and defeated them only in 1955. Reese retired with a lifetime World Series average of .272, along with 46 hits, 2 home runs, 20 runs scored, and 5 stolen bases.

Pee Wee became a coach for Los Angeles in 1959, then briefly became a broadcaster and went to work for Hillerich & Bradsby, makers of the Louisville Slugger.

Reese was inducted into the Hall of Fame in 1984, and the Dodgers retired his uniform number 1 the same year. Pee Wee died in Louisville in 1999.

Awards/Honors

1984 Hall of Fame

Cal Ripken, Jr.

Retired Number: 8 (Baltimore Orioles, 2001)
Shortstop/Third Baseman
Playing Career: Baltimore Orioles 1981–2001

Lou Gehrig's successor to the title of "Iron Man," Cal Ripken, Jr. will forever be remembered for "The Streak"—the 2632 consecutive games in which he played between 1982 and 1998.

A Maryland native, Cal came from a baseball family. His father, Cal, Sr., coached and later managed the Baltimore Orioles, and his brother Billy was a major league second baseman. For a time in the 1980s and 1990s, all three were with the Orioles at the same time.

Cal was born in 1960 and reached the major leagues with Baltimore in 1981 as a shortstop. He played only 23 games and was still considered a rookie when he became the Orioles' regular at that position in 1982. He batted .264 that season with 28 home runs, 93 runs batted in, and 32 doubles, good enough to be named the American League's Rookie of the Year.

With unusual power — and size, at 6-feet-4 — for a shortstop, Ripken hit 21 or more home runs for 10 seasons in a row, and for 12 total. He followed up his outstanding debut season with one that was even better, hitting .318 in 1983 with 27 homers and 102 RBIs, while leading the American League with 211 hits, 47 doubles, and 121 runs scored. This time he was the league's Most Valuable Player, and he batted .400 in the playoffs to lead Baltimore to the World Series, then took home a ring to signify the ultimate championship.

He hit .304 in 1984, but his average began to slip after that although he continued to hit home runs. He bottomed out in 1990 when he hit .250, and his high during that four-year stretch was .264 in 1988. Pundits had begun to criticize The Streak and counseled sitting him down for a rest. But that rest would come only in the form of a rare inning off here or there; between June 5, 1982, and September 14, 1987, Cal played not only every game, but also every inning, reaching 8243 straight innings before being rested.

He silenced his critics in 1991 with full-season career-high numbers of a .323 average, 34 home runs, and 114 RBIs, while also collecting 210 hits and 46 doubles. As a result he won his second MVP Award, and he was recognized for his fielding excellence by being awarded the first of two consecutive Gold Gloves. On October 6, he became the last batter ever at Baltimore's Memorial Stadium, grounding into an unfortunate double play in a loss to the Detroit Tigers.

His average fell into the .250s during his first two seasons at Oriole Park at Camden Yards, but in 1994 he hit .315. In 1995 he batted .262, but no one was focused on his offensive statistics. On September 6 at Baltimore, Ripken broke Gehrig's record of 2130 consecutive games played. The game was stopped in the fifth inning, once it became an official contest, and the new record was greeted with great fanfare.

Gehrig's record was the major league benchmark, but it was not actually the *professional* benchmark. That record belonged to Sachio Kinugasa, who had played in 2215 consecutive games with the Hiroshima Carp of the Japanese Central League. On June 14, 1996, Ripken played in his 2216th straight game at Kansas City to eclipse the world record, with Kinugasa, graciously in attendance, offering his congratulations.

Cal slugged 26 homers that year while knocking in 102 runs and adding 40 doubles. In 1997 he was moved to third base, a shift that caused a stir among the major league faithful but that Cal accepted with his typical grace. He continued The Streak at that position, and would reach

2632 games in a row before benching himself on September 20, 1998. The Streak had had many close calls, surviving a twisted knee in 1993 during a brawl with the Seattle Mariners; a photo shoot incident prior to the 1996 All-Star Game during which Roberto Hernandez of the Chicago White Sox slipped and, in attempting to regain his balance, accidentally rammed his forearm into Cal's face, breaking his nose; back problems that began to plague Cal during the 1997 season; and numerous frightening fastballs that happened to clip Cal in one place or another. In the end, Ripken had brought The Streak to an end on his own terms.

Back problems limited Cal to 86 games in 1999, but he hit .340 and belted 18 home runs in the process. He played only 83 games in 2000, but on April 15, in the top of the seventh inning at Minnesota's Metrodome, he singled off Hector Carrasco of the Twins for his 3000th career hit. He retired following the 2001 season. In addition to his consecutive games record, he had a .276 lifetime batting average, 3184 hits, 603 doubles, and 431 home runs.

Ripken was always a fan favorite, and he often stayed long after a game ended to sign autographs. He was meticulous about making sure that, once he started signing, no one would leave without getting his signature. He was heralded for his work ethic, for his natural ability, and for the class with which he played the game and with which he carried himself both on and off the field.

The Orioles retired his number in 2001. Cal and his brother, Billy, later became the owners of the minor league Aberdeen IronBirds, who took their nickname from Cal and who played at none other than Ripken Stadium.

Awards/Honors

1982 American League Rookie of the Year
1983 American League Most Valuable Player
1991 American League Most Valuable Player
1991 American League Gold Glove Shortstop
1992 American League Gold Glove Shortstop

Phil Rizzuto

Retired Number: 10 (New York Yankees, 1985)
Shortstop
Playing Career: New York Yankees 1941–42, 1946–56

Phil Rizzuto, or "Scooter," was born in New York in 1917 and played his entire major league career with his hometown Yankees.

An outstanding defensive shortstop, Phil could also hold his own at the plate. In his rookie season of 1941 he hit .307 with 20 doubles, and the following season batted .284 and contributed 24 two-baggers. He did not have much power, never hitting more than 7 home runs in a season, but he was good at getting on base and twice scored more than 100 runs in a season.

Rizzuto served in the military from 1943 through 1945, like many of his contemporaries. He came back in 1946, and the following season batted a solid .273 with 26 doubles. In 1949 he hit .275 and scored 110 runs, but he had his most outstanding season by far in 1950. That year he hit .324 with 200 hits, 36 doubles, 125 runs scored, and 92 bases on balls, all career highs, and he was named the American League Most Valuable Player. On February 2, before the season began, he had even been the first mystery guest on the premier of the television program *What's My Line?*

Phil hit over .300 twice, and he contributed at least 20 doubles eight times during his 13-year career. Five of those came consecutively, between 1949 and 1953, and in 1951 he followed up his MVP season with a .274 average and 21 two-baggers.

Rizzuto had a terrible season in 1954, batting only .195, and he was used in a backup role after that. He played only 31 games in 1956 before retiring, and he did so with a .273 career average and 239 lifetime doubles.

Phil had participated in nine World Series with the Yankees, and in four of them he was outstanding. Oddly, he hit in the .200s only once, in 1955 when he batted .267 in a seven-game Series. He was usually a person of World Series extremes at the plate, hitting in the .100s four times and in the .300s another four.

He won World Championships with the Yanks in 1941, 1947, and from 1949–53. One of his best Series performances came in 1942, when he batted .381 with eight hits, a home run, and two runs scored during a five-game loss to the St. Louis Cardinals. He retired with 45 Series hits in his career, 21 runs scored, 30 walks, and 10 stolen bases.

After his retirement, Phil became a long-time broadcaster. The Yankees retired his number in 1985, and he was inducted into the Hall of Fame by the Veterans Committee in 1994.

Awards/Honors

1950 American League Most Valuable Player
1994 Hall of Fame

Robin Roberts

Retired Number: 36 (Philadelphia Phillies, 1962)
Pitcher
Playing Career: Philadelphia Phillies 1948–61; Baltimore Orioles 1962–65; Houston Astros 1965–66; Chicago Cubs 1966

Robin Evan Roberts was one of the most outstanding pitchers in major league history, and was the ace of the Philadelphia Phillies' staff for a good portion of his 19-year career.

He was born in Springfield, Illinois, in 1926, and was recruited by Michigan State as a basketball player. He also played baseball, however, and showed true talent as a pitcher, even hurling a no-hitter against Michigan. He was signed by the Phillies in 1948 and briefly pitched for their Wilmington Blue Rocks farm team in the Inter-State League before being called up to Philadelphia.

Roberts went 7–9 in his first major league season in 20 games, but posted a decent 3.19 earned run average. After winning 15 in 1949, he won at least 20 games for the next six seasons in a row.

He was a durable pitcher, leading the National League in starts those six seasons, and during the last five he also led in innings pitched. He started every Opening Day for the Phillies from 1950 through 1961. His 1950 record was 20–11, and he topped the circuit with 5 shutouts (along with three other pitchers) while leading the Phillies to their first World Series appearance since 1915 and giving Philadelphia its first 20-game winner since 1917. He put up a sparkling 1.64 ERA in that Series, but nevertheless lost his only decision in extra innings as the Phillies were swept by the New York Yankees. Roberts' one weakness was a penchant for giving up home runs — he even set several major league records in that category — and his gopher ball to Joe DiMaggio in the tenth inning of Game 2 proved to be the deciding factor in that contest.

After going 21–15 in 1951, Robin led the league in victories for the next four years in a row. His 28 wins in 1952 were the most in the National League since 1935, and beginning that year, he led the league in complete games for the next five in a row.

He won 23 games during each of the next three seasons. His victories in 1953 tied him with Warren Spahn, his 2.75 ERA was second in the league, and he led with 198 strikeouts, just missing the pitching Triple Crown. In 1954 he led in strikeouts again with 185, and on May 13 he very nearly pitched a perfect game against the Cincinnati Redlegs. Giving up a leadoff home run to Bobby Adams, he proceeded to retire the next 27 batters in a row, winning the game by an 8–1 score.

In 1956 Roberts led the league with 18 losses, although he won 19. He led in that dubious category again in 1957, this time faltering to 10–22. He won 17 in 1958 and then began to struggle. After posting a 1–10 record in 1961, he was sold to the New York Yankees, but he was released before even pitching a game. He then signed with the Baltimore Orioles, with whom he spent three fair seasons, even winning 14 games in 1963. He was released during the 1965 season and signed with the Houston Astros, then was released by them during the 1966 campaign and went to the Chicago Cubs. The Cubs released him again following the 1966 season. Still not ready to retire, he signed with the Reading Phillies of the Eastern League for the 1967 campaign, but he would not return to the major leagues.

Retiring with 286 career victories, a 3.41 ERA, and 2357 strikeouts, Roberts later became head coach for the University of Florida and then served as an instructor in the Phillies organization.

The Phillies retired his number in 1962, the year following his departure from Philadelphia, and Robin was inducted into the Hall of Fame in 1976.

Awards/Honors

1976 Hall of Fame

Brooks Robinson

Retired Number: 5 (Baltimore Orioles, 1977)
Third Baseman/Coach
Playing Career: Baltimore Orioles 1955–77
Coaching Career: Baltimore Orioles 1977

Arkansas native Brooks Robinson, who was born in 1937 in Little Rock, spent his entire 23-year career with the Baltimore Orioles as one of the best — if not *the* best — defensive third basemen ever to play the game.

Discovered by the Orioles playing in a church league, Robinson made his major league debut in six games in 1955 and played only a few more the next two seasons with the big club. He became the O's regular third baseman in 1958, but batted only .238. Two years later he finally established himself, hitting .294 in 1960 with 14 home runs and winning the first of 16 consecutive Gold Gloves. His defensive work was dazzling, and he would eventually set major league career marks at his position for games, chances, putouts, assists, double plays, and fielding percentage.

In 1962 Brooks hit .303, one of only two seasons in which he would top the .300 mark. He also swatted 23 home runs. In 1964 he did better, batting .317, hitting a career-high 28 home runs, and leading the league with 118 runs batted in en route to being named the American League's Most Valuable Player.

He hit .297 in 1965 and drove in 100 runs in 1966. The Orioles won their division in 1969 and Robinson hit .500 in the League Championship Series, but he had a terrible World Series at the plate — managing only a single in 19 official at-bats, good for a dismal .053 average — as the Orioles fell to the New York Mets.

It was in the 1970 postseason that he truly shone, however. After hitting .583 in a three-game sweep of the Minnesota Twins to help win the American League pennant, Robinson batted .429 in a five-game win over the Cincinnati Reds in the World Series, hitting home runs in Games 1 and 4 and putting on a defensive clinic at third base that dazzled fans — and players — across the country. Frustrating the Cincinnati offense again and again, he was eventually named the Series' MVP.

Brooks hit only .201 in 1975, although he won his sixteenth and final Gold Glove, and he was used in a part-time role the next two seasons before becoming a coach with the Orioles in 1977. The O's retired his number 5, which he wore as a tribute to Joe DiMaggio, the same year. He had previously worn numbers 6 and 34 early in his career.

Brooks retired with a .267 lifetime average and 268 home runs. He became a broadcaster for the Orioles, and was inducted into the Hall of Fame in 1983.

Awards/Honors

1960 American League Gold Glove Third Baseman
1961 American League Gold Glove Third Baseman
1962 American League Gold Glove Third Baseman
1963 American League Gold Glove Third Baseman
1964 American League Most Valuable Player
1964 American League Gold Glove Third Baseman
1965 American League Gold Glove Third Baseman
1966 American League Gold Glove Third Baseman
1967 American League Gold Glove Third Baseman
1968 American League Gold Glove Third Baseman
1969 American League Gold Glove Third Baseman
1970 American League Gold Glove Third Baseman
1971 American League Gold Glove Third Baseman
1972 American League Gold Glove Third Baseman
1973 American League Gold Glove Third Baseman

1974 American League Gold Glove Third Baseman
1975 American League Gold Glove Third Baseman
1983 Hall of Fame

Frank Robinson

Retired Number: 20 (Baltimore Orioles, 1972; Cincinnati Reds, 1998)
Outfielder/First Baseman/Designated Hitter/Manager/Coach
Playing Career: Cincinnati Redlegs 1956–58; Cincinnati Reds 1959–65; Baltimore Orioles 1966–71; Los Angeles Dodgers 1972; California Angels 1973–74; Cleveland Indians 1974–76
Managerial Career: Cleveland Indians 1975–77; San Francisco Giants 1981–84; Baltimore Orioles 1988–91; Montreal Expos 2002–
Coaching Career: California Angels 1977; Baltimore Orioles 1978–80, 1985–87

Texan Frank Robinson was born in Beaumont in 1935 and reached the major leagues with the Cincinnati Redlegs at the age of 20. He made a huge impact his rookie season, batting .290 with 38 home runs and 83 runs batted in 1956 while leading the National League with 122 runs scored, and he was named the league's Rookie of the Year.

He was a major force with Cincinnati — who returned to their previous name of Reds in 1959 — for the first 10 years of his career, leading the league in slugging percentage three years in a row, hitting over .300 five times, and hitting no fewer than 21 home runs all 10 seasons.

He contributed to the Reds' 1961 pennant drive with a .323 average, a league-leading .611 slugging percentage, 37 homers, and 124 RBIs. He also scored 117 runs and was named the NL's Most Valuable Player. The following year he hit an even better .342 with 39 home runs and a career-best 136 RBIs, and he led the league with 51 doubles and with 134 runs scored.

Robinson was no slouch defensively, having won a Gold Glove as a left fielder in 1958. But it was with his bat that he continued to make the most noise, and he would eventually hit over 20 home runs in a season 17 times in his 21-year career, and would drive in over 100 runs on six occasions.

Despite his .296 average and 33 homers in 1965, the Reds believed he had peaked and traded him to the Baltimore Orioles. Frank responded by winning the American League's Triple Crown, batting .316 with 49 home runs and 122 RBIs, while also topping the loop with a .637 slugging percentage and 122 runs scored. He was named the league's Most

Valuable Player, and remains the only player to win that award in both leagues.

He battled injuries the next few years, but still succeeded in hitting over .300 three of the next four and dropping below 25 homers only once. Despite a .281 average and 28 home runs in 1971, however, the Orioles traded him to the Los Angeles Dodgers.

Robinson spent only one year in Los Angeles, and during that season the Orioles retired his uniform number 20. Frank was traded to the California Angels for the 1973 season and belted 30 home runs, then, toward the end of the 1974 campaign, was traded to the Cleveland Indians. In 1975 the Indians named him their player/manager, making him the first black manager in major league history.

Robinson played sparingly the next two seasons, and turned strictly to managing in 1977. He ended his playing days with a .294 lifetime batting average, 586 home runs, and 1812 RBIs.

He had guided the Indians to consecutive fourth-place finishes in 1975 and '76, and they were faring worse in 1977 when he was fired and replaced by Jeff Torborg. He finished the season coaching for the Angels, then went to the Orioles as a coach for the next three seasons.

In 1981 he was named manager of the San Francisco Giants. Two third-place finishes in the next three years were not enough to keep his job, however; in sixth place in 1984, he was fired and replaced by Danny Ozark. He then returned to the Orioles as a coach, and was named that team's manager in 1988 after the team had started the season 0–6 under Cal Ripken, Sr. The club eventually set a record by losing their first 21 games in a row, and they finished in last place, but in 1989 they rebounded with 87 wins and vaulted into second place, finishing only two games behind the Toronto Blue Jays. Both the Associated Press and the Baseball Writers Association of America named Robinson the Manager of the Year, and the AP presented only one award to cover both leagues.

The Orioles finished fifth in 1990, and were only 13–24 in 1991 when Robinson was replaced by Johnny Oates.

Frank had been inducted into the Hall of Fame in 1982. In 1998, the Reds followed the Orioles' example and retired his uniform number 20, making him one of only eight men to have his number retired by more than one team.

Frank eventually went to work for Major League Baseball, at one point becoming the Vice President of On-Field Operations. When MLB assumed control of the Montreal Expos franchise in 2002, he was named the team's manager and brought the club in second in his first year at the helm.

Awards/Honors

1956 National League Rookie of the Year
1958 National League Gold Glove Left Fielder
1961 National League Most Valuable Player
1966 American League Most Valuable Player
1982 Hall of Fame
1989 Manager of the Year (AP)
1989 American League Manager of the Year (BBWAA)

Jackie Robinson

Retired Number: 42 (Los Angeles Dodgers, 1972; Major League Baseball, 1997)
First Baseman/Second Baseman/Outfielder/Third Baseman
Playing Career: Brooklyn Dodgers 1947–56

One of the greatest all-around athletes in history, Jackie Robinson was born in Cairo, Georgia, in 1919. At UCLA he lettered in four sports — baseball, football, basketball, and track — all in the same year (1941), and was also a competitive swimmer and tennis player. The event for which he is most noted, however, is his breaking of the color barrier in major league baseball in 1947. That single, pivotal achievement has made him not only a famous sports figure, but an American historical icon as well.

The last two black players in major league baseball had been brothers. Moses Fleetwood Walker and Welday Walker both played for the Toledo Blue Stockings of the American Association in 1884. From that point on, however, there was an unwritten rule barring blacks from major league play, a rule that would not be broken until 63 years later, when Robinson took the field for the Brooklyn Dodgers.

Brooklyn General Manager Branch Rickey began a deliberate search to find the right player to break the color line. He wanted someone not only with athletic ability, but also with a temperament that would allow him to face the inevitable bias, controversy, and loneliness that would accompany his introduction into major league baseball's ranks while remaining competitive and having the courage *not* to fight back. Scout Clyde Sukeforth found Robinson playing shortstop for the Kansas City Monarchs of the Negro American League, where he batted .387 in 1945. Amid much publicity, Rickey signed Robinson to a contract and assigned him to the Montreal Royals of the International League for the 1946 season. Robinson won the league's batting title and helped the Royals to the league's Little World Championship, and was called up to Brooklyn for the historic 1947 campaign.

Jackie struggled with the Dodgers at first, undoubtedly, at least in part, because of racist comments, petitions, slurs, epithets, and even death threats on the part of not only baseball fans, but opposing players and even teammates as well. The Dodgers' popular Pee Wee Reese made a special point of making Robinson feel welcome, at one point even putting his arm around Jackie on the field in a show of support.

Robinson played first base for the Dodgers that season, and he did come around as he ended up batting .297 with 31 doubles and scoring 125 runs while also leading the National League with 29 stolen bases. As a result he was named baseball's very first Rookie of the Year. For the first two years, the award was given to only a single player representing both leagues.

Moved to second base in 1948, Robinson had a similar season, hitting .296 and stealing 22 bases, then he had a sensational 1949. Winning the NL batting title with a .342 average, he hit 16 home runs, drove in a career-high 124 runs, and led the league with 37 steals while scoring 122 runs of his own. He accumulated 203 hits and was named the National League Most Valuable Player.

Beginning with that year, Robinson hit over .300 for six seasons in a row, and he continued to steal a lot of bases and twice reached career highs of 19 home runs in a season. He was used primarily in the outfield in 1953 and 1954, and primarily at third base in 1955 and 1956. His frequent defensive shifts were a result of his great versatility.

The Dodgers sold Jackie to the New York Giants following the 1956 campaign, but Robinson retired instead with a .311 lifetime average, 273 doubles, and 197 steals in a 10-year career. He had participated in six World Series with Brooklyn but had hit only .234 in postseason play, although he scored 22 runs and drew 21 walks. The Dodgers lost each of those Series to the New York Yankees, except in 1955 when they won one in seven games.

Jackie was inducted into the Hall of Fame in 1962. Ten years later, he died in Stamford, Connecticut, and the Dodgers retired his uniform number 42.

In 1987 Major League Baseball named the Rookie of the Year Award after him in celebration of the fortieth anniversary of his breaking the color barrier. When the fiftieth anniversary came around in 1997, Commissioner Bud Selig announced that *all* teams would retire Jackie's number 42, making him the first player in any sport to be so honored. He thus became one of only eight men to have his number retired by more than one team, and the only one to have his number retired by more than three. Players already wearing the number were allowed to continue wearing it for the rest of their careers, and more than one commented that the downside to this universal retirement was that players who idolized Robinson would no longer be able to honor him by donning his number. On the positive side, all major league baseball teams now honor the number, creating a constant reminder of Jackie's achievements.

Somewhat oddly, the universal number retirement also extended to the minor league affiliates of Major League Baseball's teams.

Robinson's effect on baseball remains a rather obvious one. Without his courageous, lone crusade to shatter the inherent racism that had permeated the sport, the baseball world might never have experienced the spectacular, historic moments afforded by players such as Hank Aaron, Willie Mays, Frank Robinson, Bob Gibson, Roy Campanella, Ken Griffey, Jr., and countless others.

Robinson's career made a definite statement to the domain of sports. But, perhaps even more importantly, it made a statement to the entire nation as well.

Awards/Honors

1947 Rookie of the Year
1949 National League Most Valuable Player
1962 Hall of Fame

Babe Ruth

Retired Number: 3 (New York Yankees, 1948)
Pitcher/Outfielder/Coach
Playing Career: Boston Red Sox 1914–19; New York Yankees 1920–34; Boston Braves 1935
Coaching Career: Brooklyn Dodgers 1938

George Herman "Babe" Ruth was a bigger-than-life athlete with a bigger-than-life personality to match. His, in fact, is probably the most recognizable name in baseball — if not all of sports — history.

Ruth was born in Baltimore in 1895 and was raised at a boarding school. A gifted athlete, he was signed by minor league Baltimore Orioles owner Jack Dunn. It was in the spring of 1914 that Ruth received his nickname, because his Oriole teammates began to refer to him as "Jack Dunn's new babe."

Later that year he was purchased by the Boston Red Sox. Originally a pitcher, Ruth was outstanding in six seasons with Boston. After appearing in only 4 games in 1914, he went 18–8 the following season and posted a 2.44 earned run average. In 1916 he became a 20-game winner, going 23–12 and leading the American League with a 1.75 ERA and 9 shutouts while striking out 170 batters. In Game 2 of the World Series against the Brooklyn Robins, he gave up an inside-the-park home run in the first inning and then did not allow another run. The game went 14 innings, and Ruth pitched all 14 and came away with a 2–1 victory. His ERA for the Series was 0.64, and the Red Sox became World Champions in five games.

In 1917 he posted a 24–13 record with a 2.01 ERA while leading the AL with 35 complete games. The Red Sox were noticing his strong hitting, however — he had a .304 lifetime average as a pitcher — and began to use him more and more in the outfield. As a result Ruth pitched only 20 games in 1918, winning 13 of them, and in a victorious World Series against the Chicago Cubs he won two more, even pitching a shutout in Game 1. At the plate he led the league with 11 home runs (tying him with Tilly Walker of the Philadelphia Phillies) and a .555 slugging percentage.

Babe pitched 17 games in 1919 and won 9 of them, while playing 111 games in the outfield. He set a new major league record that year with 29 home runs, and also led the league with 114 runs batted in, 103 runs scored, and a .657 slugging percentage.

Red Sox owner Harry Frazee was a theatrical producer who cared more about his Broadway plays than about baseball. In January of 1920, he sold Ruth to New York Yankees owner Jacob Ruppert for $125,000. Ruppert also provided Frazee a $300,000 loan to help finance his productions.

The rest is legend. Ruth immediately shattered his own home run record by hitting an unimaginable 54 in 1920, and had an .847 slugging percentage. No major league *team* hit that many home runs that year except for the Philadelphia Phillies, who hit 64. Babe pitched only one game that season and won it. In 1921 he broke his own record again by hitting 59 home runs; he pitched two games and won them, but he was now, for all practical purposes, a full-time outfielder.

In all, in 22 years Ruth would lead the league in home runs 12 times, in RBIs 6 times, in runs scored 8 times, in bases on balls 11 times, and in slugging percentage 13 times. He would hit over .300 seventeen times. His 1921 performance — a .378 batting average, 59 home runs, 171 RBIs, 177 runs scored, 144 walks, and an .846 slugging percentage — led the Yankees to their first of a multitude of pennants, and his presence over the years would contribute significantly to what would become baseball's biggest dynasty.

In 1923 Babe batted a career-high .393. He won the League Award, which was that era's version of the Most Valuable Player Award, on the strength of that average plus league-leading totals of 41 homers, 131 RBIs, 151 runs scored, and 170 walks.

He won his only batting title in 1924, when he hit .378. His 1927 season, however, was one of his best, as it was for many of the Yankees. He hit an unprecedented 60 home runs that year, setting a record that would stand until Roger Maris broke it 34 years later, and he had 164 RBIs. He also batted .400 in the World Series as the Yankees swept the Pittsburgh Pirates.

Ruth loved to cater to his young fans, and was noted for his generosity to children. He also loved to party, however, and after a while his off-the-field antics — late nights, carousing, drunkenness, and an appetite that caused him to gain too much weight — began to catch up with him. In 1934 he hit .288 with 22 home runs — good numbers for most players, but tiny compared to Babe's abilities — and he was released at the end of the season and signed with the Boston Braves for 1935. Babe played only 28 games with the Braves and batted a mere .181, but he finished his playing career with a flourish by hitting three home runs in one game at Pittsburgh's Forbes Field. One of them, in fact, was the longest ball ever hit out of the park.

Ruth retired with a .342 lifetime batting average, and with a then-record 714 home runs and 2211 RBIs, as well as with 2174 runs scored and 2056 walks. Additionally, he had hit .326 in 10 World Series with 15 homers and 33 RBIs. As a pitcher he was 94–46 with a career ERA of 2.28, and was 3–0 and 0.87 in two World Series.

Babe had always wanted to manage a major league team, but he turned down offers to begin at the minor league level and never did become a big-league skipper. In 1936 he became one of the first five men inducted into the brand new Hall of Fame. He then signed on as a coach with the Brooklyn Dodgers in 1938, but that was mainly for publicity purposes and he had few real duties with the club.

The Yankees were the first team to wear uniform numbers regularly; they instituted the practice in 1929. At that time Ruth was assigned number 3 because he batted third in the lineup. After Babe retired, at least nine other Yankees wore the number, but in 1948 they retired it in his honor. Two months later, Ruth died of throat cancer.

Awards/Honors

1923 League Award
1936 Hall of Fame

Nolan Ryan

Retired Number: 30 (Anaheim Angels, 1992)
Retired Number: 34 (Texas Rangers, 1996; Houston Astros, 1996)
Pitcher
Playing Career: New York Mets 1966, 1968–71; California Angels 1972–79; Houston Astros 1980–88; Texas Rangers 1989–93

A native of Refugio, Texas, born in 1947, Nolan Ryan is one of only eight men to have his uniform number retired by more than one team; along with Carlton Fisk, is one of only two to have two *different* numbers retired; and, other than Jackie Robinson, is the only one to have his number retired by at least three teams.

A fireballing right-hander, Ryan ironically never won a Cy Young Award, a Most Valuable Player Award, or any other major award. What he did do was set record after record for strikeouts, pitch an unbelievable seven no-hitters, and put together a 27-year career that earned him induction into the Hall of Fame.

A hard-throwing but wild high school pitcher, Ryan was drafted by the New York Mets and began striking out batters at a record-setting pace with the minor league Greenville Mets. He pitched two games in New York in 1966, spent most of 1967 in the military, then returned to New York in 1968 and struck out 133 batters in 134 innings. Used as both a starter and reliever with the Mets, Ryan did not like the spotlight in New York and requested a trade after the 1971 season.

The Mets obliged, sending him to the California Angels in December along with three other players in exchange for Jim Fregosi. The Angels made him primarily a starter, and in 1972 Ryan won 19 games and led the American League with 329 strikeouts and 9 shutouts. That was the first of 15 times in which he would strike out at least 200 batters in a season, and the first of 6 in which he would whiff over 300.

He was a 20-game winner twice. In 1973 he went 21–16 and set a new major league record by striking out 383 batters, and in 1974 was 22–16 with a league-leading 367 Ks and 333 innings pitched. In his career he would top the league in strikeouts 11 times. Like most hard throwers, he was also prone to wildness, and would lead the league in bases on balls a total of eight times.

Ryan led the league in losses in 1976, going 17–18, but he was best in the league with 327 strikeouts and 7 shutouts. He won 19 games in 1977, and finished in a three-way tie for league leadership with 5 shutouts in 1979.

In November of that year Nolan became a free agent and returned to his home state of Texas, signing with the Houston Astros. In 1981 he led the National League with a 1.69 earned run average, but would not lead the NL in strikeouts until 1987. He did so two years in a row, also leading with a 2.76 ERA in 1988, then he became a free agent again and signed with the Texas Rangers.

Nolan won 16 in 1989 with Texas, topping the AL with 301 strikeouts, the third of four consecutive years in which he was his respective league's best in that category. On August 22 against the Oakland Athletics he whiffed Rickey Henderson to record his 5000th career strikeout, an unprecedented mark.

Ryan pitched into the 1993 season, then retired when he injured his arm. He won 324 games, struck out 5714 batters, pitched 61 shutouts, and had a career ERA of 3.19. He is the only pitcher to strike out over 2000 batters in each league. His record seven no-hitters came with three different teams: the Angels (four), the Astros (one), and the Rangers (two). He also pitched 12 one-hitters.

The Angels retired his number 30 in 1992. The Rangers retired the number 34 he had worn with them in 1996, and the Astros followed suit exactly two weeks later.

Ryan was inducted into the Hall of Fame in 1999. With his sons, he later became the owner of the minor league Jackson Generals, whom he moved to Round Rock, Texas. In a name-the-team contest, the club was renamed the Round Rock Express after Ryan's own nickname, "The Ryan Express."

Awards/Honors

1999 Hall of Fame

Ron Santo

Retired Number: 10 (Chicago Cubs, 2003)
Third Baseman/Designated Hitter
Playing Career: Chicago Cubs 1960–73; Chicago White Sox 1974

A 1940 native of Seattle, Washington, Ron Santo debuted with the Chicago Cubs at third base in Jume of 1960 and would become the team's regular at the hot corner for the next 13 seasons. A power hitter with a short temper, Santo had occasional run-ins with opponents, managers, the media, and even teammates, but he was a fierce competitor who hated to lose. He hit 24 doubles in only 95 games in 1960, and reached the 20 mark

12 times in his 15-year career. He hit at least 20 home runs 11 times, topping out at 33 in 1965. Santo batted .313 in 1964, his best season. He led the National League with 13 triples and 86 bases on balls that year while also slugging 30 home runs and driving in 114. He was no slouch defensively, either, winning the first of five consecutive Gold Gloves at third base.

Ron drove in 101 runs in 1965, and the following season he batted .312 with another 30 homers and 94 RBIs. He led the NL with 95 walks, and would lead again with 96 in 1967 and an equal number the following year. His .300 average in '67 was supplemented by 31 home runs, 98 RBIs, and 23 doubles. He also set a new major league record at third base with 393 assists. In 1969 he drove in 123 runs, his personal best, and knocked home 114 the following year. On July 6, 1970, he hit a two-run homer to win the first game of a doubleheader, then hit two more out of the park in the second game while driving in an incredible eight runs. He hit .302 in 1972, and the following season cracked 20 home runs. Nevertheless, in December of 1973 the Cubs traded him across town to the Chicago White Sox for Steve Stone, Ken Frailing, Steve Swisher, and Jim Kremmel. He hit only .221 in his new league in 1974, mainly as a designated hitter, then the nine-time All-Star retired with a .277 lifetime average and 342 career home runs.

Santo became a Cubs broadcaster following his playing career, and would be much-loved by Chicago fans. He was diagnosed with diabetes in his teens, and eventually had both legs amputated because of complications from the disease. He had his prostheses designed to look like Cubs uniforms — one a home version and the other a road — and both bore his familiar number 10. He has served on the board of directors for the Juvenile Diabetes Foundation and has raised a great deal of money for the organization through his annual Ron Santo Walk for the Cure walk-a-thon. The Cubs retired his number on September 28, 2003. Santo was thrilled by the honor, and he stated, "There's nothing more important to me in my life than this happening. I'm a Cubbie. I'll always be a Cubbie."

Awards/Honors

1964 National League Gold Glove Third Baseman
1965 National League Gold Glove Third Baseman
1966 National League Gold Glove Third Baseman
1967 National League Gold Glove Third Baseman
1968 National League Gold Glove Third Baseman

Mike Schmidt

Retired Number: 20 (Philadelphia Phillies, 1990)
Third Baseman/First Baseman
Playing Career: Philadelphia Phillies 1972–89

Dayton, Ohio native Mike Schmidt was drafted out of Ohio University by the Philadelphia Phillies in 1971, and after two full minor league seasons he broke in with Philadelphia at the end of 1972 at the age of 22. He struggled a bit at the plate at first, hitting only .196 in 1973, but in 1974 he began to hit his stride. Having hit a promising 18 home runs in '73 in spite of his low average, he upped that total to a National League–leading 36 the following year and would top the league for three years in a row. On June 10 he hit a ball off a speaker hanging from the roof in the Astrodome, over 300 feet from home plate and 100 feet off the ground. In play, the ball fell back to the field for one of the longest singles in history.

Between 1974 and 1987 Schmidt would never hit fewer than 21 home runs in a season. He led the league 8 times in that category during an 18-year career, and led in runs batted in 4 times. Additionally, he was a stellar-fielding third baseman, winning 10 Gold Gloves, the first 9 of which were consecutive. Strikeouts were always a problem for him, and he led the league in that category four times as well.

Mike hit exactly 38 home runs three years in a row, beginning in 1975. He played a well-rounded game; having stolen 23 bases in 1974, he stole 29 in '75.

On July 17, 1976, he hit four home runs in a game against the Chicago Cubs at Wrigley Field. The Phillies won that game, 18–16, in 10 innings. He hit .308 in the League Championship Series, but the Phillies were swept in three games by the Cincinnati Reds.

Mike had something of a down year in 1978, hitting 21 homers, but he rebounded with 45 in 1979. He drove in 114 runs and also led the league for the first of four times in bases on balls with 120.

In 1980 Schmidt won the National League Most Valuable Player Award by hitting .286 with a league-leading 48 home runs, which broke Eddie Mathews' record for most by a third baseman in a season. He also led the loop with a career-high 121 RBIs and a .624 slugging percentage, while scoring 104 runs. The Phillies went to the World Series and defeated the Kansas City Royals in six games, and Schmidt was the Series MVP as well, as he batted .381 with two home runs and seven RBIs.

Mike repeated as the league MVP in 1981. He hit .316, and despite the fact that the season was shortened by a players' strike, he led the NL with 31 homers, 91 RBIs, 73 walks, and 78 runs scored.

Schmidt hit a league-best 40 home runs in 1983; it was the last time he would achieve that mark, but he would top the loop twice more. In a losing World Series effort against the Baltimore Orioles, he hit a miserable .050, managing only a single in 20 at-bats.

He was moved to first base in 1985 to make room for Rick Schu, but by the end of the season he was back at third. He had a third MVP season in 1986, hitting .290 and leading the league with 37 home runs, 119 RBIs, and a .547 slugging percentage. He hit 35 more homers in 1987, then injured his rotator cuff in 1988 and played only 108 games. He was batting a mere .203 in May of 1989 when he decided it was time to retire. The Phillies retired his number the following year.

Schmidt came away with 548 lifetime home runs and 1595 RBIs. He was a 12-time All-Star, and was inducted into the Hall of Fame in 1995.

Awards/Honors

1976 National League Gold Glove Third Baseman
1977 National League Gold Glove Third Baseman
1978 National League Gold Glove Third Baseman
1979 National League Gold Glove Third Baseman
1980 National League Most Valuable Player
1980 National League Gold Glove Third Baseman
1981 National League Most Valuable Player
1981 National League Gold Glove Third Baseman
1982 National League Gold Glove Third Baseman
1983 National League Gold Glove Third Baseman
1984 National League Gold Glove Third Baseman
1986 National League Most Valuable Player
1986 National League Gold Glove Third Baseman
1995 Hall of Fame

Red Schoendienst

Retired Number: 2 (St. Louis Cardinals, 1996)
Outfielder/Second Baseman/Coach/Manager
Playing Career: St. Louis Cardinals 1945–56, 1961–63; New York Giants 1956–57; Milwaukee Braves 1957–60

Coaching Career: St. Louis Cardinals 1963–64, 1979–95; Oakland Athletics 1977–78
Managerial Career: St. Louis Cardinals 1965–76, 1980, 1990

Albert Fred "Red" Schoendienst was born on February 2, 1923, in Germantown, Illinois. He was signed by the St. Louis Cardinals in 1942 for $75 a month, and in 1943 played for their Rochester Red Wings farm team in the International League and won the league's Most Valuable Player Award. He was in the Army in 1944, and made his debut with the Cardinals in 1945, playing mostly in the outfield. He hit a solid .278 that first season, and led the National League with 26 stolen bases.

Schoendienst was moved to second base in 1946 and hit .281, but his average fell significantly the following year. He was a slick fielder, eventually leading the NL in fielding percentage seven times.

In 1950 his 43 doubles were best in the NL. Two years later he cracked the .300 mark for the first of seven times, hitting .303. He upped that mark to .342 in 1953, and added 15 home runs to the mix while scoring 107 runs.

During the 1956 season the Cardinals traded Schoendienst to the New York Giants. Red finished the season at .302, and during the next season he was traded again, this time to the Milwaukee Braves. He finished that year at .309.

In 1958 he suffered several injuries and played only 106 games, then he came down with tuberculosis and lost part of a lung. He played only 5 games in 1959, and 68 in 1960.

He returned to the Cardinals in 1961, and although he played only on a part-time basis for his final three years, he hit .300 in '61 and then .301 in 1962, when he led the league with 22 pinch hits. He would bat .303 in his career as a pinch hitter.

He played only six games in 1963 before becoming a Cardinals coach. His lifetime batting average for a 19-year career was .289, and he had played in three World Series with the Cardinals and Braves.

Schoendienst was named the Redbirds' manager in 1965. The team played approximate .500 ball his first two seasons at the helm, then won the National League pennant in 1967 by 10½ games over the San Francisco Giants. In the World Series they defeated the Boston Red Sox in seven games, and Schoendienst was named the NL Manager of the Year by the Associated Press.

The Cards repeated as league champions in 1968, outdistancing the Giants by nine games, but this time they dropped the Series to the Detroit Tigers. The AP once again named Red its Manager of the Year for the NL.

Over the next eight seasons the Cardinals would not win another pennant, but they would manage three second-place finishes. Red was fired following the 1976 campaign, and he became a coach with the Oakland Athletics for the next three years. He returned to the Cardinals as a coach in 1979, and would remain in that capacity until he retired in 1995. In 1980 he was called upon to take the reins on an interim basis when manager Whitey Herzog became the team's general manager. He managed the last 37 games, winning 18 and losing 19, as the Redbirds finished fourth. He was again made interim manager in 1990, again to replace Whitey Herzog, and managed another 24 games before being succeeded by Joe Torre.

Schoendienst was inducted into the Hall of Fame in 1989. He originally wore number 6 in 1945 as a player, but when Stan Musial returned from the war and reclaimed it in 1946 he switched to number 2 and would keep that for the rest of his St. Louis career. The Cards retired the number in 1996.

Awards/Honors

1967 National League Manager of the Year (AP)
1968 National League Manager of the Year (AP)
1989 Hall of Fame

Mike Scott

Retired Number: 33 (Houston Astros, 1992)
Pitcher
Playing Career: New York Mets 1979–82; Houston Astros 1983–91

Californian Mike Scott was born in Santa Monica in 1955 and made his major league debut with the New York Mets in 1979 as a hard-throwing right-handed pitcher. He struggled during his years in New York, however, making his entrance in 18 games that first year and compiling a 1–3 record with an unimpressive 5.37 earned run average. He surrendered 59 hits in 52 innings, and his performance would be somewhat typical of his time with the Mets.

In six games in 1980 he was 1–1, his ERA 4.34, and he gave up 40 hits in 29 innings. After posting poor records the next two seasons, he was traded to the Houston Astros for Danny Heep. It was in Houston that he would hit his stride.

He went 10–6 in his first season with the Astros and put up a decent 3.72 ERA. After struggling in 1984, he rebounded to go 18–8 the next year with a 3.29 ERA. In 1986 he was truly outstanding, posting an 18–10 record and leading the National League with a 2.22 ERA as he helped lead the Astros to the NL Western Division title. His 306 strikeouts — the only time he would top the 300 mark — were also best in the league, as were his 5 shutouts (tying him with Bob Knepper) and 275⅓ innings pitched. He pitched a no-hitter against the San Francisco Giants in the game that clinched the division for Houston, and won the National League Cy Young Award. He struck out 14 batters in Game 1 of the League Championship Series against the Mets, although New York would eventually win the series, four games to two. Scott did his part for Houston, winning the two games he pitched and coming away with a microscopic ERA of 0.50 with 19 total strikeouts.

He won 16 more games in 1987 while striking out 233 batters, and he won 14 the next season. In 1989 he became a 20-game winner — the only one in the league that year, in fact — as he turned in a 20–10 mark and posted an ERA of 3.10.

He was never the same pitcher after that, and played only one more full season. In 1990 he fell off to 9–13, and after pitching only 2 games in 1991, and giving up 11 hits in 7 innings, he retired. The Astros retired his number the following season.

Awards/Honors

1986 National League Cy Young Award

Tom Seaver

Retired Number: 41 (New York Mets, 1988)
Pitcher
Playing Career: New York Mets 1967–77, 1983; Cincinnati Reds 1977–82; Chicago White Sox 1984–86; Boston Red Sox 1986

Tom Seaver was signed by the New York Mets through a lottery. Pitching at the University of Southern California, he was offered $40,000 to sign with the Atlanta Braves, but Commissioner William Eckert and the NCAA voided the offer and made him, in effect, a free agent. Any team was allowed to match the Braves' offer, and the names of any who did would be placed in a hat and a winner would be selected. Three teams joined the Braves — the Mets, the Cleveland Indians, and the Philadelphia Phillies — and the Mets' name was drawn.

Seaver was born in 1944 in Fresno, California. He pitched immediately for the Mets as a part of the starting rotation in 1967, and he proved his worth by going 16–13 with a 2.76 earned run average and winning the

National League Rookie of the Year Award. The following season was the first of 9 in a row and 10 overall in which he would strike out over 200 batters, and he led the league in that category 5 times. He led the NL in victories in 1969, and his 25–7 record was good for a league-best .781 winning percentage. He won the first of three Cy Young Awards, and helped take the Mets all the way to a World Championship in a five-game series over the Baltimore Orioles.

In 1970 he won 18 and led the league with a 2.81 ERA. On April 22 he struck out 19 San Diego Padres in a 9-inning game, including the last 10 in a row.

He was a 20-game winner for the second time in 1971 as he posted a 20–10 mark, and he once again led the NL in ERA at 1.76. His league-best 289 strikeouts were also his career high.

After posting a 21–12 mark in 1972, he won 19 games in '73 and led the league with a 2.08 ERA, 18 complete games (tying him with Steve Carlton), and 251 strikeouts en route to his second Cy Young Award and another National League pennant for the Mets. This time, however, the club dropped a seven-game World Series to the Orioles.

A sore hip plagued Seaver in 1974, but in 1975 "Tom Terrific" led the league in victories with a 22–9 record. It was the second of three times in which he would lead the NL in wins, and the fourth of five times in which he would win at least 20 games in a season. He won his third and last Cy Young Award that year.

Seaver had been feuding with Mets general manager M. Donald Grant over issues related to Seaver's salary and to the Mets as a whole, and on June 15, 1977, Grant stunned the New York faithful by trading Tom to the Cincinnati Reds for four players. Seaver continued his winning ways in Cincinnati, finishing the season with a 21–6 record and leading the league with 7 shutouts. He won 16 in 1978, and on June 16, after many near-misses, he pitched his only no-hitter, a 4–0 victory over the St. Louis Cardinals.

He won 16 games in 1979 while leading the league with a .727 winning percentage and finishing in a three-way tie with 5 shutouts. The 1981 season was shortened by a players' strike, but despite starting only 23 games, Seaver went 14–2 to lead the NL in victories, as well as in winning percentage at .875.

He fell to a 5–13 record in 1982, and in December the Reds traded him back to the Mets for three players. He went only 9–14 upon his return to New York, but the last-place Mets' offense was among the worst in the league. Seaver became a free agent in 1984 and signed with the Chicago White Sox, and he went 15–11 and 16–11 in his two full seasons with them.

On August 4, 1985, he recorded his 300th career win, a 4–1 victory over the New York Yankees. In June of 1986, he was only 2–6 when the Sox traded him to their crimson counterparts, the Boston Red Sox, for Steve Lyons. Seaver finished the season with a lowly 7–13 mark and a 4.03 ERA.

He attempted another comeback with the Mets during spring training of 1987, but did not pitch well and decided to retire. He did so with a lifetime record of 311–205, a 2.86 ERA, 3640 strikeouts, and 61 shutouts.

The Mets retired his number in 1988, and Seaver went into broadcasting that year. He was inducted into the Hall of Fame in 1992.

Awards/Honors

1967 National League Rookie of the Year
1969 National League Cy Young Award
1973 National League Cy Young Award
1975 National League Cy Young Award
1992 Hall of Fame

Enos Slaughter

Retired Number: 9 (St. Louis Cardinals, 1996)
Outfielder
Playing Career: St. Louis Cardinals 1938–42, 1946–53; New York Yankees 1954–55, 1956–59; Kansas City Athletics 1955–56; Milwaukee Braves 1959

Originally a tobacco farmer from North Carolina, where he was born in 1916, Enos Slaughter bore the nickname "Country" and was one of the fiercest competitors ever to play the game.

He began his major league career in 1938 with the St. Louis Cardinals, and he became a regular the next year. He would hit over .300 for the next five seasons in a row — although he would lose the years from 1943 through 1945 due to military service in World War II — and would accomplish the feat 10 times in his 19-year career. His batting average was .320 in his first full season, and he led the National League with 52 doubles.

He hit .311 the next year, then in 1942 batted .318 and led the NL with 188 hits and 17 triples.

Returning from the war in 1946, he never broke stride. He hit .300 and paced the circuit with 130 runs batted in, clubbing a career-high 18 home runs while scoring 100 runs himself. It was the second of three seasons in a row in which he would score exactly 100. What was probably the most famous play of Slaughter's career came during the World Series that year, when the Cardinals were facing the Boston Red Sox. In Game 5 he was hit by a pitch that broke his elbow, yet he continued to play. In the eighth inning of Game 7 he was on first base when teammate Harry Walker hit a double, and Slaughter never hesitated as he rounded second and third and went all the way home to score what ultimately proved to be the winning run. The play has forever been known as Slaughter's "Mad Dash." He hit .320 in that Series overall.

In 1949 Enos batted .336, his career best, and he tied Stan Musial for the league lead in triples with 13. The following season he drove in 101 runs and in 1952 he hit an even .300, the last time he would reach that mark with St. Louis.

In April of 1954 the Cardinals dealt Slaughter to the New York Yankees for Bill Virdon, Mel Wright, and minor leaguer Emil Tellinger. Enos did not fare well in his first go-round in New York, batting .248 in 69 games, and he was hitting a lowly .111 the following season when, in May, the Yankees traded him to the Kansas City Athletics. Slaughter finished the season with a .315 mark and led the American League with 16 pinch hits, but in August of 1956 the A's sold him back to the Yankees.

Slaughter performed better this time. He was now being used in a part-time role, mostly as a pinch hitter, and he hit .281 in 1956 and batted .350 in the World Series as he played the outfield in all six games to contribute to the Yankees' seven-game championship over the Brooklyn Dodgers. In 1958 he batted .304.

The next year, however, he had trouble connecting at all, and in September the Yankees sold him to the Milwaukee Braves. Slaughter finished out the season — and his career — in 11 games with Milwaukee. He retired with an even .300 lifetime batting average, 2383 hits, and a .291 average in five World Series.

Enos was inducted into the Hall of Fame in 1985, and the Cardinals retired his number in 1996. Slaughter died in North Carolina in 2002.

Awards/Honors

1985 Hall of Fame

Ozzie Smith

Retired Number: 1 (St. Louis Cardinals, 1997)
Shortstop
Playing Career: San Diego Padres 1978–81; St. Louis Cardinals 1982–96

Osborne Earl Smith was born on the day after Christmas in 1954 in Mobile, Alabama. He was originally drafted in 1976 by the Detroit Tigers, but chose to remain in school and signed in 1977 with the San Diego Padres.

He hit .303 with the Walla Walla Padres of the Northwest League in 1977, but it was not his offense that caught the attention of scouts. Smith was an acrobatic, gymnastic shortstop who made difficult plays look easy and who made impossible plays possible.

Ozzie's trademark was a backflip that he would perform before each game when he ran out to his position for the first time. Eventually known as "The Wizard of Oz," he would dazzle spectators and players alike with his plays and would be valued more for the opposing runs he prevented than for those he produced.

Smith became the Padres' regular shortstop in 1978, and while he batted only .258, he led the National League with 28 sacrifices and stole 40 bases. He would steal at least 21, in fact, for the first 16 years of his 19-year career.

That .258 average would be his highest in San Diego, as he batted a mere .211 in 1979 although he managed 28 steals. In 1980, he raised his average to a still-unimpressive .230, but he stole 57 bases and, more importantly, won the first of 13 consecutive Gold Gloves.

In December of 1981 the Padres included him in a six-player deal with the St. Louis Cardinals, a trade that sent Garry Templeton to San Diego. Smith blossomed in St. Louis.

In 1982 he batted only .248, but hit .556 in the League Championship Series and helped the Cardinals to an eventual World Championship. For a time his average slowly began to climb. In 1985 he hit .276 to help lead the Cardinals to the National League Eastern Division crown. Facing the Los Angeles Dodgers in the NL Championship Series, he batted .435 with a rare home run, a shot that happened to come in the bottom of the ninth inning of Game 5 to win the game. The Cardinals eventually went on to the World Series, although they would lose in seven games to the Kansas City Royals. Smith was named the Most Valuable Player of the NLCS.

Ozzie hit .280 in 1986, then he cracked the .300 mark with a .303 average in 1987. He had 182 hits and scored 104 runs while stealing 43 bases. The Cardinals went to the Series, but lost in seven to the Minnesota Twins.

Ozzie's fielding remained spectacular throughout his career. He was an eventual 15-time All-Star, and set numerous fielding records for a shortstop. Retiring after the 1996 season, he had a .262 lifetime batting average, 2460 hits, and 580 stolen bases, but his record numbers for his position included 8375 assists, 1590 double plays, 12,624 total chances, 8 years with 500 or more assists, and 8 years leading the league in assists and total chances.

The Cardinals retired his number in 1997, and Ozzie was inducted into the Hall of Fame in 2002.

Awards/Honors

1980 National League Gold Glove Shortstop
1981 National League Gold Glove Shortstop
1982 National League Gold Glove Shortstop
1983 National League Gold Glove Shortstop
1984 National League Gold Glove Shortstop
1985 National League Gold Glove Shortstop
1986 National League Gold Glove Shortstop
1987 National League Gold Glove Shortstop
1988 National League Gold Glove Shortstop
1989 National League Gold Glove Shortstop
1990 National League Gold Glove Shortstop
1991 National League Gold Glove Shortstop
1992 National League Gold Glove Shortstop
2002 Hall of Fame

Duke Snider

Retired Number: 4 (Los Angeles Dodgers, 1980)
Outfielder
Playing Career: Brooklyn Dodgers 1947–57; Los Angeles Dodgers 1958–62; New York Mets 1963; San Francisco Giants 1964

Duke Snider was one-third of the topic of many a New Yorker's conversation in the 1950s. A star center fielder when he played for the Brooklyn Dodgers, his talent was often compared to that of New York's two other center fielders—Mickey Mantle of the Yankees and Willie Mays of the Giants.

Born in 1926 in Los Angeles, Snider made his debut in Brooklyn in 1947, but did not play regularly until 1949. He hit .292 with 23 home runs that year, but he also led the National League in strikeouts with 92. He would eventually lead three times in that category, but would easily make up for it in many other ways.

In 1950 Duke broke the .300 mark for the first of seven times, batting .321 and topping the NL with 199 hits while belting 31 home runs.

His power was consistent, as he would slug at least 20 home runs 10 times in his first 11 full seasons.

He hit .303 in 1952 and had a sensational World Series, batting .345 and cracking four home runs in a losing effort against the Yankees.

He put together a strong 1953 campaign, hitting .336 with 42 home runs and 126 runs batted in, and he led the league with a .627 slugging percentage and with 132 runs scored. He led the league in runs three years in a row, in fact, and in 1954 his .341 batting average was his career best.

He hit at least 40 home runs for five years in a row, from 1953 through 1957, and his 43 in 1956 led the league. In 1955 he hit 42 and topped the NL with 136 RBIs and 126 runs scored, and in the World Series batted .320 and once again hit four roundtrippers. He thus became the only player in baseball history to hit four home runs in a World Series twice. The Dodgers went on to the World Championship that year, besting the Yankees in seven games.

On September 22, 1957, Snider hit two home runs against the Philadelphia Phillies, and those would be the last two hit out of Brooklyn's Ebbets Field. The Dodgers moved to Los Angeles the following season, and Snider went with them.

On April 23, 1958, Duke attempted to hurl a ball out of Los Angeles Coliseum and ended up injuring his arm. He was fined by the Dodgers, but more importantly, was able to play only 106 games that season. He was relegated to part-time duty by 1960, and in April of 1963 he returned to New York when the Dodgers sold him to the Mets.

Snider batted only .243 upon his return, and in April of 1964 the Mets sold him to the San Francisco Giants. After a .210 season, Duke retired. He had a lifetime batting average of .295 with 407 home runs and 2116 hits. In six World Series he had hit .286 with 11 homers, 26 RBIs, and 21 runs scored.

He later became a scout for the Dodgers and the San Diego Padres, and he managed in the minor leagues before becoming a broadcaster for the Montreal Expos. The Dodgers retired his number in 1980, and Snider was inducted into the Hall of Fame the same year.

Awards/Honors

1980 Hall of Fame

Warren Spahn

Retired Number: 21 (Atlanta Braves, 1965)
Pitcher/Coach

Playing Career: Boston Braves 1942, 1946–52; Milwaukee Braves 1953–64; New York Mets 1965; San Francisco Giants 1965
Coaching Career: New York Mets 1965; Cleveland Indians 1972–73

Warren Edward Spahn was born in Buffalo, New York, on April 23, 1921. He was signed as a left-handed pitcher by the Boston Braves, and after going 17–13 with a 1.96 earned run average with the Hartford Bees of the Eastern League in 1942, finished the season by pitching 4 games with Boston.

Immediately thereafter he joined the Army and was a foot soldier during World War II, where he earned the Bronze Star and a Purple Heart. He returned to the Braves in 1946 and went 8–5 while posting an ERA of 2.94. A third of his appearances were out of the bullpen.

In 1947 Spahn became a regular starter, and he became a 20-game winner for the first of an incredible 13 times. He went 21–10 that season while leading the National League with a 2.33 ERA, as well as with 7 shutouts and 289⅔ innings pitched. After winning 15 in 1948, he topped the league with 21 wins the next two seasons, and he won 22 more in 1951. Between 1949 and 1952 he topped the NL every year in strikeouts, his high being 191 in 1950. His seven shutouts were best in the league in 1951, and although he slipped to a 14–19 record in '52, the Braves' last season in Boston, he still put up a more-than-solid 2.98 ERA.

The Braves moved to Milwaukee for the 1953 season, and Spahn brought his dominating ways with him. His 23 victories tied Robin Roberts for the NL lead that year, and he also paced the circuit with an ERA of 2.10. He won 21 in 1954, and "only" 17 the following season.

Beginning in 1956 Warren won at least 20 games for six seasons in a row, and he led or tied for the National League lead in victories for the last five of them. In 1957 he won the NL Cy Young Award by going 21–11 with a 2.69 ERA and leading the league with 18 complete games. He was 22–11 in 1958, and his .667 winning percentage (tying him with teammate Lew Burdette), 23 complete games, and 290 innings pitched were all best in the NL. He posted a 2.20 ERA in the World Series that year, which was his third; the Braves had lost in '48 and had won in '57, but they lost again in 1958.

Spahn was extremely durable. He led the National League in complete games every year between 1957 and 1963, and accumulated 382 in his career. In both 1959 and 1961 he tied for the league lead with four shutouts.

On September 16, 1960, he won his 20th game of the season by pitching a no-hitter against the Philadelphia Phillies in a game that the Braves won by a 4–0 score. He pitched a second no-hitter on April 28, 1961, when, at the age of 40, he bested the San Francisco Giants, 1–0. He won his 300th career game on August 11 of that year, a 2–1 victory over the Chicago Cubs.

Spahn went 23–7 in 1963, becoming the oldest 20-game winner in history at the age of 42. It was his thirteenth 20-win season, tying the major league mark previously set by Christy Mathewson.

Spahn declined abruptly after that. He was only 6–13 in 1964 with a horrendous 5.29 ERA, and in November the Braves sold him to the New York Mets. The Mets employed him as a player/coach, but after he went 4–12 for them they released him and he signed with the San Francisco Giants. He posted a 3–4 record in San Francisco before being released again.

He then pitched in Mexico and in the minor leagues before retiring in 1967. He won 363 games in his career with a lifetime ERA of 3.09 and 63 shutouts. From 1972–73 he coached for the Cleveland Indians, and in '73 was inducted into the Hall of Fame.

Spahn wore number 16 with the Braves in 1942, but donned number 21 upon his return from World War II. The Braves retired the number in 1965, while they were still in Milwaukee. Spahn died in 2003.

Awards/Honors

1957 National League Cy Young Award
1973 Hall of Fame

Willie Stargell

Retired Number: 8 (Pittsburgh Pirates, 1982)
Outfielder/First Baseman/Coach
Playing Career: Pittsburgh Pirates 1962–82
Coaching Career: Pittsburgh Pirates 1985; Atlanta Braves 1986–88

An Oklahoma native who was born in 1940, Willie Stargell played his entire 21-year career with the Pittsburgh Pirates and became the team's primary leader, both on the field and in the clubhouse.

Originally an outfielder, Willie broke in with Pittsburgh in 10 games in 1962. In 1964 he belted 21 home runs, and on July 22 he hit for the cycle in a 13–2 win over the St. Louis Cardinals. By 1965 he was a regular, and he crushed 27 home runs that year and drove in 107 runs. On June 24 he hit three home runs against the Los Angeles Dodgers, and he would bang three homers in a game on three other occasions during his career.

Stargell hit 33 home runs in 1966. Between 1964 and 1976, in fact, he never hit fewer than 20. He also batted .315 in '66, the first of three times he would break the .300 mark. In 1969 he did it again, batting .307 with 29 home runs and 92 RBIs.

In 1970 Willie helped the Pirates to the National League Eastern Division championship, and he hit .500 in the League Championship Series in a losing effort against the Cincinnati Reds. The Pirates were back in '71, however, and Stargell was a big part of their drive as he led the NL with 48 home runs, drove in 125, and scored 104. He went hitless in the LCS against the San Francisco Giants, but his teammates picked up the slack and the Bucs won anyway. He had a mediocre World Series, but the Pirates prevailed over the Baltimore Orioles to win the championship.

At Dodger Stadium in 1972, Willie hit a home run off Claude Osteen that was estimated to have traveled 506 feet. In 1973 his 44 home runs, 119 RBIs, 43 doubles, and .646 slugging percentage were all best in the National League.

Knee and leg injuries had begun to plague Stargell; he had played mostly at first base in 1972, and was moved to that position permanently in 1975. In 1977 he appeared in only 63 games because of a broken arm he suffered while breaking up a fight between teammate Bruce Kison and Mike Schmidt of the Philadelphia Phillies. He bounced back in 1978 to hit .295 with 28 homers and 97 RBIs, numbers good enough to win him the Comeback Player of the Year Award.

Willie's most memorable season, however, was 1979. He hit .281 during the year and launched 32 home runs while driving in 82, and he was the co-winner of the NL Most Valuable Player Award with Keith Hernandez of the St. Louis Cardinals. The Pirates went to the postseason, where they faced the Reds in the NLCS, and Willie batted .455 with two home runs as the Pirates swept Cincinnati. Stargell was named MVP of the series. The Bucs then went to the World Series, where they bested the Orioles in seven games, and Willie batted .400 with three homers to become MVP of *that* series. He thus became the only player to win all three MVP awards in the same season.

Injuries continued to exact their toll after that, and Stargell was reduced to a part-timer. He played three more seasons, then retired in 1982 with a .282 lifetime average, 475 home runs, and 1540 RBIs. He had a .315 average with three home runs in World Series play. The Pirates retired his number the same year he retired.

Stargell returned to the Pirates as a coach in 1985, then performed the same function with the Atlanta Braves from 1986 through 1988. In '88, he was also inducted into the Hall of Fame.

Willie passed away in 2001.

Awards/Honors
1979 National League co-Most Valuable Player
1988 Hall of Fame

Rusty Staub

Retired Number: 10 (Montreal Expos, 1993)
First Baseman/Outfielder/Designated Hitter
Playing Career: Houston Colt .45s 1963–64; Houston Astros 1965–68; Montreal Expos 1969–71, 1979; New York Mets 1972–75, 1981–85; Detroit Tigers 1976–79; Texas Rangers 1980

Rusty Staub was the first player to appear in 500 games with at least four different teams, and also the first to stroke 500 hits with four different teams.

Staub hailed from New Orleans, where he was born in 1944, to make his debut with the Houston Colt .45s in 1963. He struggled a bit his first three seasons, but found his stroke in 1966 when he hit .280 for Houston, whose team was now called the Astros. In 1967 he batted .333 and led the National League with 44 doubles.

In January of 1969, the Astros traded Staub to the Montreal Expos, and Rusty responded with a .302 average and 29 home runs. The following season he hit 30 roundtrippers, his career high, and drove in 94 runs. He upped his average to .311 in 1971, but in April of 1972 the Expos dealt him to the New York Mets in exchange for Tim Foli, Ken Singleton, and Mike Jorgensen.

A broken hand relegated him to only 66 games his first year in New York, but in 1973 he was a big part of the Mets' pennant drive as he batted .279 and clubbed 15 homers. He separated his shoulder hitting the outfield wall during the League Championship Series against the Cincinnati Reds, but continued to play and, in a World Series loss against the Oakland Athletics, batted .423.

In December of 1975 the Mets traded Staub to the Detroit Tigers, and Rusty hit .299 his first season in Detroit. He slugged 22 and 24 homers the next two seasons, but in July of 1979 the Tigers traded him back to the Expos.

Upon his arrival back in Montreal, Staub discovered that Andre Dawson was now wearing his previous number 10. He offered Andre $2000 for the number, but Dawson refused. In 1993, the Expos would retire the number for Staub, but they would add Dawson's name to that retirement in 1997.

Rusty played only 38 games during his second stint in Montreal, and in March of 1980 the Expos traded him to the Texas Rangers. Staub hit .300 his only season in Texas, then became a free agent and returned to the Mets. He hit .317 in 70 games in strike-shortened 1981, but struggled the following season. He became a free agent after the 1982 campaign and very nearly signed with the Baltimore Orioles, but he changed his mind at the last minute and re-signed with the Mets. He continued to play in New York, mostly as a pinch hitter, through 1985. When he hit his only home run of the 1984 season, he became the only player other than Ty Cobb to homer both as a teenager *and* in his 40s.

Staub retired with a .279 lifetime average, 292 home runs, and 2716 hits. He had collected 792 hits with the Astros, 709 with the Mets, 582 with the Tigers, and 531 with the Expos.

Having retired number 10 for both Staub and Dawson, the Expos are one of only two teams to have retired the same number for two different players. The other is the New York Yankees, who have retired number 8 for Bill Dickey and Yogi Berra.

Casey Stengel

Retired Number: 37 (New York Mets, 1970; New York Yankees, 1970)
Outfielder/Coach/Manager
Playing Career: Brooklyn Dodgers 1912–13; Brooklyn Robins 1914–17; Pittsburgh Pirates 1918–19; Philadelphia Phillies 1920–21; New York Giants 1921–23; Boston Braves 1924–25
Coaching Career: Brooklyn Dodgers 1932–33
Managerial Career: Brooklyn Dodgers 1934–36; Boston Bees 1938–40; Boston Braves 1941–43; New York Yankees 1949–60; New York Mets 1962–65

Casey Stengel received his nickname from his hometown of Kansas City, Missouri ("KC"), where he was born in 1890. He spent 54 years in professional baseball, and turned a successful 14-year playing career into a legendary one as a manager.

Originally an outfielder with the Brooklyn Dodgers, Stengel hit .316 in 17 games in 1912. In his very first game on September 17, he collected four singles and a walk and stole two bases. He played for Brooklyn through 1917, hitting .316 again in 1914, when the team was renamed the Robins for manager Wilbert Robinson. In 1916 the Robins went to the World Series, and Casey batted .364 in a losing effort against the Boston Red Sox.

He was traded to the Pittsburgh Pirates in January of 1918, and was used in a part-time role for two seasons before being dealt to the Philadelphia Phillies. He hit .292 in 1920, but in July of 1921 the Phillies traded him to the New York Giants. As a bench player, Stengel hit .368 in 1922 and .339 in 1923. He appeared in two games in the '22 World Series and hit .400 as the Giants bested the New York Yankees, and played all six games in the 1923 Fall Classic and batted .417 with two home runs in a loss to those same Yankees. His first homer was of the inside-the-park variety, and came in the bottom of the ninth inning of Game 1 to win that contest.

In November Casey was traded to the Boston Braves, and he hit .280 in 1924 as he played somewhat regularly, but batted only .077 in 12 games in 1925. He retired from playing with a .284 lifetime average and a .393 average in World Series play.

From 1926 until 1931 he managed the Toledo Mud Hens of the American Association, then was hired as a coach by the Brooklyn Dodgers in 1932. In 1934 he was elevated to team manager to replace the departed Max Carey, and thus began one of the most successful and colorful managerial careers in history.

In three years at Brooklyn's reins Stengel achieved no better than a fifth-place finish, but in 1938 he was hired to manage the Boston Bees (formerly the Braves). After finishing fifth that first year, the team came in seventh for four years in a row, and then sixth in 1943. Stengel missed the first 46 games of the 1943 season because he had been hit by a cab and suffered a broken leg. Bob Coleman had taken his place on an interim basis. Stengel was fired at the end of the season, at a time when the club was once again called the Braves.

Casey returned to the minor leagues, where he managed the Milwaukee Brewers to a first-place finish in the American Association in 1944, the Kansas City Blues to a seventh-place finish in the AA in 1945, and the Oakland Oaks to second-, fourth-, and first-place finishes in the Pacific Coast League from 1946 through 1948.

Stengel was hired to manage the Yankees in 1949, and he immediately created a buzz in the major leagues by winning five straight American League pennants. In the World Series those years, the Yankees defeated the Dodgers in 1949, swept the Phillies in 1950, defeated the Giants in 1951, defeated the Dodgers again in 1952, and defeated the Dodgers yet again in 1953 to cap off a string of five consecutive World Championships.

In 1954 the Yankees finished 8 games behind the Cleveland Indians when the Tribe won 111 games during the regular season. They then came back to win four more pennants in a row, however, and in the World

Series they lost to the Dodgers in 1955, beat the Dodgers in 1956, lost to the Milwaukee Braves in 1957, and beat the Braves in 1958.

After a third-place finish in 1959, the Yankees won the pennant again in 1960, but they dropped the World Series to the Pirates. In a 12-year span, Stengel had guided his team to an astounding 10 pennants and 7 World Championships.

The Yankees reasoned that Stengel was getting too old to manage, and they fired him a few days after the Series. Casey's response was, "I'll never make the mistake of being seventy again."

In 1962 he was hired to manage the expansion New York Mets. He experienced three consecutive tenth-place finishes, which was typical of expansion teams at that time, and was mired in tenth place in 1965 when he broke his hip and decided to retire. He had won 1905 games in his career as a manager and had a .508 winning percentage. In 10 World Series he had won 37 games against 26 losses, good for a winning percentage of .587.

Stengel was inducted into the Hall of Fame in 1966. Both the Mets and the Yankees retired his uniform number in 1970, and he is one of only eight men to have had his number retired by more than one team. Casey died in Glendale, California, in 1975 at the age of 85.

Awards/Honors

1966 Hall of Fame

Don Sutton

Retired Number: 20 (Los Angeles Dodgers, 1998)
Pitcher
Playing Career: Los Angeles Dodgers 1966–80, 1988; Houston Astros 1981–82; Milwaukee Brewers 1982–84; Oakland Athletics 1985; California Angels 1985–87

Right-hander Don Sutton was born in Alabama in 1945 and pitched in the major leagues until he was 43 years of age.

He spent 16 years of his 23-year career with the Los Angeles Dodgers. He first broke in in 1966 and went 12–12 with a solid 2.99 earned run average. His 209 strikeouts turned a lot of heads, and were the most strikeouts by a rookie since Grover Cleveland Alexander had struck out 227 in 1911.

In 1968 Sutton posted a 2.60 ERA. The following season he struck out 217 batters, then whiffed 201 more in 1970.

In spite of his performances he had losing records those first few years, but in 1970 he started a string of nine consecutive years above the .500 mark. After going 15–13, he posted a 17–12 record in 1971, and went 19–9 in 1972 with a 2.08 ERA. He struck out 207 batters and led the National League with 9 shutouts.

He won 19 games in 1974, won 2 more in the National League Championship Series while posting a 0.53 ERA, and recorded the only Dodgers' win in the World Series against the Oakland Athletics.

In 1976 Sutton became a 20-game winner for the only time in his career by going 21–10. A four-time All-Star, he made his final appearance in the 1977 Midsummer Classic and completed a string of not having allowed an earned run in eight All-Star innings. He was named Most Valuable Player of the 1977 contest.

In 1980 Don led the NL with a 2.21 ERA. In December he became a free agent and signed with the Houston Astros, and he won 11 games for Houston in strike-shortened 1981. Toward the end of the following season he was traded to the Milwaukee Brewers and finished the season at 17–9.

In December of 1984 the Brewers traded him to the Athletics, but he pitched only 29 games for Oakland before being dealt to the California Angels in September. He finished the season at 15–10, and won 15 more games in 1986. He won his 300th career game that year, and on June 28, when he faced Phil Niekro of the Cleveland Indians, it was the first matchup of 300-game winners since Tim Keefe and Pud Galvin went head-to-head in 1892.

Sutton pitched for the Angels through 1987, then returned to the Dodgers for one last hurrah in 1988. He retired with 324 career victories, a 3.26 ERA, and 3574 strikeouts. He had won at least 15 games in a season 12 times, and had struck out at least 200 batters on 5 occasions.

After his retirement, Sutton went into broadcasting, and he was inducted into the Hall of Fame in 1998. The Dodgers retired his number the same year.

Awards/Honors

1998 Hall of Fame

Bill Terry

Retired Number: 3 (San Francisco Giants, 1985)
First Baseman/Manager
Playing Career: New York Giants 1923–36
Managerial Career: New York Giants 1932–41

An excellent hitter and an outstanding defensive first baseman, Bill Terry played his entire 14-year career with the New York Giants, the last 5 as player/manager.

An Atlanta native who was born in 1896, Bill broke in with the Giants in 1923 in three games, and played on a part-time basis in 1924. He went 6-for-14 in the World Series that year, good for a .429 average, and blasted a home run in a losing cause as the Giants fell to the Washington Nationals in five games. He played regularly in 1925 and batted .319, and after hitting .289 in 1926 he would never again fail to hit over .300.

As the Giants' regular first baseman in 1927, Terry hit .326 and powered 20 home runs while driving in 121 runs. He would hit at least 20 home runs only three times in his career, but would record over 100 RBIs for six straight seasons and would score at least 100 runs for six straight and seven total.

In 1929 he batted .372, and in a doubleheader on June 18 he collected nine hits. He won his only batting title in 1930 with an incredible .401 average, becoming the last player in the National League to break the .400 mark. His 254 hits were best in the circuit, and he would collect at least 200 hits in a season on six occasions.

Terry led the NL in 1931 with 20 triples and tied Chuck Klein with 121 runs scored. In 1932 the Giants were 17–23 when ailing manager John McGraw stepped down, and Terry was named the club's player/manager. The team finished sixth that year despite Bill's .350 average and career-high 28 home runs, but the following season they outpaced the Pittsburgh Pirates by five games to take the NL pennant. This time they turned the tables on the Nationals in the World Series, winning four games to one.

After second-and third-place finishes the next two years, during which Terry continued to produce at his usual prolific pace, Bill became a part-timer in 1936 and, with a .310 batting average, guided the Giants to the pennant by five games over the Chicago Cubs and St. Louis Cardinals. The Giants lost the World Series in six games to the New York Yankees, however.

Terry retired as a player with a .341 lifetime batting average and 2193 hits in 14 seasons. He hit .295 in three World Series. His hitting overshadowed his fielding prowess, for he had also led NL first basemen in fielding percentage twice, in double plays three times, in putouts five times, in assists five times, and in total chances per game nine times.

Having stepped down as a player, Terry continued to manage. He won another pennant in 1937, coming in three games ahead of the Cubs, but his club was again bested by the Yankees in the World Series. He went on managing through the 1941 season, but never again finished better than third. He retired with 823 wins in his career and a winning percentage of .555. Terry was inducted into the Hall of Fame in 1954.

Bill had worn number 4 when the Giants first donned uniform numbers in 1932, but switched to 3 the next season. When he became solely a manager in 1937, he changed to number 30. The Giants retired number 3, the digit he wore the longest as a player, in 1985. Terry died in Jacksonville, Florida, in 1989.

Awards/Honors

1954 Hall of Fame

Pie Traynor

Retired Number: 20 (Pittsburgh Pirates, 1972)
Shortstop/Third Baseman/Manager
Playing Career: Pittsburgh Pirates 1920–35, 1937
Managerial Career: Pittsburgh Pirates 1934–39

Harold Joseph Traynor, probably nicknamed "Pie" because of his fondness for that particular pastry as a child, was born in Framingham, Massachusetts, on November 11, 1899. He was signed by the Pittsburgh Pirates as a shortstop, and played 17 games there during his major league debut season in 1920, but he was moved primarily to third base in 1921 and would eventually make his mark at the hot corner.

Traynor became a regular in 1922, and in 1923 he batted .338 and tied teammate Max Carey for the National League lead with 19 triples. He would hit over .300 ten times in his 17-year playing career.

In 1925 he contributed a .320 average with 106 runs batted in and 114 runs scored to help the Pirates to the NL pennant. In the World Series he batted .346 with a home run and two triples as the Bucs defeated the Washington Nationals in seven games.

Pie's average climbed to .342 in 1927 as the Pirates once again topped the league. This time Traynor faltered in the World Series, and the Pirates were swept by the New York Yankees.

Pie never hit a lot of home runs, but he drove in over 100 runs seven times and scored over 100 twice. He hit a lot of doubles and triples, peaking with 39 two-baggers in 1925 and 19 three-baggers in 1923.

In 1930 he reached a career-high batting average of .366, and he drove in 119 runs. He hit "only" .298 in 1931, but topped the .300 mark for the next three seasons in a row. A third of the way through the 1934 season he was named player/manager to replace George Gibson, and he hit .309 and guided the Bucs to a fifth-place finish.

He began to play on a part-time basis after that, appearing in only 57 games in 1935 as the Pirates finished in fourth place. He did not play at all in 1936, then played a mere five games in 1937. The Pirates finished fourth and third, respectively.

Traynor became a full-time manager in 1938. He retired as a player with a .320 lifetime batting average, 371 doubles, and 164 triples. He had been an excellent-fielding third baseman, accumulating 2288 putouts, 6134 total chances, and 308 doubles plays at that position.

His best season as a manager was 1938, when he brought the Pirates in in second place, only two games behind the Chicago Cubs. After a sixth-place finish in 1939, he was replaced by Frankie Frisch and became a long-time Pirates scout.

Traynor was inducted into the Hall of Fame in 1948. He had worn number 20 when the Pirates first donned uniform numbers in 1932, although he had later sported 34 and 35 during his last two years as manager. Pie died in Pittsburgh in 1972, and the Pirates retired number 20 in his honor later that season.

Awards/Honors

1948 Hall of Fame

Jim Umbricht

Retired Number: 32 (Houston Astros, 1964)
Pitcher
Playing Career: Pittsburgh Pirates 1959–61; Houston Colt .45s 1962–63

A 1930 native of Chicago, Illinois, Jim Umbricht attended the University of Georgia, where he played both baseball and basketball, and where, in 1951, he was named an All-Southeastern Conference shortstop.

Umbricht began to pitch professionally and broke into the big leagues with the Pittsburgh Pirates in 1959. He made a single, inauspicious start that year, going seven innings and giving up seven hits while walking four and striking out three. His earned run average for that one appearance was a disappointing 6.43.

He was back in 1960 for 17 games, working mainly out of the bullpen, and surrendered 40 hits in 40⅔ innings. He struck out 26 batters but walked 27, and recorded a 1–2 record with a 5.09 ERA for the season. He pitched but a single game for the big club the following year, and in three and one-third innings posted a 2.70 ERA.

Baseball expanded in 1962, and Umbricht was selected by the new Houston Colt .45s (later the Astros), who paid Pittsburgh $50,000 for his contract. The Colt .45s made Umbricht a regular out of their bullpen, and Jim responded beautifully, posting a 4–0 record and a 2.01 ERA. In 67 innings he struck out 55 and walked only 17.

Umbricht was diagnosed with cancer shortly thereafter, and on March 7, 1963, he underwent a six-hour operation. He was in uniform by Opening Day and pitched the entire season, appearing in 35 games total — starting 3 of them — and going 4–3 with a 2.61 ERA. In 76 innings he struck out 48 batters against 21 walks.

Jim was back with the club for spring training of 1964, but the cancer had begun to get the best of him. On April 8, he died in Houston at the age of 33.

In his brief 5-year major league career Umbricht had pitched 88 games, winning 9 and losing 5 while compiling a 3.06 ERA. His record as a reliever was 9–1, and he had 3 saves to his credit.

Umbricht had worn number 37 with the Pirates but number 32 with the Colt .45s. During the 1964 season, the same year that Jim had died, the Colt .45s retired the number in his honor.

Honus Wagner

Retired Number: 33 (Pittsburgh Pirates, 1956)
Outfielder/First Baseman/Third Baseman/Shortstop/Manager/Coach
Playing Career: Louisville Colonels 1897–99; Pittsburgh Pirates
    1900–17
Managerial Career: Pittsburgh Pirates 1917
Coaching Career: Pittsburgh Pirates 1933–51

One of the greatest and most versatile players in baseball history, Honus Wagner was supposedly discovered throwing rocks near his Pennsylvania home, where he was born on February 24, 1874. The story goes that scout Ed Barrow was actually on hand to look at Honus' brother Al, but signed Honus on the spot.

Wagner began his major league career with the Louisville Colonels of the National League in 1897 and played mostly in the outfield. He played primarily at first and third base the next two seasons, but was also used at second and in the outfield. He batted .338 in 1897 and .336 in 1899, but after that season the National League consolidated from 12 to 8 teams and the Colonels were eliminated. Louisville owner Barney Dreyfuss bought the Pittsburgh Pirates and brought Wagner with him. Honus responded in 1900 by winning the NL batting title with a .381 average, and also led the league with 45 doubles, 22 triples, and a .573 slugging percentage. It was the first of eight batting titles he would win in his career.

Wagner was a speedy runner, winning the stolen base crown five times and earning himself the nickname "The Flying Dutchman." In 1901 he batted .353 and drove in 126 runs, the first of four times he would top the NL in runs batted in, and his 49 steals were also best in the circuit.

Honus won the batting title in 1903 with a .355 average while also leading the league with 19 triples, and the Pirates went to the very first modern World Series, although they lost there to the Boston Americans, five games to three, in what was then a best-of-nine series.

Wagner won four of his batting crowns consecutively, from 1906 through 1909, and in 1908 he led the league with 201 hits. In 1909 the Pirates went back to the World Series, and Honus hit .333 and stole six bases this time around as the Bucs defeated the Detroit Tigers, four games to three.

On June 9, 1914, Wagner hit a ninth-inning double off Erskine Mayer of the Philadelphia Phillies at the Baker Bowl to become only the second player in history (after Cap Anson) to reach 3000 career hits.

Wagner played until 1917, and he hit over .300 sixteen times in his career. He led the league in hits twice, in doubles seven times, in triples three times, and in runs scored twice. He topped the 100-RBI mark on 9 occasions and stole at least 20 bases 18 times.

Many of his contemporaries called Wagner the best player they ever saw. He hit for a very high average, drove in runs prolifically, stole bases with abandon, and fielded his position almost flawlessly. At one point or another he played every position during his career, even pitching on two occasions. He hurled three innings in 1900 and five and a third in 1902 and, despite walking six batters, also struck out six and did not allow an earned run. He did not become a full-time shortstop until 1903, and then became one of the best — if not *the* best — ever to play the position.

In 21 years Wagner hit .327 with 3418 hits, 643 doubles, 252 triples, 1732 RBIs, and 722 stolen bases. He helped turn 964 double plays.

Wagner played only 74 games in 1917, then the Pirates named him their manager to replace Nixey Callahan. Honus managed only five games, winning one and losing four, before deciding he did not like the job and stepping down. He was replaced by Hugo Bezdek. He then became a semi-pro player for the next seven years.

In 1933 Wagner returned as a Pirates coach, and he would remain in that position until 1951. In 1936, he became one of the first five inductees in baseball's brand new Hall of Fame.

The Pirates did not adopt uniform numbers until 1932, so Wagner never wore one as a player. When he returned to the club as a coach in 1933, he was first given number 36. He wore that number for a few years and switched briefly to 35 before going back to 36. In 1940 he switched to number 33, and he would wear that number for the rest of his career as a coach. That was the number the Pirates retired for him in 1956, a year after his death in Pennsylvania.

Honus' brother, Al (also known as Butts Wagner), played a single season in the National League in 1898, a season he split between the Washington Statesmen and the Brooklyn Bridegrooms.

Awards/Honors

1936 Hall of Fame

Earl Weaver

Retired Number: 4 (Baltimore Orioles, 1982)
Coach/Manager
Coaching Career: Baltimore Orioles 1968
Managerial Career: Baltimore Orioles 1968–82, 1985–86

Earl Weaver was a rarity in that he was a long-time major league manager who never *played* a game at the major league level.

Born in St. Louis in 1930, Weaver was a minor league second baseman who played in the systems of the St. Louis Cardinals and Pittsburgh Pirates from 1948 through 1957. Following his playing career he became a minor league manager, and continued in that capacity through the 1967 season. In 1968 he was made a coach with the Baltimore Orioles, and midway through the season he was named manager to replace Hank Bauer. The O's were in third place when Weaver took the reins, and they finished in second, 12 games behind the Detroit Tigers.

Earl, or "The Earl of Baltimore," as he eventually became known, then managed his club to three consecutive first-place finishes. In 1969 they won 109 games and topped the American League Eastern Division by 19 games over the Tigers, then swept the Minnesota Twins in the League Championship Series. They fell in a five-game World Series, however, to the New York Mets.

The Orioles repeated as division champions in 1970, winning 108 games, and they once again swept the Twins to take the American League pennant. This time they captured the World Championship by dominating a five-game World Series against the Cincinnati Reds.

In 1971 the O's finished 12 games ahead of the Tigers, won a third straight pennant by sweeping the Oakland Athletics, and then lost an exciting seven-game World Series to the Pittsburgh Pirates.

After a third-place finish in 1972, Weaver led his club to two more consecutive division titles. In 1973 the Birds finished eight games ahead of the Boston Red Sox, and although they lost the pennant to the A's, three games to two, the Associated Press named Weaver its American League Manager of the Year. The following season the team finished two games up on the New York Yankees, but once again lost the pennant to Oakland.

The Orioles then experienced three straight second-place finishes, but in 1977, coming in two and a half games behind the Yankees in a tie with the Red Sox, Weaver once again got the nod as the AP's American League Manager of the Year.

Two years later Weaver's Orioles won yet another AL Eastern Division crown, winning 102 games and finishing eight games ahead of the Milwaukee Brewers. They took the AL pennant by defeating the California Angels, three games to one, but lost yet another seven-game World Series to the Pirates. The AP named Weaver its AL Manager of the Year for the third time.

Weaver never experienced another first-place finish, but he was often in the spotlight. He was notorious for his feuds with umpires, and in his career was thrown out of an estimated 91 games and was suspended 4 times. After coming in second in 1982, only a single game behind the Brewers, Weaver decided to retire. The Orioles retired his number the same year.

The Birds coaxed him out of retirement a third of the way through the 1985 campaign, after firing Joe Altobelli. Earl took over a club that was not the former, competitive squad to which he had become accustomed. The O's finished fourth, and Weaver's temper, as usual, flared many times and at one point he was thrown out of both games of a doubleheader. His club finished seventh in 1986, and Earl then retired for good. He won 1480 games in his career against 1060 losses, good for a remarkable .583 winning percentage.

Weaver was inducted into the Hall of Fame in 1996.

Awards/Honors

1973 American League Manager of the Year (AP)
1977 American League Manager of the Year (AP)
1979 American League Manager of the Year (AP)
1996 Hall of Fame

Frank White

Retired Number: 20 (Kansas City Royals, 1995)
Shortstop/Second Baseman/Coach
Playing Career: Kansas City Royals 1973–90
Coaching Career: Boston Red Sox 1994–96; Kansas City Royals 1998–2001

Frank White hailed from Greenville, Mississippi, where he was born in 1950, and made his major league debut in 51 games with the Kansas City Royals in 1973. White played primarily at shortstop that first season, but over the ensuing years began playing more and more at second base and eventually became one of the most adept fielders at that position in baseball history.

Frank was never a strong hitter; his highest average was .298, a mark he reached in 1982, but his lifetime average was .255. He had good speed on the basepaths, however, and was adept at stretching singles into doubles. He hit 21 two-baggers in 1977, then 24 the following year, then 26, then 23. In 1982 he stroked 45, and added 35 the next season.

White's fielding prowess was duly noted in 1977 as he won the first of six consecutive Gold Gloves. He would win eight in his career, and he led the league in fielding percentage three times.

Frank batted a solid .275 in 1978, and the next season he stole a career-high 28 bases. In 1980 he committed only 10 errors all season, and was charged with only 6 in strike-shortened 1981. In the 1980 American League Championship Series, he batted .545 in three games with a double and a home run as the Royals swept the New York Yankees. He faltered in the World Series, however, going only 2-for-25 as Kansas City fell to the Philadelphia Phillies.

In 1985 White clubbed a career-high 22 home runs; he had hit 17 the previous season, but otherwise had never hit more than 11. He then duplicated the feat in 1986 and recorded a personal-best 84 runs batted in. He also hit three doubles and a home run in the 1985 World Series as the Royals defeated the St. Louis Cardinals in seven games.

In 1988 he committed only 4 errors in 150 games for a fielding percentage of .994.

White retired in 1990 after an 18-year career, having collected 2006 hits, 407 of which were doubles, with a lifetime .983 fielding percentage.

He became a coach for the Boston Red Sox from 1994–96, and midway through that stint, in 1995, the Royals retired his number 20. He returned as a coach with Kansas City from 1998 through 2001.

Awards/Honors

1977 American League Gold Glove Second Baseman
1978 American League Gold Glove Second Baseman
1979 American League Gold Glove Second Baseman
1980 American League Gold Glove Second Baseman
1981 American League Gold Glove Second Baseman
1982 American League Gold Glove Second Baseman
1986 American League Gold Glove Second Baseman
1987 American League Gold Glove Second Baseman

Billy Williams

Retired Number: 26 (Chicago Cubs, 1987)
Outfielder/First Baseman/Designated Hitter/Coach
Playing Career: Chicago Cubs 1959–74; Oakland Athletics 1975–76
Coaching Career: Chicago Cubs 1980–82, 1986–87, 1992–2001; Oakland Athletics 1983–85

Billy Williams was an Alabama native who was born in 1938 and who played briefly with the Chicago Cubs in 1959 and 1960 before becoming a regular. Playing mainly in the minor leagues since 1956, he was tutored by Rogers Hornsby in 1960, and he emerged as a full-time major leaguer the following season.

Williams had many strong seasons with the Cubs, beginning in 1961 when he hit .278, blasted 25 home runs, and was named the National League's Rookie of the Year. He hit 22 and 25 homers the next two seasons, respectively.

In an 18-year career, Billy hit at least 20 home runs 14 times. He hit over .300 on 5 occasions, and drove in at least 90 runs 10 times.

His first .300 season was in 1964, when he hit .312 while accumulating 201 hits. He hit 33 homers, drove in 98 runs, and scored an even 100. He batted .315 the next season, amassing 203 hits, clubbing 34 homers, knocking in 108, and scoring 115.

Those were only slightly better than a typical Billy Williams season. He was a solid producer for some Cubs teams that did not give him much hope of postseason glory. He continued to shine, however, and on July 17, 1968, he hit for the cycle. He hit two home runs in a game on September 8, then three more in the next game, on September 10, to total five in two consecutive games. On April 9, 1969, he hit four consecutive doubles.

Billy had a great season in 1970, hitting .322 and leading the National League with 205 hits (tying him with Pete Rose) and with 137 runs scored.

He hammered a career-high 42 home runs and drove in a lifetime-best 129. He also ended a streak of 1117 consecutive games played — an NL record at the time — that had lasted from September 22, 1963, until September 2, 1970.

In 1972 Williams won his only batting title with a .333 average. He also paced the circuit with a slugging percentage of .606, while hitting 37 home runs and collecting 122 runs batted in. On July 11 he went 8-for-8 in a doubleheader, and he finished second in voting for the league's Most Valuable Player Award to Johnny Bench of the Cincinnati Reds.

In October of 1974 the Cubs traded Billy to the Oakland Athletics in exchange for Darold Knowles, Bob Locker, and Manny Trillo. Williams contributed 23 home runs to Oakland's first-place drive in 1975 and finally made a postseason appearance. The A's, coming off three consecutive World Championships, were nevertheless swept in the American League Championship Series by the Boston Red Sox, and Williams went 0-for-8 in the three games.

After hitting only .211 in 1976, Williams retired from the playing field. He had a .290 lifetime batting average, 426 home runs, and 2711 hits. In 1980 Billy returned to the Cubs as a coach. After three years, he made his way back to the A's in the same role, then came back to the Cubs from 1986 to 1987.

Williams had originally worn number 4, but wore 26 for the majority of his career. The Cubs retired the number in '87, and Williams was inducted into the Hall of Fame the same year. He went to work in Chicago's front office for a time, then returned to coaching from 1992 through 2001.

Awards/Honors

1961 National League Rookie of the Year
1987 Hall of Fame

Ted Williams

Retired Number: 9 (Boston Red Sox, 1960)
Outfielder/Manager
Playing Career: Boston Red Sox 1939–42, 1946–60
Managerial Career: Washington Senators 1969–71; Texas Rangers 1972

Ted Williams was perhaps the greatest pure hitter who ever lived. If he was not, he was certainly among the top five.

Born in 1918, Williams was signed by his hometown San Diego Padres of the Pacific Coast League at the age of 17. By 1939 he was playing for the Boston Red Sox, and in a 19-year career he *failed* to hit over .300 only once. He hit over .400 three times, although only once did he do so in a full season. He won six batting titles, four home run crowns, and two Triple Crowns.

Williams hit .327 his rookie season and led the American League with 145 runs batted in, and he batted .344 the next year. In 1941 he became the last major leaguer to bat .400 for a season when he hit .406. On the final day of that season, his average stood at .39955, which would have been rounded to .400. His manager, Joe Cronin, offered Ted the opportunity to sit out that day's doubleheader and thus finish with a technical .400 average, but Williams refused. He played both games of the twinbill, went 6-for-8, and finished at .406. (If sacrifice flies had not counted as official at-bats at that time, he would have hit .412.) He also led the AL that year with 37 home runs, 135 runs scored, 145 walks, and a .735 slugging percentage, and he drove in 120 runs. Nevertheless, the league's Most Valuable Player Award went to Joe DiMaggio of the New York Yankees, who had hit in 56 consecutive games that season.

In 1942 Ted won the first of his two Triple Crowns with a .356 average, 36 homers, and 137 RBIs. The MVP Award, however, went to the Yankees' Joe Gordon. Meaning no disrespect toward Gordon, whose .322-18-103 numbers were good but not Williams material, many began to speculate whether Williams' poor relationship with the media was costing him the coveted awards.

World War II took three full seasons away from Ted, as he served in the Navy as a flight instructor from 1943–45. He came back in 1946 to hit .342, slugging 38 homers and driving in 123 runs. He led the AL with 142 runs scored, 156 walks, and a .667 slugging percentage, and was finally named the league's MVP. He appeared in his only World Series that year, but batted only .200 as the Red Sox fell to the St. Louis Cardinals in seven games.

Ted won his second Triple Crown in 1947. He hit .343, blasted 32 homers, and amassed 114 RBIs, but the MVP Award once again went to Joe DiMaggio.

After winning another batting crown and leading the league in doubles in 1948, he won his second MVP Award in 1949 when he hit .343 and topped the loop with 43 homers, 159 RBIs (tying him with Vern Stephens), 150 runs scored, 162 walks, 39 doubles, and a .650 slugging percentage. He fractured his elbow in the 1950 All-Star Game by colliding with the wall chasing down a fly ball at Comiskey Park and appeared in only 89 games that season, but he still finished with 28 home runs and 97 RBIs.

After playing only six games in 1952 and hitting .400, Williams was called back to the military to serve in the Korean War. He flew as a fighter pilot, and at one point was even shot down but escaped serious injury. He contracted pneumonia and was sent home, and he recovered and played 37 games in 1953, batting .407.

He began to battle various injuries from that point on, and was limited to 117 games in 1954 and only 98 the next year. In 1957 he won his fifth batting title with a .388 average, and took his sixth the following year by hitting .328.

In 1959 he batted only .254 — the only time he failed to reach the .300 threshold — but he bounced back in 1960 to hit a more typical .316. In the final at-bat of his career, he hit a home run at Fenway Park. Williams retired after the 1960 season sporting a .344 lifetime batting average with 521 home runs and 2654 hits. One can only speculate on what those totals might have been had Ted not lost so much time to military service.

In addition to his six batting crowns, Williams in his career had led or tied for the league lead in home runs four times, in RBIs four times, in doubles twice, in runs scored six times, in bases on balls eight times, and in slugging percentage nine times.

The Red Sox retired his number in 1960, and Ted was inducted into the Hall of Fame in 1966. In 1969 he was named manager of the Washington Senators, and the club's fourth-place finish would be his best at the helm. The Associated Press even named him its American League Manager of the Year. The Senators came in sixth (and last) in 1970, and fifth in 1971 before moving to Texas and becoming the Rangers. Williams managed one final season in Texas, and after the team finished last again, he retired with a .429 winning percentage.

Williams died in Florida in 2002.

Awards/Honors

1946 American League Most Valuable Player
1949 American League Most Valuable Player
1966 Hall of Fame
1969 American League Manager of the Year (AP)

Don Wilson

Retired Number: 40 (Houston Astros, 1975)
Pitcher
Playing Career: Houston Astros 1966–74

Louisiana native Don Wilson was a troubled pitcher who spent his all-too-brief nine-year career with the Houston Astros.

After pitching six innings of a single game in 1966 at the age of 21, Wilson became a member of the starting rotation the following season, making 28 starts in 31 total appearances. He went 10–9 for a team that won only 69 games and finished in next-to-last place; his earned run average was a solid 2.79. On June 18, he pitched the first of two career no-hitters against the Atlanta Braves.

Wilson had a losing record in 1968, and the Astros finished in last place in the National League, but the team's offense was third-last in producing runs to support its pitchers. On July 14, Wilson struck out 18 Cincinnati Reds in a nine-inning game.

Don won 16 games in 1969, although, ironically, his ERA ballooned to 4.00. He struck out 235 batters and hurled 13 complete games. On May 1 he pitched a no-hitter against the Reds, getting revenge for a no-hitter Cincinnati's Jim Maloney had pitched against Houston the previous day.

He had what was probably his best season in 1971, as he posted a 16–10 record with a 2.45 ERA, 180 strikeouts, and 18 complete games.

Wilson had an almost identical 15–10 record in 1972, posting a 2.68 ERA and recording 172 strikeouts as the Astros finished in second place behind the Reds. The club quickly reverted to normal, however, coming in in fourth place in both 1973 and 1974.

Wilson won 11 games in each of those two seasons, but his strikeout numbers had been tailing off since their peak in 1969. In 1974 he struck out only 112 batters in 205 innings. On September 4 of that year, he very nearly pitched a third no-hitter. He had thrown eight innings of no-hit ball against Cincinnati, but was trailing 2–1 when Astros manager Preston Gomez pulled him for a pinch hitter. Reliever Mike Cosgrove gave up a leadoff single to Tony Perez in the ninth, and that was the end of that.

On January 5, 1975, Wilson shocked the baseball world by committing suicide in the garage of his home. He died of carbon monoxide poisoning.

Wilson had started out wearing number 23 during his first season, 1966, but he switched to number 40 later that year and wore that number for the rest of his career. The Astros retired the number in April of 1975, shortly after his death.

Dave Winfield

Retired Number: 31 (San Diego Padres, 2001)
Outfielder/Designated Hitter

Playing Career: San Diego Padres 1973–80; New York Yankees 1981–88, 1990; California Angels 1990–91; Toronto Blue Jays 1992; Minnesota Twins 1993–94; Cleveland Indians 1995

Dave Winfield was an outstanding college athlete who probably could have played practically any sport that he chose professionally.

He was born in St. Paul, Minnesota, in 1951, and was drafted by the Baltimore Orioles in 1969. He instead decided to go to college on a baseball scholarship, and he played both baseball and basketball at the University of Minnesota. He was named Most Valuable Player of the 1973 College World Series, and was drafted that year by the Atlanta Hawks of the National Basketball Association, the Utah Stars of the American Basketball Association, the Minnesota Vikings of the National Football League (despite the fact that he had not played college football), and the San Diego Padres of the National League. Winfield chose baseball and the Padres, and he joined the team immediately and never played a game in the minor leagues.

In 1974, his first full season, Winfield hit 20 home runs and drove in 75. He would hit at least 20 homers 15 times in his 22-year career. In both 1978 and 1979 he hit .308; he clubbed 24 home runs in '78 with 97 RBIs, then hit 34 in '79 and led the league with 118 knocked in. He also won the first of seven Gold Gloves in 1979; he would win two in the National League and five in the American.

In December of 1980 Dave became a free agent and signed with the New York Yankees, and he immediately hit .294 and contributed to the club's American League pennant drive. He had a rough World Series, however, going 1-for-22 as the Yanks fell to the Los Angeles Dodgers.

In 1982 Winfield hit a career-high 37 home runs, and with 106 RBIs he marked the first of five consecutive seasons in which he would drive in at least 100, becoming the first Yankee to accomplish that feat since Joe DiMaggio. He also won the first of five AL Gold Gloves. He hit .340 in 1984, his career best, and narrowly missed the batting title as he lost to his teammate, Don Mattingly, who hit .343. Yankees' owner George Steinbrenner attempted to trade him to the Texas Rangers during the season, but Winfield exercised a no-trade clause in his contract and vetoed the deal.

Dave averaged 27 home runs a year with the Yankees, and after driving in 97 runs in 1987 he managed 107 in 1988, the sixth of seven years in which he reached the 100 mark.

He suffered a herniated disk in 1989 and missed the entire season, but he came back in 1990. He was struggling through 20 games, however, when the Yankees traded him to the California Angels for Mike Witt.

Winfield managed 21 home runs that season and hit 28 the next, and on June 24, 1991, he became the oldest man to hit for the cycle when he accomplished the feat against the Kansas City Royals. After the season he became a free agent again and signed with the Toronto Blue Jays.

Winfield hit .290 for Toronto with 26 home runs and 108 RBIs, and helped the team to the American League pennant and to Canada's first World Championship in a six-game series over the Atlanta Braves. He went home to Minnesota in 1993, signing with the Twins, and he spent two seasons there. He cracked 21 roundtrippers in '93, and on September 16 he collected his 3000th career hit, a single off Dennis Eckersley of the Oakland Athletics.

He played as a part-timer in 1994, and signed with the Cleveland Indians in 1995. After hitting only .191 in 46 games, he retired. His lifetime batting average was .283, and he had accumulated 3110 hits and 465 home runs. He had been a 12-time All-Star.

Winfield was inducted into the Hall of Fame in 2001, and the Padres retired his number the same year.

Awards/Honors

1979 National League Gold Glove Outfielder
1980 National League Gold Glove Outfielder
1982 American League Gold Glove Outfielder
1983 American League Gold Glove Outfielder
1984 American League Gold Glove Outfielder
1985 American League Gold Glove Outfielder
1987 American League Gold Glove Outfielder
2001 Hall of Fame

Carl Yastrzemski

Retired Number: 8 (Boston Red Sox, 1989)
Outfielder/First Baseman/Designated Hitter
Playing Career: Boston Red Sox 1961–83

An 18-time All-Star, Carl Yastrzemski played his entire 23-year career with the Boston Red Sox and proved a suitable successor to the legendary Ted Williams.

"Yaz" was born in Southampton, New York, in 1939, and played basketball in high school, setting a school record at Bridgehampton in 1957 when he scored 628 points for the season. He attended Notre Dame, where he played shortstop on the baseball team, and it was there that he was signed by the Red Sox.

Carl began his major league career in 1961 as a left fielder, and in 1963, only his third year in the majors, he won the first of three batting titles as he hit .321 and led the American League with 183 hits, 40 doubles, and 95 bases on balls. He was rewarded for his fielding excellence with the first of seven Gold Gloves. Two years later he batted .312 and topped the loop with 45 doubles (tying him with Zoilo Versalles) and a .536 slugging percentage while bashing 20 home runs.

Yastrzemski led the AL in doubles for the third time in 1966 with 39, but 1967 was to be his greatest season. He captured the Triple Crown by hitting .326 with 44 home runs (matching Harmon Killebrew) and 121 runs batted in, while also leading the circuit with 189 hits, 112 runs scored, and a .622 slugging percentage. He hit 9 of his home runs in the final 39 games of the season as the Red Sox were in the midst of a pennant race with the Detroit Tigers, the Minnesota Twins, and the Chicago White Sox. In the last 12 games he hit .523 with 5 home runs, then went 7-for-8 in the last 2 games. As a result the Sox finished a single game ahead of Detroit and Minnesota and three ahead of Chicago to win the AL pennant. Carl remained hot in the World Series, batting .400 with three home runs although the Red Sox fell to the St. Louis Cardinals in seven games. As a result of his amazing season, Yastrzemski was named the American League's Most Valuable Player.

Carl won his third batting title in 1968 with a .301 average, the lowest number ever to lead a league. That season was considered a pitcher's year, and the entire league average was a mere .230. Carl was also the league leader in walks with 119, the last time he would lead in that category but also the first of six in which he would draw over 100.

In both 1969 and 1970 Yastrzemski clouted 40 home runs, and his RBI totals were 111 and 102, respectively. In '70 he topped the AL with 125 runs scored and a .592 slugging percentage, and he went 4-for-4 with two walks in the All-Star Game and was named the Midsummer Classic's Most Valuable Player.

Carl would hit .300 on only one other occasion, in 1974 when he batted .301. He would lead the AL only one more time in a major offensive category, when he scored 93 runs that same year. He would top 20 home runs on only three other occasions, although he would play through 1983. But he continued to produce effectively and steadily; in his career he hit over .300 six times, hit at least 20 home runs 8 times, and collected at least 20 doubles an incredible 21 times.

Yaz helped the Red Sox to the American League Eastern Division title in 1975, then hit .455 in the League Championship Series as Boston swept the Oakland Athletics, and he batted .310 in the World

Series although the Red Sox fell in seven games to the Cincinnati Reds.

On September 12, 1979, Yastrzemski hit a single off Jim Beattie of the New York Yankees to collect his 3000th career hit in a 9–2 Boston win. He was the first American Leaguer to reach both 3000 hits and 400 home runs, and was the third major leaguer to reach those numbers overall, joining Hank Aaron and Willie Mays. He retired following the 1983 season with a .285 lifetime average, 3419 hits, and 452 home runs.

He was inducted into the Hall of Fame in 1989, and the Red Sox retired his number 8 that same year.

Awards/Honors

1963 American League Gold Glove Outfielder
1965 American League Gold Glove Outfielder
1967 American League Most Valuable Player
1967 American League Gold Glove Outfielder
1968 American League Gold Glove Outfielder
1969 American League Gold Glove Outfielder
1971 American League Gold Glove Outfielder
1977 American League Gold Glove Outfielder
1989 Hall of Fame

Robin Yount

Retired Number: 19 (Milwaukee Brewers, 1994)
Shortstop/Outfielder/Coach
Playing Career: Milwaukee Brewers 1974–93
Coaching Career: Arizona Diamondbacks 2002–

Born on September 16, 1955, in Danville, Illinois, Robin Yount was a rare modern-day player who played his entire 20-year career with the same team.

Yount was drafted by the Milwaukee Brewers in 1973, and he became their regular shortstop in 1974 at the age of 18, one of the youngest major leaguers ever to play regularly. He had a mediocre first year, but in 1975 he stroked 28 doubles and added 34 in 1977. He briefly quit baseball in the spring of 1978, making a brief attempt to become a professional golfer. He returned to the Milwaukee lineup, however, and his .293 average was his highest to date.

Yount had something of a breakthrough season in 1980, once again hitting .293 and leading the American League with 49 doubles while clubbing 23 home runs. It was the first time he had even managed double digits in the latter power category. In 1981 he helped the Brewers to the second-half AL Eastern Division title, but in the strike-induced divisional playoffs the club lost a best-of-five series to the New York Yankees despite Robin's .316 average.

Yount had his finest season in 1982. He batted a career-high .331 and led the AL with 210 hits, 46 doubles (tying Hal McRae), and a .578 slugging percentage, while at the same time hitting 29 homers, driving in 114 runs, and scoring 129. The Brewers defeated the California Angels to take the pennant, and Yount hit a blistering .414 in the World Series although Milwaukee fell to the St. Louis Cardinals in seven games. Yount collected four hits in Game 1 on October 12, and four more in Game 5 on October 17, becoming the only player to manage four hits in a World Series game twice. Robin was named the American League Most Valuable Player and won a Gold Glove for his defense.

Yount hit .308 in 1983 and led the league with 10 triples. After the 1984 season, he needed shoulder surgery and was moved to center field in 1985.

In 1988 Yount finished in a three-way tie for the league lead in triples with 11. In 1989 he put together a second MVP season, batting .318 with 21 home runs, 103 RBIs, 101 runs scored, and 38 doubles. Along with Hank Greenberg and Stan Musial, he is one of only three players to have won an MVP Award at two different positions.

On September 4, 1992, Robin singled off Jose Mesa of the Cleveland Indians for his 3000th career hit. He played for one more season, then retired with a .285 lifetime average, 3142 hits, 251 home runs, and 583 doubles. His brother, Larry Yount, had made a single pitching appearance with the Houston Astros in 1971.

The Brewers retired Robin's number 19 in 1994, and Yount was inducted into the Hall of Fame in 1999. He became a coach with the Arizona Diamondbacks in 2002.

Awards/Honors

1982 American League Most Valuable Player
1982 American League Gold Glove Shortstop
1989 American League Most Valuable Player
1999 Hall of Fame

Team-by-Team List

Following is a team-by-team list of retired uniform numbers for every major league team and for major league umpires. An asterisk (*) indicates that the number was retired symbolically and was never actually worn by the person for whom it was retired.

American League Umpires[1]

2: Nick Bremigan
9: Bill Kunkel
16: Lou DiMuro

Anaheim Angels

11: Jim Fregosi
26: Gene Autry*
29: Rod Carew
30: Nolan Ryan
42: Jackie Robinson*
50: Jimmie Reese

Arizona Diamondbacks

42: Jackie Robinson*

Atlanta Braves

3: Dale Murphy
21: Warren Spahn
35: Phil Niekro
41: Eddie Mathews
42: Jackie Robinson*
44: Hank Aaron

Baltimore Orioles

4: Earl Weaver

1. American League umpires and National League umpires came under the joint jurisdiction of Major League Baseball in 2000. These numbers are no longer held in retirement.

5: Brooks Robinson
8: Cal Ripken, Jr.
20: Frank Robinson
22: Jim Palmer
33: Eddie Murray
42: Jackie Robinson*

Boston Red Sox

1: Bobby Doerr
4: Joe Cronin
8: Carl Yastrzemski
9: Ted Williams
27: Carlton Fisk
42: Jackie Robinson*

Chicago Cubs

10: Ron Santo
14: Ernie Banks
26: Billy Williams
42: Jackie Robinson*

Chicago White Sox

2: Nellie Fox
3: Harold Baines
4: Luke Appling
9: Minnie Minoso
11: Luis Aparicio
16: Ted Lyons
19: Billy Pierce
42: Jackie Robinson*
72: Carlton Fisk

Cincinnati Reds

1: Fred Hutchinson
5: Johnny Bench
8: Joe Morgan
18: Ted Kluszewski
20: Frank Robinson
24: Tony Perez
42: Jackie Robinson*

Cleveland Indians

3: Earl Averill
5: Lou Boudreau
14: Larry Doby
18: Mel Harder
19: Bob Feller
21: Bob Lemon
42: Jackie Robinson*

Colorado Rockies

42: Jackie Robinson*

Detroit Tigers

2: Charlie Gehringer
5: Hank Greenberg
6: Al Kaline
16: Hal Newhouser
23: Willie Horton
42: Jackie Robinson*

Florida Marlins

5: Carl Barger*
42: Jackie Robinson*

Houston Astros

25: Jose Cruz
32: Jim Umbricht
33: Mike Scott
34: Nolan Ryan
40: Don Wilson

42: Jackie Robinson*
49: Larry Dierker

Kansas City Royals

5: George Brett
10: Dick Howser
20: Frank White
42: Jackie Robinson*

Los Angeles Dodgers

1: Pee Wee Reese
2: Tom Lasorda
4: Duke Snider
19: Jim Gilliam
20: Don Sutton
24: Walter Alston
32: Sandy Koufax
39: Roy Campanella
42: Jackie Robinson
53: Don Drysdale

Milwaukee Brewers

4: Paul Molitor
19: Robin Yount
34: Rollie Fingers
42: Jackie Robinson*
44: Hank Aaron

Minnesota Twins

3: Harmon Killebrew

6: Tony Oliva
14: Kent Hrbek
29: Rod Carew
34: Kirby Puckett
42: Jackie Robinson*

Montreal Expos

8: Gary Carter
10: Rusty Staub and Andre Dawson
42: Jackie Robinson*

National League Umpires[2]

1: Bill Klem
2: Jocko Conlan
3: Al Barlick

New York Mets

14: Gil Hodges
37: Casey Stengel
41: Tom Seaver
42: Jackie Robinson*

New York Yankees

1: Billy Martin
3: Babe Ruth
4: Lou Gehrig
5: Joe DiMaggio
7: Mickey Mantle
8: Bill Dickey and Yogi Berra
9: Roger Maris

2. National League umpires and American League umpires came under the joint jurisdiction of Major League Baseball in 2000. These numbers are no longer held in retirement.

10: Phil Rizzuto
15: Thurman Munson
16: Whitey Ford
23: Don Mattingly
32: Elston Howard
37: Casey Stengel
42: Jackie Robinson*
44: Reggie Jackson
49: Ron Guidry

Oakland Athletics

27: Jim Hunter
34: Rollie Fingers
42: Jackie Robinson*

Philadelphia Phillies

None: Grover Cleveland Alexander and Chuck Klein
1: Richie Ashburn
14: Jim Bunning
20: Mike Schmidt
32: Steve Carlton
36: Robin Roberts
42: Jackie Robinson*

Pittsburgh Pirates

1: Billy Meyer
4: Ralph Kiner
8: Willie Stargell
9: Bill Mazeroski
20: Pie Traynor
21: Roberto Clemente
33: Honus Wagner
40: Danny Murtaugh
42: Jackie Robinson*

St. Louis Cardinals

1: Ozzie Smith
2: Red Schoendienst
6: Stan Musial
9: Enos Slaughter
14: Ken Boyer
17: Dizzy Dean
20: Lou Brock
42: Jackie Robinson*
45: Bob Gibson
85: August A. Busch, Jr.*

San Diego Padres

6: Steve Garvey
19: Tony Gwynn
31: Dave Winfield
35: Randy Jones
42: Jackie Robinson*

San Francisco Giants

None: Christy Mathewson and John McGraw
3: Bill Terry
4: Mel Ott
11: Carl Hubbell
24: Willie Mays
27: Juan Marichal
30: Orlando Cepeda
42: Jackie Robinson*
44: Willie McCovey

Seattle Mariners

42: Jackie Robinson*

Tampa Bay Devil Rays

12: Wade Boggs
42: Jackie Robinson*

Texas Rangers

34: Nolan Ryan
42: Jackie Robinson*

Toronto Blue Jays

42: Jackie Robinson*

Numerical List

Following is a numerical list of retired uniform numbers for every major league team and for major league umpires. An asterisk (*) indicates that the number was retired symbolically and was never actually worn by the person for whom it was retired.

None: Grover Cleveland Alexander (Philadelphia Phillies)
    Chuck Klein (Philadelphia Phillies)
    Christy Mathewson (San Francisco Giants)
    John McGraw (San Francisco Giants)

1: Richie Ashburn (Philadelphia Phillies)
   Bobby Doerr (Boston Red Sox)
   Fred Hutchinson (Cincinnati Reds)
   Bill Klem (National League Umpires)
   Billy Martin (New York Yankees)
   Billy Meyer (Pittsburgh Pirates)
   Pee Wee Reese (Los Angeles Dodgers)
   Ozzie Smith (St. Louis Cardinals)

2: Nick Bremigan (American League Umpires)
   Jocko Conlan (National League Umpires)
   Nellie Fox (Chicago White Sox)
   Charlie Gehringer (Detroit Tigers)
   Tom Lasorda (Los Angeles Dodgers)
   Red Schoendienst (St. Louis Cardinals)

3: Earl Averill (Cleveland Indians)
   Harold Baines (Chicago White Sox)
   Al Barlick (National League Umpires)
   Harmon Killebrew (Minnesota Twins)
   Dale Murphy (Atlanta Braves)
   Babe Ruth (New York Yankees)
   Bill Terry (San Francisco Giants)

4: Luke Appling (Chicago White Sox)
   Joe Cronin (Boston Red Sox)
   Lou Gehrig (New York Yankees)
   Ralph Kiner (Pittsburgh Pirates)
   Paul Molitor (Milwaukee Brewers)
   Mel Ott (San Francisco Giants)
   Duke Snider (Los Angeles Dodgers)
   Earl Weaver (Baltimore Orioles)

5: Carl Barger (Florida Marlins*)
   Johnny Bench (Cincinnati Reds)
   Lou Boudreau (Cleveland Indians)
   George Brett (Kansas City Royals)
   Joe DiMaggio (New York Yankees)
   Hank Greenberg (Detroit Tigers)
   Brooks Robinson (Baltimore Orioles)

6: Steve Garvey (San Diego Padres)
   Al Kaline (Detroit Tigers)
   Stan Musial (St. Louis Cardinals)
   Tony Oliva (Minnesota Twins)

7: Mickey Mantle (New York Yankees)

8: Yogi Berra (New York Yankees)
   Gary Carter (Montreal Expos)
   Bill Dickey (New York Yankees)
   Joe Morgan (Cincinnati Reds)
   Cal Ripken, Jr. (Baltimore Orioles)
   Willie Stargell (Pittsburgh Pirates)
   Carl Yastrzemski (Boston Red Sox)

9: Bill Kunkel (American League Umpires)

Roger Maris (New York Yankees)
Bill Mazeroski (Pittsburgh Pirates)
Minnie Minoso (Chicago White Sox)
Enos Slaughter (St. Louis Cardinals)
Ted Williams (Boston Red Sox)

10: Andre Dawson (Montreal Expos)
Dick Howser (Kansas City Royals)
Phil Rizzuto (New York Yankees)
Ron Santo (Chicago Cubs)
Rusty Staub (Montreal Expos)

11: Luis Aparicio (Chicago White Sox)
Jim Fregosi (Anaheim Angels)
Carl Hubbell (San Francisco Giants)

12: Wade Boggs (Tampa Bay Devil Rays)

14: Ernie Banks (Chicago Cubs)
Ken Boyer (St. Louis Cardinals)
Jim Bunning (Philadelphia Phillies)
Larry Doby (Cleveland Indians)
Gil Hodges (New York Mets)
Kent Hrbek (Minnesota Twins)

15: Thurman Munson (New York Yankees)

16: Lou DiMuro (American League Umpires)
Whitey Ford (New York Yankees)
Ted Lyons (Chicago White Sox)
Hal Newhouser (Detroit Tigers)

17: Dizzy Dean (St. Louis Cardinals)

18: Mel Harder (Cleveland Indians)
Ted Kluszewski (Cincinnati Reds)

19: Bob Feller (Cleveland Indians)
Jim Gilliam (Los Angeles Dodgers)
Tony Gwynn (San Diego Padres)
Billy Pierce (Chicago White Sox)
Robin Yount (Milwaukee Brewers)

20: Lou Brock (St. Louis Cardinals)
 Frank Robinson (Baltimore Orioles, Cincinnati Reds)
 Mike Schmidt (Philadelphia Phillies)
 Don Sutton (Los Angeles Dodgers)
 Pie Traynor (Pittsburgh Pirates)
 Frank White (Kansas City Royals)

21: Roberto Clemente (Pittsburgh Pirates)
 Bob Lemon (Cleveland Indians)
 Warren Spahn (Atlanta Braves)

22: Jim Palmer (Baltimore Orioles)

23: Willie Horton (Detroit Tigers)
 Don Mattingly (New York Yankees)

24: Walter Alston (Los Angeles Dodgers)
 Willie Mays (San Francisco Giants)
 Tony Perez (Cincinnati Reds)

25: Jose Cruz (Houston Astros)

26: Gene Autry (Anaheim Angels*)
 Billy Williams (Chicago Cubs)

27: Carlton Fisk (Boston Red Sox)
 Jim Hunter (Oakland Athletics)
 Juan Marichal (San Francisco Giants)

29: Rod Carew (Anaheim Angels, Minnesota Twins)

30: Orlando Cepeda (San Francisco Giants)
 Nolan Ryan (Anaheim Angels)

31: Dave Winfield (San Diego Padres)

32: Steve Carlton (Philadelphia Phillies)
 Elston Howard (New York Yankees)
 Sandy Koufax (Los Angeles Dodgers)
 Jim Umbricht (Houston Astros)

33: Eddie Murray (Baltimore Orioles)
Mike Scott (Houston Astros)
Honus Wagner (Pittsburgh Pirates)

34: Rollie Fingers (Milwaukee Brewers, Oakland Athletics)
Kirby Puckett (Minnesota Twins)
Nolan Ryan (Houston Astros, Texas Rangers)

35: Randy Jones (San Diego Padres)
Phil Niekro (Atlanta Braves)

36: Robin Roberts (Philadelphia Phillies)

37: Casey Stengel (New York Mets, New York Yankees)

39: Roy Campanella (Los Angeles Dodgers)

40: Danny Murtaugh (Pittsburgh Pirates)
Don Wilson (Houston Astros)

41: Eddie Mathews (Atlanta Braves)
Tom Seaver (New York Mets)

42: Jackie Robinson (Los Angeles Dodgers, Major League Baseball*)

44: Hank Aaron (Atlanta Braves, Milwaukee Brewers)
Reggie Jackson (New York Yankees)
Willie McCovey (San Francisco Giants)

45: Bob Gibson (St. Louis Cardinals)

49: Larry Dierker (Houston Astros)
Ron Guidry (New York Yankees)

50: Jimmie Reese (Anaheim Angels)

53: Don Drysdale (Los Angeles Dodgers)

72: Carlton Fisk (Chicago White Sox)

85: August A. Busch, Jr. (St. Louis Cardinals*)

PART II
Minor Leagues

List of Players

Hank Aaron

Retired Number: 44 (Mobile BayBears)

This number was retired symbolically for major league baseball's all-time home run king. Aaron was born in Mobile, and 44 is the number he wore with (and also had retired by) the Milwaukee/Atlanta Braves and the Milwaukee Brewers. The BayBears also play at Hank Aaron Stadium.

Tommie Aaron

Retired Number: 23 (Richmond Braves)

Tommie Aaron both played for and managed the Richmond Braves, and also had a successful major league career. The team renamed the club's Most Valuable Award the Tommie Aaron Award in his honor. Tommie was the brother of Hank Aaron.

Joe Altobelli

Retired Number: 26 (Rochester Red Wings)

Altobelli played for the Red Wings from 1963–66 as a first baseman and outfielder, and hit 47 home runs with 160 runs batted in during that period. He became the team's manager for six seasons beginning in 1971, and at the helm he won 502 games, two Governors' Cups, and the 1971 Junior World Series. He became a major league manager, where he won the Manager of the Year Award twice, then returned to Rochester and worked in the Red Wings' front office before retiring in 1996. He was inducted into the Red Wings' Hall of Fame in 1989.

Willy Ambos
Retired Number: 13 (Ogden Raptors)

Ambos was a former minor league pitcher who, at the age of 28, became the Raptors' first manager during their inaugural season of 1993. He later became a sales coordinator for a trailer sales company in Salt Lake City.

Fred Anderson
Retired Number: 1 (Modesto A's)

This number was retired symbolically for the team's former owner. Anderson was the Founder and Chairman of the Board of Pacific Coast Building Products, Inc. He was an avid sports fan and also owned the Sacramento Gold Miners and San Antonio Texans of the Canadian Football League, as well as the Sacramento Surge of the World League of American Football. He held a minority interest in the Pittsburgh Pirates, and in the Sacramento Kings of the National Basketball Association. Anderson passed away in 1997.

Carl Barger
Retired Number: 5 (Brevard County Manatees)

This number was retired symbolically for the man who played a large role in bringing major league baseball to Brevard County. The Manatees followed the example of the Florida Marlins and, upon Barger's death, retired the number 5 in his honor because Barger's favorite player had been Joe DiMaggio, who wore number 5 with the New York Yankees.

Skeeter Barnes
Retired Number: 00 (Nashville Sounds)

Barnes played with the Sounds in 1979 and again from 1988–90. He became the team's all-time leader with 514 games played, 517 hits, 94 doubles, and 1898 at-bats. In 1979 he led the team with 145 games played. In 1989 he led with a .303 batting average, 143 hits, and 39 doubles, while tying Marty Brown with 15 stolen bases. In 1990 he led with 144 games played, 548 at-bats, 83 runs scored, 156 hits, and 34 stolen bases. Barnes also played in the major leagues.

Joe Bauldree

Retired Number: 24 (Allentown Ambassadors)

This right-handed starting pitcher played for the Ambassadors in 2001, and he returned in 2002 but died in his sleep in May at the age of 25.

Yogi Berra

Retired Number: 8 (New Jersey Jackals)

The Jackals retired this number symbolically for the Hall of Fame catcher/outfielder. Berra has been a resident of Montclair, New Jersey, the Jackals' home, for over 40 years. In 1996, he received an honorary doctorate from Montclair State University, and in 1998, Yogi Berra Stadium, on the university's campus, was named for him. The Jackals call that stadium home. Additionally, in December of that year, the university opened the Yogi Berra Museum and Learning Center. The number 8 was Berra's number with the New York Yankees (and has also been retired by the Yankees).

Jim Bibby

Retired Number: 26 (Lynchburg Hillcats)

Bibby had a successful major league career before becoming a pitching coach with the Hillcats. He is a longtime resident of Lynchburg.

Tim Bishop

Retired Number: 4 (Capital City Bombers)

This Bombers outfielder was killed in a car accident early in the 1997 season. On April 18, the Bombers were scheduled to play the Hagerstown Suns in Hagerstown, Maryland, but the game was called because of poor weather and the Bombers' bus returned to Columbia, South Carolina. Bishop was riding home with teammate Randy Vickers when the car blew a tire on the interstate. Bishop got out to inspect the damage and was struck and killed by another car. He was 20 years of age.

Bobby Bragan

Retired Number: 10 (Fort Worth Cats)

Bragan's number was retired symbolically, since Bobby actually played for a previous team that was also called the Fort Worth Cats. After a seven-year major league career with the Philadelphia Phillies and Brooklyn Dodgers, Bragan was playing in 1948 when, in July, Brooklyn general manager Branch Rickey offered him the managerial job with the Cats, who were a Dodgers affiliate. Bobby accepted and became the player/manager of the Cats from 1948–52, guiding the club to Texas League titles his first two years. He also hit .295 in 1949 with 7 home runs and 60 runs batted in. His teams never finished below .500, and he eventually became a manager in the major leagues with the Pittsburgh Pirates, Cleveland Indians, and Atlanta Braves. He was known as "Mr. Baseball" in the Fort Worth community, and the current Cats retired his number during a tribute weekend from May 23–25, 2003.

Marshall Brant

Retired Number: 33 (Columbus Clippers)

Brant was voted by fans as the most popular player with the Columbus Clippers. In 1980 he hit .289 with 23 home runs and 92 runs batted in as the Clippers won their second straight International League championship, and Brant was named the league's Most Valuable Player. In 1981 he contributed 25 homers and 95 RBIs to the club's third consecutive championship. The following year the team just missed a fourth straight as Brant added 31 roundtrippers and 96 RBIs. The first baseman played three games with the New York Yankees in 1980 and five more with the Oakland Athletics in 1983.

Dave Bresnahan

Retired Number: 59 (Williamsport Crosscutters)

Bresnahan actually played for a previous team called the Williamsport Bills, who were an affiliate of the Cleveland Indians. He had a career batting average of .149 with the Bills, but the Crosscutters retired his number because of a prank he pulled during the 1987 season. In the fifth inning of Game 1 of an August doubleheader against the Reading Phillies, Bresnahan, a catcher, waited until a Phillies runner reached third base, then told the umpire something was wrong with his mitt and that he needed to obtain a new one. He went to the dugout and retrieved a mitt in which he had hidden a peeled potato. On the next pitch, which Bresnahan deliberately called outside so the batter would not swing, he caught the ball but rifled the potato, which he had switched to his throwing hand, over the third baseman's head, making it appear that he was trying to catch the runner off base. The runner, seeing what he thought was the ball sailing into the outfield, charged home, where Bresnahan easily put the tag on him with the real ball. A great deal of confusion ensued, but after some time the umpire figured out what had happened and called the runner safe. Bresnahan, his teammates, the Phillies, and even the umpires got a good laugh out of the prank, but Crosscutters manager Orlando Gomez was not amused. He removed Bresnahan from the game and fined him $50, and the Indians released their minor league catcher the next day.

George Brett

Retired Number: 5 (Spokane Indians)

This number was retired symbolically for Brett, a part-owner of the Indians. The number 5 is the number Brett wore with (and had retired by) the Kansas City Royals.

Kevin Brown

Retired Number: 45 (Hudson Valley Renegades)

Brown was a catcher who played with the Renegades during their inaugural 1994 season. He was the first Renegade to reach the major leagues, which he did in 1996 with the Texas Rangers.

Morgan Burkhart

Retired Number: 16 (Richmond Roosters)

Burkhart played for the Roosters from 1995–98 and set numerous Frontier League records. He set single-season records with 36 home runs,

98 runs batted in (tied with Scott Pinoni), 241 total bases, 55 extra-base hits, 85 bases on balls, an .861 slugging average, and a .557 on-base percentage, as well as becoming the league's all-time home run king with 86 in his career. He won the league's Most Valuable Player Award three times and then had the award named for him. He was the first position player from the league to reach the major leagues, where he played for the Boston Red Sox beginning in 2000.

Roy Campanella

Retired Number: 39 (Nashua Pride)

This number was retired symbolically for Campanella, who played for a previous team in Nashua when the Brooklyn Dodgers had a farm club there. The number 39 is the number Campanella wore with (and had retired by) the Dodgers.

Jose Canseco

Retired Number: 44 (Huntsville Stars)

Canseco played for the Stars in 1985, and was named the Southern League's Most Valuable Player when he put together a .318 batting average, 25 home runs, and 80 runs batted in in just 58 games. He became the American League Rookie of the Year the following season and thus began a very successful major league career.

Ollie Carnegie

Retired Number: 6 (Buffalo Bisons)

Ollie Carnegie became a professional ballplayer at the age of 30 when he lost his railroad job in 1931. The Bisons' retirement is symbolic, since Carnegie actually played for a previous franchise by the same name. Ollie had a long career with the Bisons, hitting .345 in 15 games in 1931, and the following season slugging 36 home runs with 140 runs batted in. In 1933 he hit .317 with 29 homers and 123 RBIs, then batted .335 the next year with 31 roundtrippers and 136 knocked in. In 1938, at the age of 39, he hit .330 with 45 homers (a new Bisons' record) and 136 RBIs. Ollie played through the 1941 season and amassed more than 1300 hits, 1000 runs scored, and 250 home runs with Buffalo.

Chin-Feng Chen

Retired Number: 43 (Inland Empire 66ers)

Chen's number was retired when the 66ers were called the San Bernardino Stampede. Chin-Feng was the second player from Taiwan to play professionally in the United States. In 1999 with the Stampede this outfielder hit .316 with 31 home runs, 123 runs batted in, 22 doubles, 10 triples, and 31 stolen bases on his way to being named the California League's Most Valuable Player. He reached the major leagues in 2002 with the Los Angeles Dodgers.

Jack Clark

Retired Number: 22 (River City Rascals)

After a successful major league career, Clark became the manager of the Rascals during their inaugural season of 1999 and guided them to a 39–45 finish. He later became a major league coach, and the Rascals retired his number on May 31, 2001, in recognition of his role in making the club a success during that first year.

Tony Clark

Retired Number: 33 (Trenton Thunder)

Tony Clark played for the AA Thunder in 1994 and hit .279 with 21 home runs, 86 runs batted in, and 25 doubles before moving up to AAA and eventually the major leagues with the Detroit Tigers. The Thunder retired his number in 1997.

Alan Cockrell

Retired Number: 31 (Colorado Springs Sky Sox)

Cockrell played for the Sky Sox in 1990, in 1992, and from 1994–96. He retired as the team's all-time leader with 494 games played, 478 hits, 91 doubles, 286 runs batted in, and 183 bases on balls, as well as being second with 63 home runs and 269 runs scored. He hit at least .300 four of the five seasons he was in Colorado Springs, and hit .304 with the club overall. In 1990 he hit .330 with 17 home runs and 70 RBIs and was named a Pacific Coast League All-Star. Cockrell eventually reached the major leagues, and he was inducted into the Sky Sox Hall of Fame on September 2, 1996, the same day the team retired his number.

Brian Cole

Retired Number: 6 (St. Lucie Mets)

Cole was an outfielder who played for the St. Lucie Mets in 2000, and was killed in an automobile accident in the spring of 2001. In 2000 he hit .312 with 54 stolen bases, and between St. Lucie and the Binghamton Mets overall he had a combined 19 home runs, 86 runs batted in, and 69 steals. In 2001 he was driving home from spring training in Florida to his home in Meridian, Mississippi, to drop off his truck before flying to Binghamton to join the AA Mets for the start of the season. His truck was hit by another vehicle near the Florida-Alabama border, killing him almost instantly. Cole was 22 years of age.

Gene Cook

Retired Number: 1 (Toledo Mud Hens)

This number was retired symbolically for Cook, who served as the Mud Hens' general manager from 1978–98 and then on the team's Board of Directors. He passed away in February of 2002, and the club expressed the sentiment that he would always be remembered as number one.

Rich Dauer

Retired Number: 25 (Inland Empire 66ers)

This number was originally retired symbolically for Dauer by a previous team called the San Bernardino Spirit. When the Spirit relocated to Rancho Cucamonga, the new San Bernardino Stampede (now the Inland Empire 66ers) picked it up. Dauer was a native of San Bernardino, and had a successful major league career with the Baltimore Orioles, with whom he wore uniform number 25.

Darren Doucette

Retired Number: 50 (Adirondack Lumberjacks)

Doucette was a big left-handed slugger from Dartmouth College who was originally drafted by the St. Louis Cardinals in 1992 and eventually became a player/coach with the Lumberjacks. The Lumberjacks have since moved to Bangor and no longer honor this number.

Brian Duva

Retired Number: 5 (Winnipeg Goldeyes)

This second baseman played for the Goldeyes from 1995–2000. He set numerous club and Northern League records and was a league All-Star in both 1997 and 1998. He was also named to the league's postseason All-Star team and to *Baseball America*'s All-Independent Second Team both years.

Dale Earnhardt

Retired Number: 3 (Kannapolis Intimidators)

This number was retired symbolically for the team's late part-owner and race car driver. Earnhardt and two friends purchased the Piedmont Boll Weevils in November of 2000 and renamed the team after Earnhardt's own NASCAR nickname, "The Intimidator." Dale was killed in a crash on the racetrack in February of 2001 before he got to see his team play a game. The number 3 was the number Earnhardt bore on his race car, and the Intimidators retired the number in his honor on May 15, 2002.

Luke Easter

Retired Number: 25 (Buffalo Bisons)
Retired Number: 36 (Rochester Red Wings)

Luke Easter is the only individual (other than Jackie Robinson) to have his number retired by more than one minor league team. The Bisons' retirement is symbolic, since Easter actually played for a previous franchise by the same name. After playing in the Negro National League with the Washington Homestead Grays from 1947–48 and then in the American League with the Cleveland Indians from 1949–54, he joined the Bisons in 1956 at the age of 41 and became Buffalo's first black player since Frank Grant in 1888. He batted .306 that year and led the International League with 35 home runs and 106 runs batted in. In 1957 he led the league again with 40 home runs and 128 RBIs, and in 1958 slugged 38 homers and drove in 109. In 1959 he was released because the Bisons began to look for young talent and Easter was 43 years old. He joined the Red Wings and was with them for six years as a player and coach, hitting 67 home runs and 76 doubles in 499 games. In 1979, as the chief union steward for the Aircraft Workers Alliance, he was approached by two men in a bank parking lot in Euclid, Ohio, while carrying $40,000 in union funds. The men demanded the money, and when Easter refused to hand it over, one of them shot him in the chest with a shotgun and killed him instantly. Easter posthumously became a charter member of the Red Wings' Hall of Fame in 1989.

Matt Erwin

Retired Number: 29 (Sioux Falls Canaries)

This catcher played for the Canaries in 1997. In September of that year, at the age of 24, he was shot to death after following his estranged wife into her apartment.

Fans of the Orlando Rays

Retired Number: 26 (Orlando Rays)

The Rays retired this number symbolically for their fans. Most baseball rosters consist of 25 players, and the club's fans were seen as the "26th man" who made the team a success. The Anaheim Angels did something similar for owner Gene Autry. The team no longer honors this number, however.

Mal Fichman

Retired Number: 4 (Boise Hawks)

When the former Tri-City Triplets were purchased by a group of New York investors and moved to Boise in 1986, Fichman was named the first manager of the franchise under its new identity. The club played as an unaffiliated team in the Northwest League until 1990, when it signed an agreement with the California Angels. The Angels replaced Fichman as manager, and the team retired his number 4. For some reason, however, the club has begun to reissue the number in recent years and no longer honors its retirement.

Rafael Furcal

Retired Number: 2 (Myrtle Beach Pelicans)

This number was retired in September of 2001 during the Legends of Baseball game for Furcal, who played for the Pelicans in 1999 before joining the Atlanta Braves in 2000 and winning the National League's Rookie of the Year Award.

Nomar Garciaparra

Retired Number: 5 (Trenton Thunder)

Garciaparra played for the Thunder in 1995 and hit .267 with 8 home runs and 47 runs batted in before beginning a successful major league career with the Boston Red Sox. His number was retired in 1998 when the Red Sox went to Trenton for an exhibition game against the Thunder, who were then one of their minor league affiliates.

Jeremi Gonzalez

Retired Number: 41 (Williamsport Crosscutters)

Gonzalez actually played for a previous team called the Williamsport Cubs, and became the first Cub to appear in the major leagues. The Crosscutters retired the number symbolically.

Mark Grace

Retired Number: 17 (Peoria Chiefs)

Mark Grace played for the Chiefs in 1986, his first professional season, and hit .342 with 15 home runs and 95 runs batted in. In 1988 he began a very successful major league career with the Chicago Cubs. The Chiefs retired his number on July 8, 2000.

Brett Gray

Retired Number: 27 (London Werewolves)

On June 3, 2000, Gray struck out 25 batters in a 9–1 victory for the Werewolves over the Chillicothe Paints. The team retired his number on

May 30, 2001, and his jersey went to the Canadian Baseball Hall of Fame. The Werewolves eventually became the Canton Coyotes and are now the Mid-Missouri Mavericks. They no longer honor this number.

Ken Griffey, Jr.

Retired Number: 24 (Inland Empire 66ers)

This number was retired symbolically for Griffey, who actually played for a previous team in San Bernardino called the San Bernardino Spirit. Griffey was with the Spirit in 1988 and hit .338 with 11 home runs, 42 runs batted in, and 32 stolen bases in only 58 games before eventually reaching the major leagues with the Seattle Mariners.

Roger Hanners

Retired Number: 50 (Chillicothe Paints)

This manager guided the Paints from 1993, their inaugural season, until he was forced to retire at the end of the 2000 campaign because of declining health. He died on January 24, 2002, at the age of 70. Hanners had a lifetime record of 292–272 for a winning percentage of .518. His squad won divisional titles in 1994, 1996, and 1998, and was a wild card entry in 1999. He won the Frontier League's Manager of the Year Award in 1996 and managed four All-Star teams. At the time of his death, Hanners had managed more games, achieved more victories, and won more postseason titles than any other manager in Frontier League history.

Ryan Hawblitzel

Retired Number: 21 (Colorado Springs Sky Sox)

Hawblitzel was with the Sky Sox for four seasons and, when he left the team, was the all-time franchise leader with 30 wins, 308 strikeouts, and 528⅓ innings pitched, as well as being second with 104 games pitched. On July 27, 1995, he pitched the only no-hitter in Sky Sox history, hurling nine no-hit innings against the Vancouver Canadians before giving up a hit and a run in the tenth and losing the game, 1–0. He won three games in the 1995 playoffs, including the deciding Game 5 against the Salt Lake Buzz. Hawblitzel was the first pitcher inducted into the Sky Sox Hall of Fame.

Mark Hindy

Retired Number: 40 (Ogden Raptors)

Hindy was a pitcher for the Raptors who was killed in the World Trade Center attack on September 11, 2001. After his baseball career Mark had become an equity trader at Cantor Fitzgerald, and had gone to work that day on the 104th floor of the North Tower in the World Trade Center. He was 28 years of age.

Gil Hodges

Retired Number: 14 (Brooklyn Cyclones)

The Cyclones retired this number symbolically for the late Brooklyn Dodger, who had an outstanding major league career in Brooklyn and also managed the New York Mets. The number 14 is the number Hodges wore with both the Dodgers and Mets, and that the Mets have retired in his honor.

Mitch House

Retired Number: 27 (Chillicothe Paints)

House spent three years with the Paints and was named to the Frontier League All-Star team all three seasons. He was selected by Chillicothe fans as the third baseman on the Paints' 10th Anniversary Dream Team.

Trenidad Hubbard

Retired Number: 4 (Colorado Springs Sky Sox)

Hubbard spent parts of four seasons with the Sky Sox from 1993–96 and set all-time team records with a .334 batting average, 25 triples, 304 runs scored, and 104 stolen bases. In 1995 he hit .340 with 163 hits, 102 runs scored, and 37 steals and was named to the Pacific Coast League All-Star team. He was inducted into the Sky Sox' Hall of Fame in 2002.

Adam Hyzdu

Retired Number: 16 (Altoona Curve)

Hyzdu joined the Curve for two seasons beginning in 1999, and in 2000 was named the Eastern League's Most Valuable Player. The Curve retired his number following the last game of the 2000 season, and that same year Hyzdu made his major league debut with the Pittsburgh Pirates.

Sam Jethroe

Retired Number: 5 (Erie SeaWolves)

This number was retired symbolically for Jethroe, who formerly resided in Erie and who had a successful career in the Negro Leagues as well as with the Boston Braves and Pittsburgh Pirates. The number 5 is the number he wore with the Braves when he won the National League Rookie of the Year Award in 1950.

Charles Johnson

Retired Number: 35 (Kane County Cougars)

Johnson played for the Cougars in 1993 and hit .275 with 19 home runs and a Midwest League-leading 94 runs batted in. He was a Midwest League All-Star and the team's Most Valuable Player, and was named the number one prospect in the league by *Baseball America*. He later went on to a successful major league career.

Brad Kelley

Retired Number: 34 (Princeton Devil Rays)

Kelley was the team's pitching coach in 1994, when the club was called the Princeton Reds and won the Appalachian League championship. He became the team's manager the following year and guided the club to a second-place finish, and was active in promoting professional baseball in Princeton. He later became a scout in the Chicago Cubs organization.

Hub Kittle

Retired Number: 34 (New Jersey Cardinals)

This one-time pitching coach for the New Jersey Cardinals enjoyed a legendary career. Kittle was a minor league pitcher from 1936 through 1955, then became a minor league manager. In a 20-year managerial career, he would eventually win 1329 games. In a game with the Savannah Senators in 1969 he ran out of pitchers and inserted himself for two innings, at the age of 52. He later became a coach with the Houston Astros, and at the age of 56 was allowed by manager Leo Durocher to pitch an inning in an exhibition game against the Detroit Tigers at the Astrodome. He retired three straight batters and earned a save. Having thus pitched professionally in five decades, he got the idea of pitching in six. In 1980 he was a pitching coach with the Springfield Cardinals, and on August 27 the club signed him to a one-dollar playing contract and inserted him into a contest against the Iowa Cubs on, appropriately, Senior Citizens Night. The 63-year-old retired the side on nine pitches in the first inning and got an out on one pitch in the second before going back into retirement. He thus became not only the oldest player in organized baseball, but the only one to pitch in six different decades as well. He later became a special assignment coach with the Seattle Mariners.

Matt LaChappa

Retired Number: 20 (Rancho Cucamonga Quakes)

This relief pitcher with the Quakes suffered a massive heart attack during a game on April 6, 1996, while warming up in the bullpen. The event ended LaChappa's career, but quick action by the team's trainer, Jim Daniel, helped save his life.

Tom Lasorda

Retired Number: 11 (Albuquerque Dukes)

Lasorda managed the Dukes to the Pacific Coast League championship in 1972 before becoming a longtime manager with the Los Angeles Dodgers (who have retired his number 2 at the major league level). The Dukes have since become the Portland Beavers, and the team no longer honors this number in Portland.

Greg Legg

Retired Number: 14 (Scranton/Wilkes-Barre Red Barons)

Legg played for the Red Barons from 1989–95 before becoming a coach in 1996. He hit .308 in 1990, .290 in 1991, and .298 in 1994. He later became a minor league manager.

Lou List

Retired Number: 7 (New Haven Ravens)

List was a popular player with the Ravens in 1994 and 1995. He later died of Hodgkin's Disease at the age of 32.

Jeff Manto

Retired Number: 30 (Buffalo Bisons)

Jeff Manto played four seasons for the Bisons and hit 79 home runs, putting him in fifth place in franchise history. He retired as the all-time minor league home run leader with 243. When his number was retired, he was presented a jersey, a video of his highlights with the Bisons, and a five-day trip to Rome, which he used to help celebrate his tenth wedding anniversary. Manto spent over four years in the major leagues and, upon his retirement, became a minor league coach.

Charlie Manuel

Retired Number: 41 (Colorado Springs Sky Sox)

Manuel managed the Sky Sox for two and a half years and led them to three consecutive playoff appearances. In 1992 his team won the Pacific Coast League championship, and Manuel was named the league's Manager of the Year. He had previously played in the major leagues and in Japan, and was the first American ever to win a Most Valuable Player Award in Japanese baseball. He later managed the Cleveland Indians, and on September 4, 1994, was inducted into the Sky Sox Hall of Fame.

Rocky Marciano

Retired Number: 49 (Brockton Rox)

This number was retired symbolically for the heavyweight boxing champion, who was born in Brockton in 1923. Nicknamed the "Brockton Blockbuster," Marciano was a huge baseball fan who actually attempted a baseball career before turning to boxing. The Rox were named, at least in part, in his honor. The number 49 represents Marciano's still-standing record of 49 consecutive professional victories.

Roger Maris

Retired Number: 8 (Fargo-Moorhead RedHawks)

The RedHawks retired this number symbolically for Maris, who actually wore the number with a previous team called the Fargo-Moorhead Twins. Roger was signed to a contract by the Cleveland Indians in 1953 and was assigned to the Twins, who were at that time a Class C team. He hit .325 with nine home runs, helped the club to the Northern League championship, and was named the league's Rookie of the Year. He eventually had a successful major league career, hitting 61 home runs in 1961 to break Babe Ruth's record of 60 home runs in a season, and had his major league number 9 retired by the New York Yankees.

Don Mattingly

Retired Number: 18 (Nashville Sounds)

The Sounds retired this number on August 12, 1999. Mattingly played for Nashville in 1981 and hit .315 with 7 home runs and 98 runs batted in before going on to a successful major league career. His number 23 was retired at the major league level by the New York Yankees.

Gator McBride

Retired Number: 20 (Chillicothe Paints)

McBride played a year and a half with the Paints, with whom he hit .403 in 1998, an all-time club record. He was batting .450 during the first half of the 1999 season when he was signed by the Boston Red Sox. He eventually became a coach with the Paints from 2000–02.

Luis Medina

Retired Number: 11 (Colorado Springs Sky Sox)

Medina played more than four seasons with the Sky Sox and won two Pacific Coast League home run titles. In his time in Colorado Springs, Luis collected 388 hits, 76 home runs, and 251 runs batted in, and became the first inductee in the Sky Sox Hall of Fame on September 7, 1992.

Brad Mills

Retired Number: 9 (Colorado Springs Sky Sox)

Mills was the second manager ever inducted into the Sky Sox Hall of Fame. He played 106 games at the major league level in parts of four seasons with the Montreal Expos before taking the helm in Colorado Springs for four years. He guided the club to the postseason in 1994, where the Sox lost to the Albuquerque Dukes in the Southern Division Championship Series, then took them all the way to the Pacific Coast League championship in 1995 by defeating the Salt Lake Buzz. It was the second league championship in Colorado Springs history.

Joe Morgan

Retired Number: 18 (Durham Bulls)

"Little Joe" played for the Bulls in 1963 before launching a Hall of Fame career at the major league level. In 95 games that season he hit .332 with 13 home runs, 43 runs batted in, 20 doubles, 91 bases on balls, 107 hits, and 74 runs scored. He was the first Bull to reach the Hall of Fame, and also had his number 8 retired by the Cincinnati Reds.

Don Newcombe

Retired Number: 36 (Nashua Pride)

This number was retired symbolically for Newcombe, who played for a previous team in Nashua when the Brooklyn Dodgers had a farm club there. The number 36 is the number Newcombe wore with the Dodgers.

Rick Patterson

Retired Number: 12 (South Bend Silver Hawks)

This former manager was at the helm when the club was called the South Bend White Sox. In 1989 he guided the team to the Midwest League championship with an 85–47 record, then in 1990 took them to the playoffs again as the club went 77–57.

Scott Pinoni

Retired Number: 30 (Chillicothe Paints)

Pinoni played for the Paints in 1996 and from 1998–99. He was named "Star of Stars," the highest award presented by the Frontier League, twice. In 1998, along with Morgan Burkhart, he set the league record by driving in 98 runs in a season. He was selected as the first baseman on the Paints' 10th Anniversary Dream Team.

Jim Reinebold

Retired Number: 4 (South Bend Silver Hawks)

Reinebold was a legendary high school baseball coach with South Bend Clay who later became a coach with the South Bend White Sox, now called the Silver Hawks. In 1979 he was inducted into the Indiana Baseball Hall of Fame as the winningest coach in the state, with 646 victories, 289 defeats, and 4 ties. His number 4 was also retired by South Bend Clay.

Robin Roberts

Retired Number: 36 (Wilmington Blue Rocks)

The Blue Rocks retired this number symbolically for Roberts, who actually played for a previous team by the same name. After being signed by the Philadelphia Phillies in 1948, Robin was assigned to the Wilmington Blue Rocks of the Inter-State League and spent two months with the club, going 9–1 with a 2.06 earned run average and 121 strikeouts. He later went on to a legendary Hall of Fame career with the Phillies. On June 23, 1998, he became the first member of the Blue Rocks Hall of Fame and had his number retired. The number 36 is the number he wore with — and also had retired by — Philadelphia.

Jackie Robinson

Retired Number: 42 (All teams affiliated with Major League Baseball; Nashua Pride)

The number 42 that Robinson wore with the Brooklyn Dodgers was retired by Major League Baseball in 1997 in celebration of the fiftieth anniversary of Jackie's breaking the color barrier. That retirement also extended to the minor league affiliates of all major league clubs. The Nashua Pride, a team in the independent Atlantic League, also retired it.

Joe Rudi

Retired Number: 26 (Modesto A's)

Rudi played for Modesto in 1966, when the team was called the Modesto Reds, and hit .297 with 24 home runs, 85 runs batted in, 113 hits, 19 doubles, and 4 triples. He and some of his teammates, such as Reggie Jackson and Rollie Fingers, went on to create the Oakland Athletics dynasty of the early 1970s.

F. P. Santangelo

Retired Number: 31 (Ottawa Lynx)

Santangelo played for the Lynx from 1993–95 and for two games in 1998. In 1993 he hit .274 with 21 doubles and 18 stolen bases, and set an all-time club record by scoring 86 runs in a season. The following year he hit .252 with 28 doubles, and batted .255 in 1995. He began his major league career that same year with the Montreal Expos.

Hank Sauer

Retired Number: 9 (Syracuse SkyChiefs)

This number was retired symbolically. The SkyChiefs were previously called the Syracuse Chiefs, and Sauer played for a previous team by that same name. The "Chief of Chiefs," as he was known, played in Syracuse from 1942–43 and from 1946–47. In 1947 Sauer hit .336 with a franchise-high 50 home runs and 141 runs batted in en route to being named the Minor League Player of the Year. He later had a successful major league career and became the National League Most Valuable Player in 1952 while with the Chicago Cubs. On July 25, 1998, he had his number retired by Syracuse and became one of the first inductees into the Syracuse Baseball Wall of Fame. He was eventually named to Syracuse Baseball's All-Millennium Team, and the restaurant at P & C Stadium, the home of the SkyChiefs, was named The Hank Sauer Room. Hank passed away on August 24, 2001.

Mike Schmidt

Retired Number: 24 (Reading Phillies)

Schmidt had his number retired for what he accomplished after leaving Reading, when he embarked on a Hall of Fame career with the Philadelphia

Phillies. Mike played for Reading in 1971 and batted only .211 with 8 home runs and 31 runs batted in. After establishing his credentials in Philadelphia, however, he was later selected as the All-Time Greatest Player to have passed through Reading. The Philadelphia Phillies have also retired his number 20.

Morrie Silver and the Original Shareholders of the Rochester Red Wings

Retired Number: 8222 (Rochester Red Wings)

This is a symbolic retirement if ever there was one. The Red Wings were an affiliate of the St. Louis Cardinals when, in October of 1956, the parent club decided to fold the team. Morrie Silver, the Red Wings' former president and general manager, took action and organized a stock drive to try to establish community ownership of the franchise and save the team. Within a 72-day period, 8222 fans responded and successfully purchased the club, establishing Rochester Community Baseball Inc. The retired number represents those fans. Red Wing Stadium was renamed in Silver's honor in 1968, and Morrie continued as the team's majority stockholder until he passed away in 1974.

Bill Slack

Retired Number: 37 (Winston-Salem Warthogs)

The Warthogs retired this number for the winningest manager in Carolina League history. Slack was a resident of Winston-Salem who managed the team for 13 years off and on, taking the helm from 1963–68, 1970, 1973–74, 1978–79, and 1983–84. The club was called the Winston-Salem Red Sox during all of that time until 1984, when it was renamed the Winston-Salem Spirits. Slack won 926 games against 880 defeats, and won league championships in 1964, 1973, and 1979. He was named the Carolina League Manager of the Year in 1964 and 1979, and became a part-owner of the team in the 1970s.

John Stearns

Retired Number: 33 (Princeton Devil Rays)

This four-time major league All-Star catcher became manager of the Princeton minor league franchise, which in 1994 was called the Princeton

Reds. Stearns guided the club to the 1994 Appalachian League championship and was named the league's Manager of the Year. He later became a major league coach and then a scout.

Kirk Taylor

Retired Number: 17 (Johnstown Johnnies)

Outfielder Kirk Taylor was the Frontier League's Most Valuable Player in 2001 when he hit .350 with 17 home runs and 72 runs batted in while leading the league with a .607 slugging percentage and 45 extra-base hits. He was also the Most Valuable Player in the league's 2001 All-Star Game, and retired as the all-time leader with 404 hits (since broken). He was second in the league with 64 career home runs, and when he reached the league's age limit, became a manager with the Johnnies. The Johnnies are now the Florence Freedom, and the team no longer honors this number in Florence.

Wayne Terwilliger

Retired Number: 5 (St. Paul Saints)

Terwilliger originally played for a previous team that was also called the St. Paul Saints, and which was an affiliate of the Brooklyn Dodgers, in 1952, when he hit .312. After playing parts of nine seasons in the major leagues, Wayne became a major league coach and eventually spent eight seasons as a coach with the current St. Paul Saints beginning in 1995. His number was retired on September 2, 2002, on what St. Paul Mayor Randy Kelly proclaimed as "Wayne Terwilliger Day." Before the Saints played to a 4–2 victory over the Sioux City Explorers, Wayne, who was preparing to move to Texas, was presented cowboy boots, a 10-gallon hat, and a personally engraved belt buckle. The team also named its Most Valuable Player Award after him.

Brian Tollberg

Retired Number: 22 (Chillicothe Paints)

This pitcher was the first Paints player to reach the major leagues when he debuted with the San Diego Padres. He had the Frontier League's Pitcher of the Year Award named for him.

Bubba Trammell

Retired Number: 22 (Jamestown Jammers)

Trammell started his professional career with Jamestown in 1994 when he hit .298 with 5 home runs, 41 runs batted in, and 18 doubles before embarking on a solid major league career.

Joe Urso

Retired Number: 7 (Lake Elsinore Storm)

This second baseman played parts of four seasons with the Storm, from 1994–97. Urso left as the team's all-time leader with 326 games played, 1213 at-bats, 221 runs scored, 353 hits, 93 doubles, 146 runs batted in, and 187 bases on balls. He then served as the Storm's hitting coach during the 1997 and 1998 seasons, and eventually became a minor league manager. His number was retired on "Joe Urso Day" on May 30, 1999.

Don Werner

Retired Number: 10 (Idaho Falls Padres)

This former major league catcher became the manager of the Idaho Falls Padres for six seasons. Werner was at the helm from 1996 through 2000 and again in 2002. His record was 257–152, and he made the playoffs four straight years and won two Pioneer League championships. He was also a greatly respected citizen in the Idaho Falls community.

David Williams

Retired Number: 36 (Williamsport Crosscutters)

Williams became the first Williamsport Crosscutter to reach the major leagues when he debuted with the Pittsburgh Pirates on June 25, 2001. He pitched for the Crosscutters in 1999 and went 4–2 with a 2.56 earned run average.

Team-by-Team List

Following is a team-by-team list of retired uniform numbers for every minor league team. An asterisk (*) indicates that the number was retired symbolically and was never actually worn by the person for whom it was retired.

Aberdeen IronBirds
(New York-Penn League)
42: Jackie Robinson*

Adirondack Lumberjacks[1]
50: Darren Doucette

Akron Aeros
(Eastern League)
42: Jackie Robinson*

Albuquerque Dukes[2]
11: Tom Lasorda

Albuquerque Isotopes
(Pacific Coast League)
42: Jackie Robinson*

Alexandria Aces
(Central League)
None

---

1. The Adirondack Lumberjacks are now the Bangor Lumberjacks, and the team no longer honors this number in Bangor.
2. The Albuquerque Dukes are now the Portland Beavers, and the team no longer honors this number in Portland.

Allentown Ambassadors
(Northeast League)
24: Joe Bauldree

Altoona Curve
(Eastern League)
16: Adam Hyzdu
42: Jackie Robinson*

Amarillo Dillas
(Central League)
None

Arizona Athletics
(Arizona League)
42: Jackie Robinson*

Arizona Brewers
(Arizona League)
42: Jackie Robinson*

Arizona Giants
(Arizona League)
42: Jackie Robinson*

Arizona Rangers
(Arizona League)
42: Jackie Robinson*

Arizona Royals
(Arizona League)
42: Jackie Robinson*

Arizona Royals Rookie Advanced
(Arizona League)
42: Jackie Robinson*

Arkansas Travelers
(Texas League)
42: Jackie Robinson*

Asheville Tourists
(South Atlantic League)
42: Jackie Robinson*

Atlantic City Surf
(Atlantic League)
None

Auburn Doubledays
(New York-Penn League)
42: Jackie Robinson*

Augusta GreenJackets
(South Atlantic League)
42: Jackie Robinson*

Bakersfield Blaze
(California League)
42: Jackie Robinson*

Bangor Lumberjacks
(Northeast League)
None

Batavia Muckdogs
(New York–Penn League)
42: Jackie Robinson*

Baton Rouge River Bats
(Southeastern League)
None

Battle Creek Yankees
(Midwest League)
42: Jackie Robinson*

Beloit Snappers
(Midwest League)
42: Jackie Robinson*

Berkshire Black Bears
(Northeast League)
None

Billings Mustangs
(Pioneer League)
42: Jackie Robinson*

Binghamton Mets
(Eastern League)
42: Jackie Robinson*

Birmingham Barons
(Southern League)
42: Jackie Robinson*

Bisbee-Douglas Copper Kings
(Arizona-Mexico League)
None

Bluefield Orioles
(Appalachian League)
42: Jackie Robinson*

Boise Hawks
(Northwest League)
4: Mal Fichman[3]
42: Jackie Robinson*

Bowie Baysox
(Eastern League)
42: Jackie Robinson*

---

3. For reasons unknown the Hawks have begun to reissue this number in recent years and no longer honor it.

Bradenton Pirates
(Gulf Coast League)
42: Jackie Robinson*

Brevard County Manatees
(Florida State League)
5: Carl Barger*
42: Jackie Robinson*

Bridgeport Bluefish
(Atlantic League)
None

Bristol White Sox
(Appalachian League)
42: Jackie Robinson*

Brockton Rox
(Northeast League)
49: Rocky Marciano*

Brooklyn Cyclones
(New York-Penn League)
14: Gil Hodges*
42: Jackie Robinson*

Buffalo Bisons
(International League)
6: Ollie Carnegie*
25: Luke Easter*

30: Jeff Manto
42: Jackie Robinson*

Burlington Bees
(Midwest League)
42: Jackie Robinson*

Burlington Indians
(Appalachian League)
42: Jackie Robinson*

Camden Riversharks
(Atlantic League)
None

Cananea Miners
(Arizona-Mexico League)
None

Capital City Bombers
(South Atlantic League)
4: Tim Bishop
42: Jackie Robinson*

Carolina Mudcats
(Southern League)
42: Jackie Robinson*

Casper Rockies
(Pioneer League)
42: Jackie Robinson*

Cedar Rapids Kernels
(Midwest League)
42: Jackie Robinson*

Charleston Alley Cats
(South Atlantic League)
42: Jackie Robinson*

Charleston RiverDogs
(South Atlantic League)
42: Jackie Robinson*

Charlotte Knights
(International League)
42: Jackie Robinson*

Chattanooga Lookouts
(Southern League)
42: Jackie Robinson*

Chillicothe Paints
(Frontier League)
20: Gator McBride

22: Brian Tollberg
27: Mitch House
30: Scott Pinoni
50: Roger Hanners

Clearwater Phillies
(Florida State League)
42: Jackie Robinson*

Clinton LumberKings
(Midwest League)
42: Jackie Robinson*

Coastal Bend Aviators
(Central League)
None

Colorado Springs Sky Sox
(Pacific Coast League)
4: Trenidad Hubbard
9: Brad Mills
11: Luis Medina
21: Ryan Hawblitzel
31: Alan Cockrell
41: Charlie Manuel
42: Jackie Robinson*

Columbus Clippers
(International League)
33: Marshall Brant
42: Jackie Robinson*

Cook County Cheetahs
(Frontier League)
None

Danville Braves
(Appalachian League)
42: Jackie Robinson*

Dayton Dragons
(Midwest League)
42: Jackie Robinson*

Daytona Cubs
(Florida State League)
42: Jackie Robinson*

Delmarva Shorebirds
(South Atlantic League)
42: Jackie Robinson*

Dunedin Blue Jays
(Florida State League)
42: Jackie Robinson*

Durham Bulls
(International League)
18: Joe Morgan
42: Jackie Robinson*

Edinburg Roadrunners
(Central League)
None

Edmonton Trappers
(Pacific Coast League)
42: Jackie Robinson*

El Paso Diablos
(Texas League)
42: Jackie Robinson*

Elizabethton Twins
(Appalachian League)
42: Jackie Robinson*

Elmira Pioneers
(Northeast League)
None

Erie SeaWolves
(Eastern League)
5: Sam Jethroe*
42: Jackie Robinson*

Eugene Emeralds
(Northwest League)
42: Jackie Robinson*

Evansville Otters
(Frontier League)
None

Everett AquaSox
(Northwest League)
42: Jackie Robinson*

Fargo-Moorhead RedHawks
(Northern League)
8: Roger Maris*

Florence Freedom
(Frontier League)
None

Fort Myers Miracle
(Florida State League)
42: Jackie Robinson*

Fort Wayne Wizards
(Midwest League)
42: Jackie Robinson*

Fort Worth Cats
(Central League)
10: Bobby Bragan*

Frederick Keys
(Carolina League)
42: Jackie Robinson*

Fresno Grizzlies
(Pacific Coast League)
42: Jackie Robinson*

Frisco RoughRiders
(Texas League)
42: Jackie Robinson*

Gary SouthShore RailCats
(Northern League)
None

Gateway Grizzlies
(Frontier League)
None

Great Falls White Sox
(Pioneer League)
42: Jackie Robinson*

Greensboro Bats
(South Atlantic League)
42: Jackie Robinson*

Greenville Braves
(Southern League)
42: Jackie Robinson*

Gulf Coast Braves
(Gulf Coast League)
42: Jackie Robinson*

Gulf Coast Dodgers
(Gulf Coast League)
42: Jackie Robinson*

Gulf Coast Expos
(Gulf Coast League)
42: Jackie Robinson*

Gulf Coast Marlins
(Gulf Coast League)
42: Jackie Robinson*

Gulf Coast Orioles
(Gulf Coast League)
42: Jackie Robinson*

Gulf Coast Phillies
(Gulf Coast League)
42: Jackie Robinson*

Gulf Coast Red Sox
(Gulf Coast League)
42: Jackie Robinson*

Gulf Coast Reds
(Gulf Coast League)
42: Jackie Robinson*

Gulf Coast Tigers
(Gulf Coast League)
42: Jackie Robinson*

Gulf Coast Twins
(Gulf Coast League)
42: Jackie Robinson*

Gulf Coast Yankees
(Gulf Coast League)
42: Jackie Robinson*

Hagerstown Suns
(South Atlantic League)
42: Jackie Robinson*

Harrisburg Senators
(Eastern League)
42: Jackie Robinson*

Helena Brewers
(Pioneer League)
42: Jackie Robinson*

Hickory Crawdads

(South Atlantic League)
42: Jackie Robinson*

High Desert Mavericks

(California League)
42: Jackie Robinson*

Houma Hawks

(Southeastern League)
None

Hudson Valley Renegades

(New York-Penn League)
42: Jackie Robinson*
45: Kevin Brown

Huntsville Stars

(Southern League)
42: Jackie Robinson*
44: Jose Canseco

Idaho Falls Padres

(Pioneer League)
10: Don Werner
42: Jackie Robinson*

Indianapolis Indians

(International League)
42: Jackie Robinson*

Inland Empire 66ers

(California League)
24: Ken Griffey, Jr.*
25: Rich Dauer*
42: Jackie Robinson*
43: Chin-Feng Chen

Iowa Cubs

(Pacific Coast League)
42: Jackie Robinson*

Jackson Senators

(Central League)
None

Jacksonville Suns

(Southern League)
42: Jackie Robinson*

Jamestown Jammers

(New York-Penn League)
22: Bubba Trammell
42: Jackie Robinson*

Johnson City Cardinals[4]
(Appalachian League)
42: Jackie Robinson*

Johnstown Johnnies[5]
17: Kirk Taylor

Joliet JackHammers
(Northern League)
None

Jupiter Hammerheads
(Florida State League)
42: Jackie Robinson*

Kalamazoo Kings
(Frontier League)
None

Kane County Cougars
(Midwest League)
35: Charles Johnson
42: Jackie Robinson*

Kannapolis Intimidators
(South Atlantic League)
3: Dale Earnhardt*
42: Jackie Robinson*

Kansas City T-Bones
(Northern League)
None

Kenosha Mammoths
(Frontier League)
None

Kingsport Mets
(Appalachian League)
42: Jackie Robinson*

Kinston Indians
(Carolina League)
42: Jackie Robinson*

Lake County Captains
(South Atlantic League)
42: Jackie Robinson*

---

4. The Johnson City Cardinals claim to have retired the number of Bobby Murcer, who played for the team in 1964 when it was called the Johnson City Yankees and won the Appalachian League championship. While the number was purportedly retired in 1991, no one with the Cardinals today can confirm the retirement or even remember what number Murcer wore.

5. The Johnstown Johnnies are now the Florence Freedom, and the team no longer honors this number in Florence.

Lake Elsinore Storm
(California League)
7: Joe Urso
42: Jackie Robinson*

Lakeland Tigers
(Florida State League)
42: Jackie Robinson*

Lakewood BlueClaws
(South Atlantic League)
42: Jackie Robinson*

Lancaster JetHawks
(California League)
42: Jackie Robinson*

Lansing Lugnuts
(Midwest League)
42: Jackie Robinson*

Las Vegas 51s
(Pacific Coast League)
42: Jackie Robinson*

Lexington Legends
(South Atlantic League)
42: Jackie Robinson*

Lincoln Saltdogs
(Northern League)
None

London Werewolves[6]
27: Brett Gray

Long Island Ducks
(Atlantic League)
None

Louisville Bats
(International League)
42: Jackie Robinson*

Lowell Spinners
(New York–Penn League)
42: Jackie Robinson*

Lynchburg Hillcats
(Carolina League)
26: Jim Bibby
42: Jackie Robinson*

Macon Peaches
(Southeastern League)
None

6. The London Werewolves are now the Mid-Missouri Mavericks, and the team no longer honors this number in Missouri.

Mahoning Valley Scrappers
(New York-Penn League)
42: Jackie Robinson*

Martinsville Astros
(Appalachian League)
42: Jackie Robinson*

Memphis Redbirds
(Pacific Coast League)
42: Jackie Robinson*

Mesa Angels
(Arizona League)
42: Jackie Robinson*

Mesa Cubs
(Arizona League)
42: Jackie Robinson*

Mid-Missouri Mavericks
(Frontier League)
None

Midland RockHounds
(Texas League)
42: Jackie Robinson*

Missoula Osprey
(Pioneer League)
42: Jackie Robinson*

Mobile BayBears
(Southern League)
42: Jackie Robinson*
44: Hank Aaron*

Modesto A's
(California League)
1: Fred Anderson*
26: Joe Rudi
42: Jackie Robinson*

Montgomery Wings
(Southeastern League)
None

Myrtle Beach Pelicans
(Carolina League)
2: Rafael Furcal
42: Jackie Robinson*

Nashua Pride
(Atlantic League)
36: Don Newcombe*
39: Roy Campanella*
42: Jackie Robinson*

Nashville Sounds
(Pacific Coast League)
00: Skeeter Barnes
18: Don Mattingly
42: Jackie Robinson*

New Britain Rock Cats
(Eastern League)
42: Jackie Robinson*

New Haven Ravens
(Eastern League)
7: Lou List
42: Jackie Robinson*

New Jersey Cardinals
(New York-Penn League)
34: Hub Kittle
42: Jackie Robinson*

New Jersey Jackals
(Northeast League)
8: Yogi Berra*

New Orleans Zephyrs
(Pacific Coast League)
42: Jackie Robinson*

Newark Bears
(Atlantic League)
None

Nogales Charros
(Arizona-Mexico League)
None

Norfolk Tides
(International League)
42: Jackie Robinson*

North Shore Spirit
(Northeast League)
None

Norwich Navigators
(Eastern League)
42: Jackie Robinson*

Ogden Raptors
(Pioneer League)
13: Willy Ambos
40: Mark Hindy
42: Jackie Robinson*

Oklahoma RedHawks
(Pacific Coast League)
42: Jackie Robinson*

Omaha Royals
(Pacific Coast League)
42: Jackie Robinson*

Oneonta Tigers

(New York-Penn League)
42: Jackie Robinson*

Orlando Rays

(Southern League)
26: Fans of the Orlando Rays*7
42: Jackie Robinson*

Ottawa Lynx

(International League)
31: F. P. Santangelo
42: Jackie Robinson*

Palm Beach Cardinals

(Florida State League)
42: Jackie Robinson*

Pawtucket Red Sox

(International League)
42: Jackie Robinson*

Pennsylvania Road Warriors

(Atlantic League)
None

Pensacola Pelicans

(Southeastern League)
None

Peoria Chiefs

(Midwest League)
17: Mark Grace
42: Jackie Robinson*

Peoria Mariners

(Arizona League)
42: Jackie Robinson*

Portland Beavers

(Pacific Coast League)
42: Jackie Robinson*

Portland Sea Dogs

(Eastern League)
42: Jackie Robinson*

Potomac Cannons

(Carolina League)
42: Jackie Robinson*

Princeton Devil Rays

(Appalachian League)
33: John Stearns

---

7. For reasons unknown, the Rays no longer honor this number.

34: Brad Kelley
42: Jackie Robinson*

Provo Angels
(Pioneer League)
42: Jackie Robinson*

Pulaski Blue Jays
(Appalachian League)
42: Jackie Robinson*

Quad City River Bandits
(Midwest League)
42: Jackie Robinson*

Quebec Capitales
(Northeast League)
None

Rancho Cucamonga Quakes
(California League)
20: Matt LaChappa
42: Jackie Robinson*

Reading Phillies
(Eastern League)
24: Mike Schmidt
42: Jackie Robinson*

Richmond Braves
(International League)
23: Tommie Aaron
42: Jackie Robinson*

Richmond Roosters
(Frontier League)
16: Morgan Burkhart

Rio Grande Valley WhiteWings
(Central League)
None

River City Rascals
(Frontier League)
22: Jack Clark

Rochester Red Wings
(International League)
26: Joe Altobelli
36: Luke Easter
42: Jackie Robinson*
8222: Morrie Silver and the original shareholders of the Rochester Red Wings*

Rockford RiverHawks
(Frontier League)
None

Rome Braves
(South Atlantic League)
42: Jackie Robinson*

Round Rock Express
(Texas League)
42: Jackie Robinson*

Sacramento River Cats
(Pacific Coast League)
42: Jackie Robinson*

St. Lucie Mets
(Florida State League)
6: Brian Cole
42: Jackie Robinson*

St. Paul Saints
(Northern League)
5: Wayne Terwilliger

Salem Avalanche
(Carolina League)
42: Jackie Robinson*

Salem-Keizer Volcanoes
(Northwest League)
42: Jackie Robinson*

Salt Lake Stingers
(Pacific Coast League)
42: Jackie Robinson*

San Angelo Colts
(Central League)
None

San Antonio Missions
(Texas League)
42: Jackie Robinson*

San Jose Giants
(California League)
42: Jackie Robinson*

Sarasota Red Sox
(Florida State League)
42: Jackie Robinson*

Savannah Sand Gnats
(South Atlantic League)
42: Jackie Robinson*

Schaumburg Flyers
(Northern League)
None

Scranton/Wilkes-Barre Red Barons
(International League)
14: Greg Legg
42: Jackie Robinson*

Shreveport Sports
(Central League)
None

Sioux City Explorers
(Northern League)
None

Sioux Falls Canaries
(Northern League)
29: Matt Erwin

Somerset Patriots
(Atlantic League)
None

South Bend Silver Hawks
(Midwest League)
4: Jim Reinebold
12: Rick Patterson
42: Jackie Robinson*

South Georgia Waves
(South Atlantic League)
42: Jackie Robinson*

Southeastern Cloverleafs
(Southeastern League)
None

Spokane Indians
(Northwest League)
5: George Brett*
42: Jackie Robinson*

Springfield/Ozark Mountain Ducks
(Central League)
None

Staten Island Yankees
(New York-Penn League)
42: Jackie Robinson*

Stockton Ports
(California League)
42: Jackie Robinson*

Syracuse SkyChiefs
(International League)
9: Hank Sauer*
42: Jackie Robinson*

Tacoma Rainiers
(Pacific Coast League)
42: Jackie Robinson*

Tampa Yankees
(Florida State League)
42: Jackie Robinson*

Tecate Brewers
(Arizona-Mexico League)
None

Tennessee Smokies
(Southern League)
42: Jackie Robinson*

Toledo Mud Hens
(International League)
1: Gene Cook*
42: Jackie Robinson*

Trenton Thunder
(Eastern League)
 5: Nomar Garciaparra
33: Tony Clark
42: Jackie Robinson*

Tri-City Dust Devils
(Northwest League)
42: Jackie Robinson*

Tri-City ValleyCats
(New York-Penn League)
42: Jackie Robinson*

Tucson Sidewinders
(Pacific Coast League)
42: Jackie Robinson*

Tulsa Drillers
(Texas League)
42: Jackie Robinson*

Vancouver Canadians
(Northwest League)
42: Jackie Robinson*

Vermont Expos
(New York-Penn League)
42: Jackie Robinson*

Vero Beach Dodgers
(Florida State League)
42: Jackie Robinson*

Visalia Oaks
(California League)
42: Jackie Robinson*

Washington Wild Things
(Frontier League)
None

West Michigan Whitecaps
(Midwest League)
42: Jackie Robinson*

West Tenn Diamond Jaxx
(Southern League)
42: Jackie Robinson*

Wichita Wranglers
(Texas League)
42: Jackie Robinson*

Williamsport Crosscutters
(New York-Penn League)
36: David Williams
41: Jeremi Gonzalez*
42: Jackie Robinson*
59: Dave Bresnahan*

Wilmington Blue Rocks
(Carolina League)
36: Robin Roberts*
42: Jackie Robinson*

Winnipeg Goldeyes
(Northern League)
5: Brian Duva

Winston-Salem Warthogs
(Carolina League)
37: Bill Slack
42: Jackie Robinson*

Wisconsin Timber Rattlers
(Midwest League)
42: Jackie Robinson*

Yakima Bears
(Northwest League)
42: Jackie Robinson*

Numerical List

Following is a numerical list of retired uniform numbers for every minor league team. An asterisk (*) indicates that the number was retired symbolically and was never actually worn by the person for whom it was retired.

00: Skeeter Barnes (Nashville Sounds)

1: Fred Anderson (Modesto A's*)
   Gene Cook (Toledo Mud Hens*)

2: Rafael Furcal (Myrtle Beach Pelicans)

3: Dale Earnhardt (Kannapolis Intimidators*)

4: Tim Bishop (Capital City Bombers)
   Mal Fichman (Boise Hawks)
   Trenidad Hubbard (Colorado Springs Sky Sox)
   Jim Reinebold (South Bend Silver Hawks)

5: Carl Barger (Brevard County Manatees*)
   George Brett (Spokane Indians*)
   Brian Duva (Winnipeg Goldeyes)
   Nomar Garciaparra (Trenton Thunder)
   Sam Jethroe (Erie SeaWolves*)
   Wayne Terwilliger (St. Paul Saints)

II. Minor Leagues

6: Ollie Carnegie (Buffalo Bisons*)
   Brian Cole (St. Lucie Mets)

7: Lou List (New Haven Ravens)
   Joe Urso (Lake Elsinore Storm)

8: Yogi Berra (New Jersey Jackals*)
   Roger Maris (Fargo-Moorhead RedHawks*)

9: Brad Mills (Colorado Springs Sky Sox)
   Hank Sauer (Syracuse SkyChiefs*)

10: Bobby Bragan (Fort Worth Cats*)
    Don Werner (Idaho Falls Padres)

11: Tom Lasorda (Albuquerque Dukes)
    Luis Medina (Colorado Springs Sky Sox)

12: Rick Patterson (South Bend Silver Hawks)

13: Willy Ambos (Ogden Raptors)

14: Gil Hodges (Brooklyn Cyclones*)
    Greg Legg (Scranton/Wilkes-Barre Red Barons)

16: Morgan Burkhart (Richmond Roosters)
    Adam Hyzdu (Altoona Curve)

17: Mark Grace (Peoria Chiefs)
    Kirk Taylor (Johnstown Johnnies)

18: Don Mattingly (Nashville Sounds)
    Joe Morgan (Durham Bulls)

20: Matt LaChappa (Rancho Cucamonga Quakes)
    Gator McBride (Chillicothe Paints)

21: Ryan Hawblitzel (Colorado Springs Sky Sox)

22: Jack Clark (River City Rascals)
    Brian Tollberg (Chillicothe Paints)
    Bubba Trammell (Jamestown Jammers)

23: Tommie Aaron (Richmond Braves)

24: Joe Bauldree (Allentown Ambassadors)
    Ken Griffey, Jr. (Inland Empire 66ers*)
    Mike Schmidt (Reading Phillies)

25: Rich Dauer (Inland Empire 66ers*)
    Luke Easter (Buffalo Bisons*)

26: Joe Altobelli (Rochester Red Wings)
    Jim Bibby (Lynchburg Hillcats)
    Fans of the Orlando Rays (Orlando Rays*)
    Joe Rudi (Modesto A's)

27: Brett Gray (London Werewolves)
    Mitch House (Chillicothe Paints)

29: Matt Erwin (Sioux Falls Canaries)

30: Jeff Manto (Buffalo Bisons)
    Scott Pinoni (Chillicothe Paints)

31: Alan Cockrell (Colorado Springs Sky Sox)
    F. P. Santangelo (Ottawa Lynx)

33: Marshall Brant (Columbus Clippers)
    Tony Clark (Trenton Thunder)
    John Stearns (Princeton Devil Rays)

34: Brad Kelley (Princeton Devil Rays)
    Hub Kittle (New Jersey Cardinals)

35: Charles Johnson (Kane County Cougars)

36: Luke Easter (Rochester Red Wings)
    Don Newcombe (Nashua Pride*)
    Robin Roberts (Wilmington Blue Rocks*)
    David Williams (Williamsport Crosscutters)

37: Bill Slack (Winston-Salem Warthogs)

39: Roy Campanella (Nashua Pride*)

II. Minor Leagues

40: Mark Hindy (Ogden Raptors)

41: Jeremi Gonzalez (Williamsport Crosscutters*)
Charlie Manuel (Colorado Springs Sky Sox)

42: Jackie Robinson
(All team affiliated with Major League Baseball,* Nashua Pride*)

43: Chin-Feng Chen (Inland Empire 66ers)

44: Hank Aaron (Mobile BayBears*)
Jose Canseco (Huntsville Stars)

45: Kevin Brown (Hudson Valley Renegades)

49: Rocky Marciano (Brockton Rox*)

50: Darren Doucette (Adirondack Lumberjacks)
Roger Hanners (Chillicothe Paints)

59: Dave Bresnahan (Williamsport Crosscutters*)

8222: Morrie Silver and the original shareholders of the Rochester Red Wings (Rochester Red Wings*)

Bibliography

American League of Professional Baseball Clubs. *American League 1994 Red Book.* New York: Sporting News Publishing, 1994.
Baseball Almanac Web site. http://baseball-almanac.com.
Baseball-Reference.com Web site. http://www.baseball-reference.com.
Brucato, Thomas W. *Major League Champions 1871–2001.* Lanham, MD: Scarecrow Press, 2002.
_____. *Major Leagues.* Lanham, MD: Scarecrow Press, 2001.
Filichia, Peter. *Professional Baseball Franchises.* New York: Facts on File, 1993.
National Baseball Hall of Fame Web site. http://www.baseballhalloffame.org.
National League of Professional Baseball Clubs. *National League 1983 Green Book.* Sherman Oaks, CA: Alfred Publishing, 1983.
_____. *National League 1995 Green Book.* New York: Sporting News Publishing, 1995.
Nemec, David, Matthew D. Greenberger, Dan Schlossberg, Dick Johnson, and Mike Tully. *Players of Cooperstown: Baseball's Hall of Fame.* Lincolnwood, IL: Publications International, 1995.
Rathgeber, Bob. *Cincinnati Reds Media Fact Book, 1977 Edition.* Cincinnati: Cincinnati Reds, Inc., 1977.
Shatzkin, Mike, ed. *The Ballplayers.* New York: Arbor House, 1990.
Stang, Mark, and Linda Harkness. *Baseball By the Numbers.* Lanham, MD: Scarecrow Press, 1997.
Thorn, John, and Pete Palmer, eds. *Total Baseball,* 2nd edition. New York: Warner, 1991.
Wolff, Rick, editorial director. *The Baseball Encyclopedia,* 9th edition. New York: Macmillan, 1993.

Index

Aaron, Hank 3, 9–11, 39, 138–139, 151, 180, 221, 223, 225, 232, 235, 269, 280
Aaron, Tommie 11, 235, 272, 279
Abbott, Glenn 72
Aberdeen IronBirds 171, 258
Adams, Bobby 173
Adirondack Lumberjacks 242–243, 258, 280
Aircraft Workers Alliance 244
Akron Aeros 258
Albuquerque Dukes 249, 252, 258, 278
Albuquerque Isotopes 258
Alexander, Dale 82
Alexander, Grover Cleveland 2, 11–12, 41, 112, 203, 226, 228
Alexander, Pete *see* Alexander, Grover Cleveland
Alexander, Roger 10
Alexandria Aces 258
Allentown Ambassadors 237, 259, 279
Alston, Walter 13–14, 118, 225, 230
Altobelli, Joe 211, 235–236, 272, 279
Altoona Curve 247, 259, 278
Altrock, Nick 144
Alvarez, Wilson 23
Amarillo Dillas 259
Ambos, Willy 236, 270, 278
American League Umpires 2, 28, 37, 53–54, 65–66, 113, 116–117, 223, 225, 228–230
American Record Corporation 20
Amsterdam Rugmakers 118
amyotrophic lateral sclerosis (Lou Gehrig's Disease) 1, 81, 101

Anaheim Angels 19, 21, 45–46, 77, 79, 150–151, 167, 183, 223, 230–232, 244
Anaheim Stadium 38
Anderson, Fred 236, 269, 277
Anheuser, Eberhard 42
Anheuser-Busch 42–43
Anson, Cap 209
Aparicio, Luis 14–17, 76, 224, 230
Appling, Luke 16–18, 224, 229
Arizona Athletics 259
Arizona Brewers 259
Arizona Diamondbacks 221–223
Arizona Giants 259
Arizona Rangers 259
Arizona Royals 259
Arizona Royals Rookie Advanced 259
Arkansas Travelers 259
Armbrister, Ed 146
Ashburn, Richie 18–19, 226, 228
Asheville Tourists 259
Astrodome 90, 186, 249
Atlanta Braves 9–11, 33, 50, 62–63, 78, 84–85, 93, 118, 130–131, 149–150, 156–157, 166, 190, 196, 198–199, 217, 219, 223, 229, 231–232, 235, 238, 245
Atlanta Hawks 218
Atlantic City Surf 259
Auburn Doubledays 259
Augusta GreenJackets 259
Autry, Gene 19–21, 223, 231, 244
Autry Museum of Western Heritage 21
Averill, Earl 21–22, 59, 224, 229
Averill, Earl Douglas 22
Azcue, Joe 68

283

Baines, Harold 22–24, 224, 229
Baker Bowl 111, 209
Bakersfield Blaze 260
Baltimore Elite Giants 43, 86
Baltimore Orioles (American Association/National League) 139–140
Baltimore Orioles (American League 1901–02) 139–140
Baltimore Orioles (American League 1954–present) 3, 14–17, 21, 23–24, 29, 38, 45–47, 52, 67, 78, 94, 101, 103–104, 107, 116, 128, 143, 147, 150–151, 153, 158–159, 161–164, 169–170, 173–177, 187, 191, 199, 201, 210–211, 218, 223–224, 229, 231–232, 242
Baltimore Orioles (International League) 180
Bangor Lumberjacks 243, 258, 260
Banks, Ernie 24–26, 224, 230
Barger, Carl 26–27, 65, 224, 229, 236, 261, 277
Barlick, Al 27–28, 54, 113, 225, 229
Barnes, Skeeter 236–237, 270, 277
Barrow, Ed 208
Baseball America 243, 248
Batavia Muckdogs 260
Baton Rouge River Bats 260
Battle Creek Yankees 260
Bauer, Hank 210
Bauldree, Joe 237, 259, 279
Bavarian Brewery 42
Baylor University 122
Beattie, Jim 221
Bell, Cool Papa 25
Beloit Snappers 260
Bench, Johnny 28–30, 214, 224, 229
Berkshire Black Bears 260
Berra, Dale 32
Berra, Yogi 3, 30–32, 61, 66, 95, 106, 129, 201, 225, 229, 237, 270, 278
Bezdek, Hugo 209
Bibby, Jim 237, 268, 279
Big Red Machine 29, 146–147, 163
Billingham, Jack 10, 47, 146
Billings Mustangs 260
Billy the Marlin 26
Binghamton Mets 242, 260
Birmingham Barons 260
Birmingham Black Barons 134
Bisbee-Douglas Copper Kings 260
Bishop, Tim 237–238, 261, 277
Blue, Vida 72
Bluefield Orioles 260
Boggs, Wade 32–34, 227, 230

Boise Hawks 244, 260, 277
Boone, Bob 49
Boston Americans 140, 209
Boston Bees 201–202
Boston Braves 12, 21–22, 35, 66, 71, 120, 130, 132, 152, 180, 182, 197, 201–202, 248
Boston Red Sox 2, 14–15, 21, 24, 27, 32–35, 38–39, 46, 49–50, 54–57, 61, 65–68, 73–74, 84, 89, 95–96, 121–122, 125–127, 141, 147, 162–163, 168, 180–181, 188, 190, 192–193, 201, 211–212, 214–216, 219–221, 224, 228–231, 240, 245, 251
Boswell, Dave 128
Boudreau Boulevard 35
Boudreau, Lou 34–35, 224, 229
Bowie Baysox 260
Boyer, Clete 35
Boyer, Cloyd 35
Boyer, Ken 35–36, 226, 230
Bradenton Pirates 261
Bradley University 165
Bragan, Bobby 152, 238, 264, 278
Brant, Marshall 238, 262, 279
Bremigan, Nick 37, 223, 228
Bresnahan, Dave 238–239, 276, 280
Brett, Bobby 39
Brett, George 37–39, 45, 64, 225, 229, 239, 274, 277
Brett, Ken 39
Brevard County Manatees 236, 261, 277
Bridgehampton High School 219
Bridgeport Bluefish 261
Bristol White Sox 261
Brock, Lou 39–40, 94, 226, 231
Brockton Rox 250, 261, 280
Broglio, Ernie 39
Brooklyn Bridegrooms 210
Brooklyn Cyclones 247, 261, 278
Brooklyn Dodgers 3, 13–14, 27, 31, 43–44, 66, 69, 86, 92–93, 114–115, 117–118, 122–123, 128, 139, 142, 168–169, 178–180, 182, 193, 195–196, 201–203, 238, 240, 247, 252–253, 256
Brooklyn Robins 181, 201
Brooklyn Superbas 139–140
Brown, Kevin 239, 266, 280
Brown, Marty 237
Brush, John T. 131
Budweiser 42–43
Buffalo Bisons (American Association/International League) 240, 243, 250, 261, 278–279

Index

Buffalo Bisons (Eastern League/International League) 28, 240, 243–244
Buford, Don 15
Bumbry, Al 45
Bunning, Jim 12, 40–42, 112, 165, 226, 230
Burdette, Lew 197
Burkhart, Morgan 239–240, 253, 272, 278
Burlington Bees 261
Burlington Indians 261
Busch, Adolphus 42
Busch, Adolphus, III 43
Busch, August A. 42
Busch, August A., Jr. 3, 42–43, 226, 232
Busch, August A., III 43
Busch (beer) 43
Busch Stadium (first) 43
Busch Stadium (second) 43
Buttram, Pat 20

Caldwell, Mike 138
California Angels 19, 21, 38, 45–46, 70, 72, 77–78, 89, 97, 103–104, 120–121, 167–168, 176–177, 183–184, 203–204, 211, 218, 222, 244
Callahan, Nixey 209
Camden Riversharks 261
Camnitz, Howie 132
Campanella, Roy 43–44, 93, 180, 225, 232, 240, 269, 279
Canadian Baseball Hall of Fame 246
Cananea Miners 261
Canseco, Jose 240, 266, 280
Canton Coyotes 246
Cantor Fitzgerald 247
Capital City Bombers 237–238, 261, 277
Carew, Rod 3, 45–46, 223, 225, 231
Carey, Andy 124
Carey, Max 202, 206
Carl Barger Baseball Complex 27
Carl Barger Player Development Person of the Year Award 27
Carlton, Steve 46–48, 191, 226, 231
Carnegie, Ollie 240, 261, 278
Carolina Mudcats 261
Carrasco, Hector 171
Carter, Gary 48–49, 225, 229
Casper Rockies 262
CBS 20
CBS Radio Network 20
Cedar Rapids Kernels 262
Cepeda, Orlando 49–51, 226, 231
Cepeda, Perucho 50

Chapman, Ben 68
Charleston Alley Cats 262
Charleston RiverDogs 262
Charlotte Knights 262
Chattanooga Lookouts 262
Chen, Chin-Feng 241, 266, 280
Chicago Cubs 11–12, 18, 22, 24–25, 34–35, 39–40, 56–60, 62, 83, 88, 91–92, 109–111, 115–116, 140, 153–154, 156, 160, 173–174, 181, 184–186, 198, 205, 207, 213–214, 224, 230–231, 245, 248, 254
Chicago White Sox 3, 13–18, 22–24, 31, 35–36, 46, 48, 53, 59, 61, 65–67, 70, 73–74, 76–78, 88, 93–95, 114, 120–123, 126, 141–145, 151, 164–165, 171, 184–185, 190–192, 220, 224, 228–230, 232
Chillicothe Paints 245–247, 251–253, 256, 262, 278–280
Chunichi Dragons 67
Cincinnati Redlegs 18, 114, 173, 176
Cincinnati Reds 10, 14, 22, 24, 28–29, 40, 47, 62, 72–73, 75, 83, 88, 91–92, 101–103, 113–115, 118–119, 127–129, 131–132, 146–148, 153, 162–164, 175–177, 186, 190–191, 199–200, 211, 214, 217, 221, 224, 228–231, 252
Clark, Jack 241, 272, 278
Clark, Tony 241, 275, 279
Clearwater Phillies 262
Clem, Hal 41
Clemens, Doug 39
Clemente, Roberto 51–52, 226, 231
Cleveland Indians 16–17, 21–24, 33–35, 46, 48, 66–67, 70, 88, 91–92, 94–97, 109–110, 120–121, 126–128, 135, 143, 145, 150–151, 155–157, 176–177, 190, 197–198, 202, 204, 218–219, 222, 224, 229–231, 238–239, 243, 250–251
Clinton LumberKings 262
Coastal Bend Aviators 262
Cobb, Ty 45, 201
Cochrane, Mickey 123
Cockrell, Alan 241–242, 262, 279
Colavito, Rocky 108
Cole, Brian 242, 273, 278
Coleman, Bob 202
College World Series 218
Collins, Eddie 40
Collins, Ripper 160
Colorado Rockies 149–150, 224
Colorado Silver Bullets 157
Colorado Springs Sky Sox 5, 241–242, 246–247, 250–252, 262, 277–280
Columbia Records 20

Columbus Clippers 238, 262, 279
Comiskey Park 70, 215
Concepcion, Dave 147
Conlan, Jocko 28, 53–54, 113, 225, 228
Cook, Gene 242, 275, 277
Cook County Cheetahs 263
Cosgrove, Mike 217
Country Music Hall of Fame 20
Craft, Harry 35
Cramer, Doc 83
Creighton University 84
Cronin, Joe 54–55, 99, 215, 224, 229
Crosley Field 10
Cruz, Hector 55
Cruz, Jose 55–57, 224, 231
Cruz, Jose, Jr. 56
Cruz, Tommy 55
Cuban Giants 112
Cunningham, Joe 143

D-Day 30
Daniel, Jim 249
Danville Braves 263
Dark, Alvin 17
Dartmouth College 242
Dauer, Rich 242, 266, 279
Dawson, Andre 3, 56–58, 200, 225, 230
Dayton Dragons 263
Daytona Cubs 263
Dean, Dizzy 58–59, 226, 230
Dean, Paul "Daffy" 58–59
Delmarva Shorebirds 263
Derringer, Paul 59
Detroit Tigers 16–17, 21–22, 40–41, 55, 59, 66–67, 80, 82–83, 85, 87–88, 94–95, 97–99, 101–102, 104, 106–107, 111, 120, 122–123, 127–128, 130–131, 151, 155–156, 161, 164–165, 170, 188, 194, 200–201, 209–211, 220, 224, 228–231, 241, 249
Dick Howser Trophy 97
Dickey, Bill 3, 32, 60–61, 95, 201, 225, 229
Dickey, George 61
Dierker, Larry 61–63, 225, 232
Dierker, Rick 63
DiMaggio, Dom 65
DiMaggio, Joe 27, 38, 63–65, 124, 145, 173, 175, 215, 218, 225, 229, 236
DiMaggio, Vince 65
DiMuro, Lou 65–66, 223, 230
DiMuro, Mike 65
DiMuro, Ray 65
Dobson, Chuck 161

Doby, Larry 66–67, 121, 224, 230
Dodger Stadium 199
Doerr, Bobby 67–68, 224, 228
Donovan, Dick 165
Doucette, Darren 242–243, 258, 280
Downing, Al 10, 36
Drabowsky, Moe 154
Dreyfuss, Barney 209
Driessen, Dan 147, 163
Drysdale, Don 69–70, 225, 232
Dunedin Blue Jays 263
Dunn, Jack 180
Durham Bulls 252, 263, 278
Durocher, Leo 53, 160, 249
Duva, Brian 243, 276–277
Dykes, Jimmy 123

Earnhardt, Dale 243, 267, 277
Easter, Luke 5, 243–244, 261, 272, 279
Ebbets Field 196
Eckersley, Dennis 219
Eckert, William 190
Edinburg Roadrunners 263
Edmonton Trappers 263
Eisenstat, Harry 22
Elizabethton Twins 4, 263
Elmira Pioneers 263
El Paso Diablos 263
Empire State Building 42
Erie SeaWolves 248, 263, 277
Erwin, Matt 244, 274, 279
Eugene Emeralds 263
Evansville Otters 264
Everett AquaSox 264

Fans of the Orlando Rays 244, 271, 279
Fargo-Moorhead RedHawks 251, 264, 278
Fargo-Moorhead Twins 251
Feller, Bob 70–71, 156, 224, 230
Fenway Park 216
Ferraro, Mike 97
Fichman, Mal 244, 260, 277
Fingers, Rollie 3, 71–73, 225–226, 232, 254
Finley, Charlie 100–101, 104
Fisk, Carlton 3, 49, 73–74, 183, 224, 231–232
Fitz Gerald, Ed 165
Fletcher, Scott 23
Flood, Curt 36, 51
Florence Freedom 256, 264, 267
Florida Marlins 26–27, 56–57, 64, 163–164, 224, 229, 236

Foli, Tim 200
Fondy, Dee 114
Forbes Field 182
Ford, Whitey 74–76, 226, 230
Ford Motor Company 165
Fort Myers Miracle 264
Fort Wayne Wizards 264
Fort Worth Cats (Central League) 238, 264, 278
Fort Worth Cats (Texas League) 238
Fortugno, Tim 38
Fosse, Ray 28
Fox, Nellie 15, 76–77, 224, 228
Foxx, Jimmie 87–88, 99
Foy, Joe 68
Frailing, Ken 185
Frazee, Harry 181
Frederick Keys 264
Fregosi, Jim 77–79, 183, 223, 230
Fresno Grizzlies 264
Frey, Jim 97
Friend, Bob 84
Frisch, Frankie 207
Frisco RoughRiders 264
Fryman, Woodie 41
Furcal, Rafael 245, 269, 277

Galvin, Pud 204
Garciaparra, Nomar 245, 275, 277
Gardner, Billy 143
Garver, Ned 120
Garvey, Steve 79–80, 226, 229
Gary SouthShore RailCats 264
Gateway Grizzlies 264
Gehrig, Lou 1, 80–82, 99, 124, 169–170, 225, 229
Gehringer, Charlie 82–84, 224, 228
Gene Autry Productions 20
Geronimo, Cesar 146
Gibson, Bob 84–85, 180, 226, 232
Gibson, George 207
Gilliam, Jim 86–87, 225, 230
Gladden, Dan 48
Go-Go Sox 76
Gomez, Lefty 92, 99
Gomez, Orlando 239
Gomez, Preston 217
Gonzalez, Jeremi 245, 276, 280
Gordon, Joe 215
Governors' Cup 236
Grace, Mark 245, 271, 278
Grant, Frank 243
Grant, M. Donald 191
Gray, Brett 245–246, 268, 279

Great Falls White Sox 264
Greenberg, Hank 64, 87–88, 168, 222, 224, 229
Greensboro Bats 264
Greensboro Hornets 133
Greenville Braves 265
Greenville Mets 183
Griffey, Ken, Jr. 180, 246, 266, 279
Griffith, Calvin 128
Griffith, Clark 54
Grim, Bob 130
Groh, Heinie 132
Guidry, Ron 89–90, 226, 232
Gulf Coast Braves 265
Gulf Coast Dodgers 265
Gulf Coast Expos 265
Gulf Coast Marlins 265
Gulf Coast Orioles 265
Gulf Coast Phillies 265
Gulf Coast Red Sox 265
Gulf Coast Reds 265
Gulf Coast Tigers 265
Gulf Coast Twins 265
Gulf Coast Yankees 265
Gwynn, Chris 91
Gwynn, Tony 33, 45, 90–91, 226, 230

Hack, Stan 102
Hagerstown Suns 237, 265
Hamilton, Steve 36
Hamilton (Hams) 112
Haney, Chris 33
Hank Aaron Award 11
Hank Aaron Stadium 235
The Hank Sauer Room 254
Hanners, Roger 246, 262, 280
Hansen, Ron 15
Harder, Mel 91–92, 224, 230
Harlem Globetrotters 84
Harris, Lum 131
Harrisburg Senators 265
Hartford Bees 197
Hawblitzel, Ryan 246, 262, 278
Hayes, Von 90
Heep, Danny 189
Hegan, Jim 110
Helena Brewers 265
Helms, Tommy 146
Henderson, Rickey 33, 40, 184
Henry, John 27
Herman, Babe 111
Hernandez, Keith 199
Hernandez, Roberto 171
Hernandez, Willie 98

Herzog, Whitey 36, 189
Hickory Crawdads 266
High Desert Mavericks 266
Hillerich & Bradsby 169
Hindy, Mark 247, 270, 280
Hiroshima Carp 170
Hodges, Gil 92–94, 225, 230, 247, 261, 278
Hollywood Walk of Fame 21
Hornsby, Rogers 45, 160, 213
Horton, Willie 94–95, 224, 231
Houma Hawks 266
House, Mitch 247, 262, 279
Houston Astros 30, 32, 55–56, 61–63, 76–77, 90, 118, 130–131, 146–147, 157, 173–174, 183–184, 189–190, 200–201, 203–204, 207–208, 216–217, 222, 224–225, 231–232, 249
Houston Buffaloes 58
Houston Colt .45s 61, 76–77, 125, 146, 200, 207–208
Howard, Bruce 15
Howard, Elston 95–96, 107, 226, 231
Howser, Dick 96–97, 225, 230
Hoyt, Waite 122
Hrbek, Kent 98–99, 225, 230
Hubbard, Trenidad 247, 262, 277
Hubbell, Carl 99–100, 111, 226, 230
Hudson Valley Renegades 239, 266, 280
Huizenga, Wayne 26–27
Hunter, Jim 100–101, 161, 163, 226, 231
Huntsville Stars 240, 266, 280
Hutch Award 103
Hutchinson, Fred 102–103, 224, 228
Hyzdu, Adam 247–248, 259, 278

Idaho Falls Padres 257, 266, 278
Indiana Baseball Hall of Fame 253
Indianapolis Clowns 9
Indianapolis Indians 17, 144, 266
Inland Empire 66ers 241–242, 246, 266, 279–280
Iowa Cubs 249, 266

Jackson, Reggie 103–105, 129, 226, 232, 254
Jackson Generals 184
Jackson Senators 266
Jacksonville Suns 266
Jamestown Jammers 257, 266, 278
Jenkins, Ferguson 101
Jethroe, Sam 248, 263, 277
Johnson, Ban 140
Johnson, Charles 248, 267, 279

Johnson, Cliff 65
Johnson, Lance 145
Johnson, Roy 83
Johnson City Cardinals 267
Johnson City Yankees 267
Johnstown Johnnies 256, 267, 278
Joliet JackHammers 267
Jones, Randy 105–106, 226, 232
Jones, Sam 154
Jorgensen, Mike 200
Junior World Series 236
Jupiter Hammerheads 267
Juvenile Diabetes Foundation 185

Kalamazoo Kings 267
Kalas, Harry 19
Kaline, Al 106–107, 224, 229
Kane County Cougars 248, 267, 279
Kannapolis Intimidators 243, 267, 277
Kansas City Athletics 16–17, 34–35, 96–97, 100–101, 103–104, 116–119, 126–128, 192–193
Kansas City Blues 142, 202
Kansas City Monarchs 25, 178
Kansas City Royals 37–38, 47, 50, 67, 78, 91–92, 96–97, 120–121, 129, 146, 148, 165, 186, 194, 212, 219, 225, 229–231, 239
Kansas City T-Bones 267
Keefe, Tim 204
Keeler, Wee Willie 140
Kelley, Brad 248, 272, 279
Kelly, Randy 256
Kenosha Mammoths 267
Keokuk Kernels 126
Killebrew, Harmon 107–109, 220, 225, 229
Kiner, Ralph 109–110, 226, 229
King, Clyde 131
Kingsport Mets 267
Kinston Indians 267
Kinugasa, Sachio 170
Kison, Bruce 199
Kittle, Hub 248–249, 270, 279
Klein, Chuck 2, 12, 41, 110–112, 160, 205, 226, 228
Klem, Bill 28, 54, 112–113, 225, 228
Klimm, Bill *see* Klem, Bill
Kluszewski, Ted 113–115, 224, 230
Knepper, Bob 190
Knowles, Darold 214
Knoxville Appalachians 142
Korean War 95, 216
Koufax, Sandy 44, 115–116, 125, 225, 231

Kremmel, Jim 185
Kuenn, Harvey 76
Kunkel, Bill 116–117, 223, 229
Kunkel, Jeff 117
KVOO 20

LaChappa, Matt 249, 272, 278
Lake County Captains 267
Lake Elsinore Storm 257, 268, 278
Lakeland Tigers 268
Lakewood BlueClaws 268
Lamp, Dennis 40
Lancaster JetHawks 268
Lansford, Carney 33
Lansing Lugnuts 268
Larsen, Don 31, 126
Lary, Lyn 55
Las Vegas 51s 268
Lasorda, Tom 117–119, 225, 228, 249, 258, 278
Laxton, Bill 41
Legg, Greg 249, 274, 278
Lemon, Bob 34, 67, 75, 97, 120–121, 129, 165, 224, 231
Lexington Legends 268
Leyland, Jim 119
Lincoln Saltdogs 268
Lindblad, Paul 72
List, Lou 250, 270, 278
Locker, Bob 214
London Werewolves 245, 268, 279
Long, Dale 135
Long Island Ducks 268
Los Angeles Angels (American League) 19, 21–22, 77–78, 114, 118
Los Angeles Angels (Pacific Coast League) 167
Los Angeles Coliseum 196
Los Angeles Dodgers 10, 13–14, 16, 35–36, 40–41, 43–44, 47–49, 53, 57, 69–70, 77, 79–80, 86–87, 89, 91–93, 101–102, 109, 114–119, 121, 125, 129, 144, 148, 150–151, 153, 165, 168–169, 176–178, 194–196, 198, 203–204, 218, 225, 228–232, 240–241, 249
Louisville Bats 268
Louisville Colonels (major American Association/National League) 208–209
Louisville Colonels (minor American Association) 168
Louisville Slugger 169
Lowell Spinners 268
Lynch, Ed 106
Lynchburg Hillcats 237, 268, 279

Lyons, Steve 192
Lyons, Ted 122–123, 224, 230

Macon Peaches 268
Mahoning Valley Scrappers 269
Maloney, Jim 217
Manning, Rick 145
Mantle, Mickey 123–125, 127–128, 151, 195, 225, 229
Manto, Jeff 250, 261, 279
Manuel, Charlie 250, 262, 280
Manush, Heinie 81–83
Marciano, Rocky 250, 261, 280
Marichal, Juan 115, 125–126, 226, 231
Maris, Roger 124, 126–127, 182, 225, 230, 251, 264, 278
Martin, Billy 31, 97, 104, 121, 127–130, 225, 228
Martinez, Dennis 166
Martinsville Astros 269
Mathews, Eddie 130–131, 186, 223, 232
Mathewson, Christy 2, 12, 131–133, 141, 198, 226, 228
Mathewson, Henry 133
Matias, John 15
Matlack, Jon 52
Mattingly, Don 133–134, 218, 226, 231, 251, 270, 278
Mauch, Gene 78
May, Dave 10
May, Lee 146, 163
Mayer, Erskine 209
Mays, Willie 134–136, 151, 180, 195, 221, 226, 231
Mazeroski, Bill 136–137, 226, 230
McBride, Gator 251, 262, 278
McCovey, Willie 137–139, 226, 232
McDowell, Sam 161
McGraw, John 2, 87, 133, 139–141, 205, 226, 228
McGwire, Mark 109–110
McLain, Denny 50, 85
McRae, Hal 45, 222
Medina, Luis 251, 262, 278
Medwick, Ducky 160
Memorial Stadium 170
Memphis Chicks 17
Memphis Redbirds 269
Menke, Denis 146
Mesa, Jose 222
Mesa Angels 269
Mesa Cubs 269
Messersmith, Andy 157
Metro, Charlie 121

Metrodome 98, 171
Metzger, Roger 146
Meyer, Billy 141–142, 226, 228
Miami-Dade Community College 46
Miami Marlins 26
Michael, Gene 97, 121
Michelob 42–43
Michigan State University 173
Mid-Missouri Mavericks 246, 268–269
Midland RockHounds 269
Mills, Brad 252, 262, 278
Milwaukee Braves 9–11, 102, 127–128, 130, 139, 152, 156, 187–188, 192–193, 197–198, 203, 235
Milwaukee Brewers (American Association) 202
Milwaukee Brewers (American League 1901) 139
Milwaukee Brewers (American League/National League 1970–present) 9–11, 21, 23, 45–46, 65, 71–72, 144–146, 203–204, 211, 221–222, 225, 229–230, 232, 235
Minneapolis Millers 134
Minnesota Twins 4, 14, 45–46, 48, 97–99, 101, 107–109, 116, 127–128, 145–146, 151, 158–159, 165–166, 171, 175, 194, 210, 218–220, 225, 229–232
Minnesota Vikings 218
Minoso, Minnie 142–144, 224, 230
Miracle Mets 93
Missoula Osprey 269
Mize, Johnny 13, 109
Mobile BayBears 235, 269, 280
Modesto A's 236, 254, 269, 277, 279
Modesto Reds 254
Molitor, Paul 144–146, 225, 229
Money, Don 41
Monroe, Marilyn 64
Montclair State University 237
Montgomery Wings 269
Montreal Expos 3, 32, 48–49, 56–58, 61–62, 66–67, 91, 118, 135, 162–163, 176–177, 196, 200–201, 225, 229–230, 252, 254
Montreal Royals 13, 86, 118, 178
Morgan, Joe 146–148, 224, 229, 252, 263, 278
Municipal Stadium 92
Munson, Thurman 104, 148–149, 226, 230
Murcer, Bobby 267
Murphy, Dale 149–150, 223, 229
Murray, Eddie 150–152, 224, 232

Murray, Rich 151
Murtaugh, Danny 152–153, 226, 232
Musial, Stan 45, 110, 153–155, 189, 193, 222, 226, 229
Myrtle Beach Pelicans 245, 269, 277

NASCAR 243
Nashua (Dodgers) 240, 252
Nashua Pride 5, 240, 252–253, 269, 279–280
The Nashville Network 20
Nashville Songwriters' Hall of Fame 20
Nashville Sounds 236, 251, 270, 277–278
National Association of Broadcasters Hall of Fame 20
National Cowboy Hall of Fame 20
National League Umpires 2, 27–28, 37, 53–54, 66, 112, 117, 223, 225, 228–229
NCAA 190
Nelson, Roger 15
Neun, Johnny 61
New Britain Rock Cats 270
New Haven Ravens 250, 270, 278
New Jersey Cardinals 248, 270, 279
New Jersey Jackals 237, 270, 278
New Orleans Zephyrs 270
New York Cubans 143
New York Giants 53–54, 60, 67, 87, 99–100, 111, 120, 131–135, 139, 140–141, 154, 159–160, 179, 187–188, 195, 201–202, 204–206
New York Highlanders 139
New York Mets 18–19, 30–33, 35–36, 41, 48–49, 52, 56, 77–78, 84–85, 91–94, 101, 105–106, 119, 134–135, 150–151, 175, 183, 189–192, 195–198, 200–201, 203, 210, 225, 230, 232, 247
New York Yankees 1–2, 13–14, 18, 27, 29–33, 36, 38–39, 44, 50–51, 54–56, 58, 60–61, 63–65, 71, 74–76, 79–82, 84, 86–87, 89–90, 93–97, 99–101, 103–107, 115–118, 120–121, 123–124, 126–130, 133–135, 137–139, 141–142, 147–149, 152, 156–157, 163, 165, 167, 169, 171–174, 179–182, 192–193, 195–196, 201–203, 205–206, 211–212, 215, 218, 221–222, 225–226, 228–232, 236–238, 251
Newark Bears 270
Newark Eagles 66
Newcombe, Don 67, 252, 269, 279
Newhouser, Hal 71, 155–156, 224, 230
Newsom, Bobo 70
Nicholson, Dave 15
Niekro, Joe 157

Niekro, Phil 156–158, 204, 223, 232
Nogales Charros 270
Norfolk Mary Janes 131
Norfolk (Tars) 30
Norfolk Tides 270
North Shore Spirit 270
Norwich Navigators 270
Notre Dame University 219

Oakland Athletics 14, 23–24, 29, 31, 50, 63–64, 71–72, 79, 94–95, 97, 100–101, 103–105, 119, 128–129, 138, 146–147, 159, 161, 163, 184, 188–189, 200, 203–204, 211, 213–214, 219–220, 226, 231–232, 238, 254
Oakland Oaks 128, 160, 167, 202
Oates, Johnny 177
Ogden Raptors 236, 247, 270, 278, 280
Oglivie, Ben 104
Ohio University 186
Oklahoma RedHawks 270
Oliva, Pedro *see* Oliva, Tony
Oliva, Tony 158–159, 166, 225, 229
Oliva, Tony (brother of player) 158
Oliver, Al 149
O'Loughlin, Silk 112
Olympic Stadium 57
Omaha (Cardinals) 84
Omaha Royals 270
Oneonta Tigers 271
Oneonta Yankees 133
Onslow, Jack 123
Oriole Park at Camden Yards 170
Orlando Rays 244, 271, 279
Ormsby, Red 53
Ott, Mel 111, 159–161, 226, 229
Ottawa Lynx 254, 271, 279
Ozark, Danny 177

P & C Stadium 254
Pacific Coast Building Products, Inc. 236
Palm Beach Cardinals 271
Palmer, Jim 101, 161–162, 224, 231
Patterson, Rick 252, 274, 278
Pawtucket Red Sox 271
Peninsula (Grays) 28
Pennsylvania Road Warriors 271
Pensacola Pelicans 271
Peoria Chiefs 245, 271, 278
Peoria Mariners 271
Perez, Tony 147, 162–164, 217, 224, 231
Perry, Gaylord 85
Pershing, John J. 67

Philadelphia Athletics 76, 82, 122–123, 132, 140–143
Philadelphia Phillies 2, 11–12, 18–19, 22, 29, 38, 40–41, 46–47, 56, 78–80, 87, 98, 103, 110–112, 119–121, 125, 141, 145–147, 149–150, 152–153, 160, 162–163, 173–174, 181, 186–187, 190, 196–197, 199, 201–202, 209, 212, 226, 228, 230–232, 238, 253–255
Piedmont Boll Weevils 243
Pierce, Billy 40, 120, 164–165, 224, 230
Pinoni, Scott 240, 252–253, 262, 279
Pittsburgh Pirates 14, 26, 29, 32, 40–41, 51–52, 54, 58, 62, 77–79, 85, 87–88, 99, 109–111, 114, 119, 132, 136–137, 140–142, 152, 163, 182, 198–199, 201–203, 205–211, 226, 228–232, 236, 238, 248, 257
Polo Grounds 53, 113, 159
Porterfield, Bob 120
Portland Beavers 249, 258, 271
Portland Sea Dogs 271
Portsmouth Cubs 13
Potomac Cannons 271
Princeton Devil Rays 248, 255, 271–272, 279
Princeton Reds 248, 255–256
Provo Angels 272
Puckett, Kirby 165–167, 225, 232
Pulaski Blue Jays 272

Quad City River Bandits 272
Quebec Capitales 272

Raines, Tim 90
Rancho Cucamonga Quakes 249, 272, 278
Reading Phillies 174, 239, 254–255, 272, 279
Red Wing Stadium 255
Reed, Jody 38
Reese, Jimmie 167–168, 223, 232
Reese, Pee Wee 88, 168–169, 179, 225, 228
Reinebold, Jim 253, 274, 277
Reynolds, Bob 21
Rice, Jim 89
Richmond Braves 235, 272, 279
Richmond Roosters 239, 272, 278
Rickey, Branch 13, 43, 178, 238
Rio Grande Valley WhiteWings 272
Ripken, Billy 169, 171
Ripken, Cal 169, 177
Ripken, Cal, Jr. 81, 98, 169–171, 224, 229

Ripken Stadium 171
River City Rascals 241, 272, 278
Rivers, Mickey 37
Rizzuto, Phil 171–172, 226, 230
Roberts, Robin 173–174, 197, 226, 232, 253, 276, 279
Robertson, Mildred 55
Robinson, Brooks 3, 38, 64, 174–176, 224, 229
Robinson, Frank 3, 176–178, 180, 224, 231
Robinson, Jackie 3–5, 27, 44, 53, 66–67, 128, 168, 178–180, 183, 223–227, 232, 243, 253, 258–276, 280
Robinson, Wilbert 201
Rochester Community Baseball Inc. 255
Rochester Red Wings 5, 188, 235–236, 243–244, 255, 272, 279–280
Rockford RiverHawks 272
Rogers, Will 20
Rolfe, Red 102
Rome Braves 273
Rommel, Eddie 122
Ron Santo Walk for the Cure 185
Roosevelt, Franklin D. 42, 53
Rosado, Jose 146
Rose, Pete 28, 145, 147, 164, 213
Roseboro, John 125
Rosen, Al 66
Round Rock Express 184, 273
Rudi, Joe 73, 254, 269, 279
Rudolph, Dick 11
Ruppert, Jacob 181
Rusie, Amos 131
Ruth, Babe 2, 10–11, 81, 99, 104, 109–110, 124, 127, 167, 180–182, 225, 229, 251
Ryan, Nolan 3, 48, 74, 78, 162, 183–184, 223–224, 227, 231–232

Sacramento Gold Miners 236
Sacramento Kings 236
Sacramento River Cats 273
Sacramento Surge 236
Sadecki, Ray 50
St. Louis Browns 53, 58–59, 70, 122, 139, 154
St. Louis Cardinals 3, 11–14, 27, 31, 35–36, 38–40, 43, 46–47, 50, 55–56, 58–59, 61–63, 68, 72, 83–85, 87, 94, 97, 102–103, 107, 118–119, 126–127, 131, 139–140, 143–145, 153–155, 160, 166–167, 172, 187–189, 191–195, 198–199, 205, 210, 212, 215, 220, 222, 226, 228–232, 242, 255
St. Lucie Mets 242, 273, 278

St. Paul Saints (American Association) 256
St. Paul Saints (Northern League) 144, 256, 273, 277
Salem Avalanche 273
Salem-Keizer Volcanoes 273
Salt Lake Buzz 246, 252
Salt Lake Stingers 273
San Angelo Colts 273
San Antonio Missions 273
San Antonio Texans 236
San Bernardino Spirit 242, 246
San Bernardino Stampede 241–242
San Diego Clippers 90
San Diego Padres (National League) 33, 62, 71–72, 79–80, 90–91, 105–106, 138–139, 157, 191, 193–194, 196, 217–219, 226, 229–232, 256
San Diego Padres (Pacific Coast League) 110, 167, 215
San Francisco Giants 2, 46, 48–52, 57, 69, 99, 125–126, 131, 133–139, 141, 146–147, 151, 153, 159, 164–165, 176–177, 188, 190, 195–199, 204, 206, 226, 228–232
San Francisco Seals 63
San Jose Giants 273
Santangelo, F. P. 254, 271, 279
Santo, Ron 184–185, 224, 230
Sarasota Red Sox 273
Sauer, Hank 110, 254, 274, 278
Savannah Sand Gnats 273
Savannah Senators 249
Sax, Steve 90
Schaumburg Flyers 273
Schenectady Blue Jays 118
Schmidt, Mike 49, 149, 186–187, 199, 226, 231, 254–255, 272, 279
Schoendienst, Red 187–189, 226, 228
Schu, Rick 187
Schultz, Joe 128
Scott, George 104
Scott, Mike 189–190, 224, 232
Scranton/Wilkes-Barre Red Barons 249, 274, 278
Seattle Angels 121
Seattle Mariners 24, 94–95, 136–137, 171, 226, 246, 249
Seaver, Tom 47, 105, 190–192, 225, 232
Seitz, Peter 101
Seitzer, Kevin 166
Selig, Bud 179
Shantz, Bobby 39
Shea Stadium 41
Shepard, Larry 153

Shippensburg University 26
Shreveport Sports 274
Silver, Morrie, and the original shareholders of the Rochester Red Wings 5, 255, 272, 280
Simmons, Al 99
Simpson, Wayne 10
Singleton, Ken 200
Sioux City Explorers 256, 274
Sioux Falls Canaries 244, 274, 279
Skinner, Joel 74
Slack, Bill 255, 276, 279
Slaughter, Enos 27, 192–193, 226, 230
Smith, Al 15, 42
Smith, Dan 91
Smith, Ozzie 193–195, 226, 228
Snider, Duke 144, 195–196, 225, 229
Snyder, Russ 15
Somerset Patriots 274
Sosa, Sammy 23
South Bend Clay 253
South Bend Silver Hawks 252–253, 274, 277–278
South Bend White Sox 252–253
South Georgia Waves 274
Southeastern Cloverleafs 274
Southern University 39
Space Coast Stadium 27
Spahn, Warren 17, 41, 48, 70, 173, 196–198, 223, 231
Spokane Indians 39, 239, 274, 277
The Sporting News 121, 142
Sportsman's Park 43
Spring, Jack 39
Springfield Cardinals 249
Springfield/Ozark Mountain Ducks 274
Stargell, Willie 198–200, 226, 229
Staten Island Yankees 274
Staub, Rusty 3, 58, 200–201, 225, 230
Stearns, John 255–256, 271, 279
Steinbrenner, George 97, 121, 129, 218
Stengel, Casey 3, 128, 201–203, 225–226, 232
Stephens, Vern 215
Stewart, Jimmy 146
Stockton Ports 274
Stone, Steve 185
Sukeforth, Clyde 178
Sutton, Don 203–204, 225, 231
Swisher, Steve 185
Syracuse Chiefs (International League) 254
Syracuse Chiefs (International League/Eastern League) 254

Syracuse SkyChiefs 254, 274, 278
Syracuse Stars 11

Tacoma Giants 138
Tacoma Rainiers 274
Tampa Bay Devil Rays 32–34, 227, 230
Tampa Yankees 275
Taylor, Kirk 256, 267, 278
Tecate Brewers 275
Tellinger, Emil 193
Temple, Johnny 18
Temple Cup 140
Templeton, Garry 194
Tennessee Smokies 275
Terry, Bill 111, 160, 204–206, 226, 229
Terry, Ralph 137
Terwilliger, Wayne 256, 273, 277
Texas Rangers 23–24, 65, 76–78, 94–95, 117, 128–129, 183–184, 200–201, 214, 216, 218, 227, 232, 239
Thomas, Gorman 104
Thomas, Tommy 122
Thomson, Bobby 9
Three Rivers Stadium 52
Tolan, Bobby 40
Toledo Blue Stockings 178
Toledo Mud Hens (American Association) 202
Toledo Mud Hens (International League) 242, 275, 277
Tollberg, Brian 256, 262, 278
Tommie Aaron Award 235
Torborg, Jeff 177
Toronto Blue Jays 24, 26, 38, 67–68, 78, 94–95, 97, 129, 145, 156–157, 166, 177, 218–219, 227
Torre, Joe 50, 85, 189
Toth, Paul 39
Trammell, Bubba 257, 266, 278
Traynor, Pie 206–207, 226, 231
Trenton Giants 134
Trenton Packers 13
Trenton Thunder 241, 245, 275, 277, 279
Tri-City Dust Devils 275
Tri-City Triplets 244
Tri-City ValleyCats 275
Trillo, Manny 214
Triton College 165
Tucson Sidewinders 275
Tulsa Drillers 275

UCLA 178
Umbricht, Jim 63, 207–208, 224, 231
U.S. House of Representatives 42

USO 20
University of Cincinnati 115
University of Florida 174
University of Georgia 207
University of Michigan 173
University of Minnesota 218
University of Southern California 190
Urso, Joe 257, 268, 278
Utah Stars 218

Vancouver Canadians (Northwest League) 275
Vancouver Canadians (Pacific Coast League) 246
Vaughan, Arky 54
Veeck, Bill 23
Vermont Expos 275
Vero Beach Dodgers 275
Versalles, Zoilo 220
Veterans Stadium 41
Vickers, Randy 238
Victor Records 20
Viola, Frank 46
Virdon, Bill 153, 193
Visalia Oaks 275
Vuckovich, Pete 162

Wagner, Al (Butts) 208, 210
Wagner, Honus 45, 208–210, 226, 232
Walker, Harry 153, 193
Walker, Moses Fleetwood 178
Walker, Tilly 181
Walker, Welday 178
Walla Walla Padres 194
Walt Disney Company 21
Ward, Pete 15
Warneke, Lon 58
Washington Homestead Grays 243
Washington Nationals 54–55, 99, 108–109, 141, 155, 205–206
Washington Senators (1901–04 1957–60), 108, 165
Washington Senators (1961–71) 76–77, 93, 143–144, 214, 216
Washington Statesmen 210
Washington Wild Things 275
Weaver, Earl 210–211, 223, 229
Wegener, Mike 135
Werner, Don 257, 266, 278
Wertz, Vic 135

West Michigan Whitecaps 276
West Tenn Diamond Jaxx 276
White, Frank 212–213, 225, 231
Whiz Kids 18
Wichita Wranglers 276
Wilhelm, Hoyt 15
Williams, Bernie 138
Williams, Billy 213–214, 224, 231
Williams, David 257, 276, 279
Williams, Ted 34, 64, 68, 124, 214–216, 219, 224, 230
Williamsport Bills 238–239
Williamsport Crosscutters 238–239, 245, 257, 276, 279–280
Williamsport Cubs 245
Wills, Maury 40
Wilmington Blue Rocks (Carolina League) 253, 276, 279
Wilmington Blue Rocks (Inter-State League) 173, 253
Wilson, Don 63, 216–217, 224, 232
Wilson, Nigel 26
Winfield, Dave 217–219, 226, 231
Winnipeg Goldeyes 243, 276–277
Winston-Salem Red Sox 255
Winston-Salem Spirits 255
Winston-Salem Warthogs 255, 276, 279
Wisconsin Timber Rattlers 276
Wise, Rick 47
Witt, Mike 218
World Trade Center 247
World War I 68, 132
World War II 20, 27, 30, 43, 53, 60, 64, 71, 102, 120, 123, 155, 168, 192, 197–198, 215
Wright, Mel 193
Wrigley Field 111, 154, 186
Wynn, Early 120
Wytheville Twins 158

Yakima Bears 276
Yankee Stadium 89–90
Yastrzemski, Carl 108, 219–221, 224, 229
Yogi Berra Museum and Learning Center 237
Yogi Berra Stadium 237
York, Rudy 88
Young, Cy (other than Cy Young Award) 41
Yount, Larry 222
Yount, Robin 221–222, 225, 230

www.ingramcontent.com/pod-product-compliance
Lightning Source LLC
Chambersburg PA
CBHW051210300426
44116CB00006B/507